The Imaginary
Institution of India

The Imaginary Institution of India

Politics and Ideas

SUDIPTA KAVIRAJ

 Columbia University Press   New York

Columbia University Press
Publishers Since 1893
New York   Chichester, West Sussex
Copyright © 2010 Sudipta Kaviraj
All rights reserved

Library of Congress Cataloging-in-Publication Data
Kaviraj, Sudipta.
The imaginary institution of India : politics and ideas /
Sudipta Kaviraj.
p. cm.
Includes bibliographical references and index.
ISBN 978-0-231-15222-8 (cloth)—
ISBN 978-0-231-15223-5 (pbk.)—
ISBN978- 0-231-52651-7(ebook)
1. Politicalscience— India—Philosophy.
2. Nationalism—India.   3. Postcolonialism—India.
4. India—Social conditions—1947–   5. India—Politics
and government—1947–   I. Title.
JA84.I4K4 2010
306.20954—dc22
2009049464

for
Nilanjana

Contents

	Introduction	1
1	On State, Society, and Discourse in India	9
2	On the Construction of Colonial Power: Structure, Discourse, Hegemony	39
3	On the Structure of Nationalist Discourse	85
4	Writing, Speaking, Being: Language and the Historical Formation of Identities in India	127
5	The Imaginary Institution of India	167
6	A State of Contradictions: The Post-colonial State in India	210
7	Government and Opposition: Fifty Years of Indian Independence	234
8	The Reversal of Orientalism: Bhudev Mukhopadhyay and the Project of Indigenist Social Theory	254
	Index	291

The Imaginary
Institution of India

Introduction

These essays were written over a long period of time, in answer to a single but vastly complex question. How does one try to understand coherently the internally diverse historical field of what we call Indian politics? Although published as academic papers, these essays were written primarily to clarify questions to myself, not to instruct others. For a long time I tried to figure out what the significant questions to ask were if someone wanted to understand modern India's political history.

It should be clear from the essays that these questions appeared to grow harder and more complicated, and that by writing them I tried to bring them under some form of intellectual control. Because these essays were written over a considerable period of time, this raises a question about their internal coherence and implicit methodological orientation. I can see in retrospect that there is a closer adherence to Marxist explanatory techniques in the essays I wrote earlier, less so in others. This is not the place to provide a full explanation for these methodological shifts or the reasons behind them: that would involve us in the fascinating but complex history of Indian Marxism and its relation to academic thinking. Authors are not always trustworthy guides to their own processes of thinking: modifying the hermeneutic paradox, it could be said that an author never quite fully understands why he thought the way he did.

In these essays, in my own understanding, there is a movement *from* Marx in a double sense. I think there are deep and enduring marks of Marxist beginnings in the shape and form of the questions that animate these enquiries into the historical nature of Indian politics. This is most clearly reflected in my conviction, which became stronger with time, that the only way to understand Indian political life was to read it through a form of historical sociology. Schematically, when I began writing partial analyses of Indian politics, Indian Marxism was marked by four specific intellectual features. The first injunction of Marxist historical theory seemed the principle of historicization: an impulse to historicize every single question, to seek the ways in which significant parts of the political were formed and previous structures unformed.

Second, Marxist analyses in the intellectual life of Kolkata in the 1960s there were marked by a deep reliance on the simple methodological technique of economic reduction. But by the end of that decade a deep unease about its shortcomings also became commonplace—though what should be done to replace it was not entirely clear.

Third, partly in tension with the second principle, in actual intellectual discussions there was an intense feeling of the primacy of the political—about the questions of the deep arrangements and organization of social power, which political practice was meant to modify and change in an egalitarian direction.

Finally, there existed a deep hermeneutic of suspicion towards established systems of social knowledge, and of the social sciences as generically 'bourgeois'—a term used with breathtakingly sweeping imprecision to characterize all forms of dominant knowledge, fraught with the idea that these were simply elaborate systematizations of the contingent epistemics of dominant, educated social classes. In consequence, there was a corresponding impulse to search for an alternative epistemology of the subaltern classes, an aspiration to build a picture of society—both in the sense of social analysis and of the construction of political ideals—from the point of view of subaltern groups in society: a hard task under any circumstance, but particularly difficult for intellectuals drawn from the middle classes. I think, except for the second, the other features retain their cognitive force, although the manner in which I have responded to these demands in these essays is unavoidably individual and contingent.

Historicism was an especially paradoxical intellectual principle. Its duality of connotation is reflected with startling clarity in the sharply discordant meanings to which this term is put in current social thought. Modern historical reflection, in one form, induces thinking about the uniqueness, specificity, and particularity of historical moments and processes, which is reflected in the German neo-Kantian conception of historicism and hermeneutics. Interestingly, subsequently thinkers like Popper use the term 'historicism' to refer to just the opposite tendency which considers the primary task of modern historical thought to observe/discern regularities across different situations. These patterns and regularities exist at various levels of scale. Even if theories which imputed to history what are derisively called 'grand narratives' have become discredited, there is no doubt that contingent facts—such as the circumstance that after the British departed the Indian state has not collapsed but has consolidated itself—exert structural pressures on the modes of calculations and actions of political agents.

These two procedures raise epistemic difficulties of different kinds. Bengali Marxist thought was overwhelmingly influenced by the second form of historicism: a belief that the cognitive superiority of Marxist theory consisted in its mastery of a small number of powerful formulae with which all historical questions could be unlocked. Historical categories commonly used for understanding Indian politics and its historical frame were usually drawn quite obviously from two common sources—either European history of the nineteenth century, implicit in Marx's texts; or structures from Russian or Chinese history embedded in the works of Lenin or Mao. A separate strand of Bengali Marxism was drawn, from the mid-1960s, to a contrasting strand in Marxism—towards Gramsci, and through him to the alternative tradition of German historicism. Students of Indian politics inside the Indian Marxist tradition were thus drawn towards both conceptions of 'historicism', between the two ways of construal of the meaning of 'historicity'.

Some of the earlier-written essays in this book show the direct influence of this second 'historicist' tendency associated with Gramsci. But the influence of Gramsci was to work out its effects in two ways, one relatively explicit, the other somewhat indirect. In certain essays I sought to draw directly upon some of Gramsci's concepts, for example in an essay I wrote on 'the passive revolution'. Over the years, I realized the workings of a deeper and less explicit influence from that tradition of Marxist historicism: by the demand for historicization, which forced me to think more closely and particularistically about the specificity of the Indian past. In the later-written essays there is an increasing engagement with the particularities of Indian history, of both its past and its present, a stress on the ways in which this history is quite different from the more widely recorded trajectories of European modernity.

With the passage of time, the essays seem to move away from explanatory reductivism towards a more complex understanding of the historical process and the persistent difficulties of explanation. It becomes clear that the capitalist social form produces a peculiar causal priority for the economic-productive moment of the social structure, which is ungeneralizable to other, pre-capitalist social forms. In any case, even in the earlier essays, economic reduction is present as an extreme belief weakly held: gradually, that methodological frame fades and is replaced by a clearer acknowledgement of the decisive causal powers of political institutions of the state in conditions of colonial history. Without reducing the significance of structural economic analysis, it can be claimed that many of the central transformations of colonial modernity were wrought by the causal force of state actions—the peculiarly concentrated and organized form of violence represented in the modern state: in fact, some of the changes in the economy were dependent on prior causal impulses from the state and the political realm.

Although the fourth element of Marxist analysis—the constant search for subaltern perspectives—is invoked occasionally, it is not a central aspect of political analysis in these essays. It is not always appreciated how difficult it is to deliver on the abstract promise of 'subaltern studies'—to dredge up from the ruins of everyday life pieces of subaltern experience, then to find a language to express them, and finally to theorize on the basis of the distinctiveness of that angle of vision.

Observers of modern political life in India will immediately note that the analytical language we all use for describing, evaluating, and understanding this field is composed of a constantly uneasy and unstable mixture of really three distinct 'languages' which possess internal coherence. To speak about modern politics we rely implicitly and constantly on the conventional language of 'social science', the language that modern Western intellectual practices have fashioned to describe analyse and evaluate modern forms of power. In the Indian life world, we necessarily have to take recourse to an older traditional language of power indigenous to Indian society—a habitual language of describing and evaluating what is involved in the exercise of power and responding to its demands. A part of this language is itself a product of mixtures between Sanskritic and Persianate 'high cultures', with the other part consisting of vernacular adaptations to power of local rulers. Finally, we need to rely quite often, unavoidably, on a third language of a very different kind: this is the evolving streetwise language of political description which simply follows new developments in political experience with constantly refashioned vocabularies—usually in a colloquial vernacular.

The task of political theory is twofold: it is primarily to describe the evolving patterns of political power in a cognitively opportunistic way, expressing its truth in whatever language is at hand, by whatever idiomatic expressions are available, which can felicitously capture the precise contours of the shifting world of political power. At the same time, its task is to observe the composite language it is itself using: to reflect upon its sources, its problems of internal consistency, its historical appropriateness or obsolescence, and particularly upon the constant combinations between these linguistic registers demanded by observed political practice. No particular essay in this book takes up this set of methodological or linguistic issues, but these can be glimpsed within the uses of the analytical language in this collection.

Taken together, the essays in this volume state four specific propositions regarding Indian politics. First, by the title of the naming essay they imply a distinction between two meanings of the term 'India'—cultural and political; it asserts that despite the venerable antiquity of a cultural sense of India, the construction of a political India is rather recent; and that this was rendered possible by the development of modern techniques of state-formation. Second, they seek to historicize the analysis of the colonial state by showing a slow historical process through which an earlier period of colonial power over scattered segments of society and culture later systematized into institutions of the colonial state. Additionally, they suggest that internal sequences are important for understanding the nature of the impact of colonialism in different parts of Indian society. Third, the essays suggest a similar historicizing of 'Indian nationalism' by rejecting an implicit teleology often contained in nationalist history-writing—of dividing periods into different forms of patriotism. They also suggest that, even in its mature stage, Indian nationalism is a complex, unstable, internally diverse body of ideas in which various strands vie for imaginative dominance. Finally, some of the essays insist on the innovativeness of the structure of Indian nationalism: one of the country's major peculiarities was the way in which institutional nationalism was able to resolve the potential conflict between regional and 'Indian' identity, and arrange them in a stratified order.

The subject that these essays explore collectively is the place in the social life of modern India of the activity named politics. All the essays are animated by a single idea, namely that what we with casual mundaneness call politics today is historically an entirely new activity, unlike its namesakes in earlier times. It is hardly surprising that this activity is often referred to as 'politics' in a vernacularized English term, precisely because, in a strict sense, it had no historical precursors. To be sure, in pre-modern India there existed activities associated with the acquisition and deployment of political power—the exercise of rule over the life of society: and correspondingly, on the opposite side, the acts of ordinary people responded to the power of the rulers. But these were quite unlike what passes under the name of politics in modern times, when politics is the name of that activity which, assuming the plasticity of the social world in which people live, seeks to reflexively affect and shape that world. Politics, in that sense, has become an activity with a universal reach, an activity which can affect, structure, and shape all others. In this sense, it is an activity which has all other forms of activity as its object.

The largest purpose of all the essays that I have written, some of which appear in the present book, has been to come to an understanding of politics in modern India. Taken as a whole the essays contain analyses of nationalism, of the nature and structure of the institutions of the state, and the peculiar processes by which democracy has become indigenous to Indian politics. This present volume (it will be succeeded by two others) deals primarily with Indian nationalist discourses. I view them as part of the genealogy of the modern Indian state. The state which emerged after Independence drew heavily from two contradictory lineages: the evolving structures of the colonial state and the ideological movements of Indian nationalism. Accordingly, two strands of arguments run parallel in this volume: the sequentially earlier essays follow the slow process through which the power of

European capitalist empires entered pre-colonial Indian society and transformed it, eventually establishing the peculiar institutions of the British Indian colonial state. Later, the essays follow the historical emergence of forms of patriotism and their gradual formation into the complex structures of Indian nationalist ideology.

The essays try to present 'Indian nationalism' as a field of ideas rather than as a doctrine—evolving, unstable, volatile, capable of sudden shifts in emphasis and political direction. They also suggest that the Nehruvian version of Indian nationalism, though politically preferable to me and many others who share my political opinions, was one among several forms. Its great political success consisted in devising a formation of 'nationalism' which was stratified, allowing expression to more local forms of patriotism, unlike the predominant European model. But such an historical sense of its achievement is also inevitably accompanied by some political anxiety about its permanence. Every form of nationalism requires a slow, insidious, continuous endorsement through arguments, a daily referendum in the minds of citizens. And I cannot hide my anxiety that this discursive justification of a pluralist nationalism has been failing in recent years. In political life, there is no guarantee that the more civilized positions will win out. Even the most morally justifiable ideological positions have to fight for their political life.

Methodologically, two types of essays are brought together in this volume. Some are primarily explorations in the history of ideas, but their differences also show how diverse the meaning of 'history of political ideas' can be. They start from a fairly straightforward analysis of how the idea and ideal of modern freedom enters Indian intellectual life—and some of the surprisingly divergent consequences this produces when it affects pre-existing cultures of political thinking—and are all studies in ideas, but ideas of very different kinds, with very different but always significant effects on political life. Some other essays deal more with the establishment of political institutions, and the structures of justification which go into their making and continuance. Clearly, political ideals and theories have a significant effect in the political lives of societies only when they crystallize into stable practices, and eventually form institutions. The study of political ideals must include analysis of thinking within at least three levels: the thinking of theorists, of political agents, and of ordinary people whose interest or indifference decides which ideas have the power to affect history.

In the years over which these essays were written I have accumulated debts to a large number of individuals whose works or conversations have provided inspiration to my thinking. Many friends and colleagues have helped me think through questions by allowing me to read their work—often before publication; through critical responses to drafts of these essays; often through long-term conversations on questions of common interest; or simply by the subtle incitement of attentive listening. For thinking about history of ideas I am particularly indebted, over many years, to conversations and suggestions from John Dunn, Sheldon Pollock, and Quentin Skinner. I have developed clarity in many of these themes in conversation over many years with Rajeev Bhargava, Partha Chatterjee, Sunil Khilnani, and Sheldon Pollock.

I am particularly grateful to Satish Saberwal for his great intellectual generosity, and for sharing with me his insights into the practice of historical sociology. I owe a special debt to the members of the Subaltern Studies collective, who have helped me understand the meaning of historicity through the always generous sharing of ideas which marked the group—although I am conscious that my work is much less concerned with the question of 'subalternity' than is that of the other members.

My ideas about the historical structures of political power in India have benefited greatly from exchanges with a large number of friends and colleagues. I am particularly grateful to Muzaffar Alam, Shahid Amin, Amitava Banerjee, Dipesh Chakrabarty, Sobhanlal Dattagupta, Ranajit Guha, Rajni Kothari, Ashis Nandy, Sanjay Palshikar, Gyan Pandey, D.L. Sheth, Bhikhu Parekh, and Asok Sen. Finally, these essays would have never seen the light of day without the encouragement and patience of Rukun Advani, my imperturbable editor.

Despite the general singleness of the question they seek to answer, these essays are a preparation for a more coherent analysis of the strange historical phenomenon of the Indian state, not a substitute.

1

On State, Society, and Discourse in India

This essay seeks to place the relation between state and society in India in a broader than usual perspective. It tries to do so in two ways. It tries first to set out the processes of modern Indian politics in terms of a long-term historical understanding, rather than pretend, as is often done, that all the causalities of politics somehow sprang up in 1947. Second, it suggests that the historical argument reveals problems of a theoretical character, and that without dealing with some of these methodological and philosophical issues it is impossible to tackle some of the difficulties faced by empirical explanations. The essay is divided into four parts. The first makes some preliminary theoretical remarks, the second assesses some of the initiatives or proposals for modernity that the colonial power set in motion, the third tries to analyse what happens to these after Independence, and the final part returns to some questions of theory.

It is often said that to use concepts like 'state' and 'society' is not helpful because of their abstractness and excessive generality. But I think that it is possible to begin at a still more radical starting point. To analyse the relation between state and society in India, it could be argued, is impossible because they do not exist in India, at least not so securely as to enable us to apply these concepts unproblematically to analysis. This may help us understand something quite fundamental. 'Society' can mean just any set of actually existing social relations, and that is the sense in which it is often used in the social science literature.

First published in *Rethinking Third World Politics*, ed. James Manor (London: Longman, 1991), pp. 72–99.

But it can also mean a specific kind of society, known often as *gesellschaft*. 'State', similarly, can mean either any system of political rule or regime, or a specific, historically indexed style of impersonal governance, and, of course, there is a close historical connection between these ways of seeing society and the state.[1] A state of this modern kind can exist, some types of social theory would assert, only on condition that it is embedded or surrounded by a 'civil society' of this kind. And it has been argued that one of the major problems for political construction in India is precisely the setting up of a modern state without the presence of a civil society.[2] So the underlying theoretical questions here would be: what are the conditions in which society and state, in the generic sense of these words, allow themselves to be shaped into states and societies in the second sense; and are these processes such that collective intentionalities, like legislation or constitution-making, are able to create them, or are they products of something more glacial, less intentional, more mysterious?

If all societies have 'structures' (in the sense in which structuralists use the term—it can be very different from the self-description of the formal organization that a society offers), and if states have to obey their logic, and adapt to its compulsions, it becomes necessary to begin the story of the Indian state somewhat earlier than the point at which it is ordinarily done. It becomes necessary to tell the story of modernity as inextricably linked to the story of colonialism. This will, as we shall see, alter the punctuation and the shape of this narrative quite significantly at some points. In order to understand some of the present political difficulties of the Indian state, it is necessary to think in ways that are undetermined by the dominant myths and narrative strategies of nationalist historiography.

But it is important to see that modernization theories also give rise to a largely parallel illusion in the analysis of social change. It is one of their serious drawbacks to encourage the notion that it is only

---

[1] For an excellent discussion of the historical stratification of the meaning of the term 'state', see Skinner 1989.

[2] The term 'civil society' is used here in Gramsci's sense. But it appears that it is used in so many distinct ways, and that there are justifications for most of these, that there should be some rigorous discussion about its many, but somewhat confusing, riches.

modernity which has institutions, and it is only modernity which is rational. It is clear that if we work with a thin theory of rationality, then many of the practices condemned as hopelessly traditional (and devoid of any possible rational justification) can be rationally justified, unless the abstract definition of rationalism itself is surreptitiously packed with presuppositions of European Enlightenment thinking. Getting people to ground their practices differently is not just dispelling a false consciousness, but a contestation of rationalities differently constructed. Similarly, modernity does not build institutions in an empty space. It has to rework the logic of existing structures, which have their own, sometimes surprisingly resilient, justificatory structures. The entry of modernity into the discourses and practices of a society depends, I shall argue, on a gradual, dialogical, discursive undermining of these historically rational grounds. And this cannot happen without extending much greater hermeneutic charity towards the practices we try to destroy. For the first condition of setting up a critical, dialogical relation with them is to identify these beliefs correctly, and to see their structures of justification.

The Structure of Traditional Society and the Space of the State[3]

Several features of the traditional construction of Indian society must be noted if we are to understand exactly where the state is placed and exactly what it can and cannot do. First, the caste system is significant not only for its great internal complexity, but also the principles on which this complexity is constructed. Unlike pre-modern European societies, which seem to have had a symmetrical hierarchy, its internal principle of the organization of inequality was an *asymmetric* one. By this I mean that if social hierarchy is a complex concept, and it is disaggregated into several different criteria of ranking individuals and groups—say, between control over economic assets, political power, and ritual status—the rank ordering in India would be asymmetric between the upper-caste groups. That is, if ritual status ranks groups as ABC, political power might rank as BCA, and control of the economy

---

[3] In this section I have simply summarized my argument in a different but related paper: Kaviraj 1989a.

CBA. Of course, caste had a history, and the *jati* system which actually functioned on the ground was quite different from the ideological self-presentation of the *varna* system. But the advantage of seeing this model as presenting a sort of faded but still discernible background ideology of social practices is that it helps account for the relative infrequency of lower-order defiance in Indian history. It makes it cognitively more difficult to identify the structure of dominance because of some dispersal of power among the superordinate groups. Second, by this dispersal, it also imposes a strong necessity of a broad coalition among the upper strata in Indian society.

A second feature is the relation between society and the state. This depended on the way in which the social groups that were given to people's immediate 'natural consciousness' were themselves structured. Since the scale of social action was small, and highly segmented—despite the recent discovery by Cambridge history of much large-scale economic activity which they call, a trifle boldly, the growth of capitalism—this had some interesting consequences for the reach, structure, and form of political power. The 'sovereignty' of the state was two-layered. (This is to indulge in something I have been criticizing: for one of the major problems of theorizing the field of power is precisely the absence of something like 'sovereignty' in modern Europe; yet let us approach the unfamiliar first through the familiar.) Often, there existed a distant, formally all-encompassing, empire, but actual political suffering was caused on an everyday basis by neighbourhood tyrants. There were also considerable powers of self-regulation by these communities. (However, calling them in some ways self-regulating does not mean romanticizing them into democratic communities, or unchanging ones. Self-regulating communities can also create and maintain hierarchies of the most debasing sort.)

Thus the state, or the upper layers of it, which the colonial and the national regimes saw themselves as historically succeeding, sat in the middle of a peculiar segmentary social arrangement. I shall call this, by a deliberate misuse of a Hegelian metaphor, a circle of circles, each circle formed by a community of a neighbourhood mix of caste, religious denomination, and occupation. The state would occupy, to extend the metaphor, a kind of high ground in the middle of this circle of circles. It enjoyed great ceremonial eminence, but in fact it had rather limited powers to interfere with the social segment's internal organization. Its classical economic relation with these communities over which it formally presided would be in terms of tax and rent. And while its rent demands would fluctuate according to its military needs and its ability to despoil, it could not (in its own interest or in the pretended interest of the whole society) restructure the productive or occupational organization of these social groups. One of our crucial points is that the conceptual language of acting 'on behalf' of the society as a whole was unavailable to this state.

Two implications follow from this. First, the eminence or the spectacular majesty of the state (at least the large state at the imperial centre) was combined with a certain marginality in terms of both time and space. Incursions by this high state were in the most literal sense spectacular—both wondrous to behold and unlikely to happen every day. The large and high state therefore had an ineradicable link with spectacle, pomp and majesty, and symbolic rituals, rather than the slovenly and malodorous business of the everyday use of power, a sort of double image which one finds in both the British period and after Independence.

But there is another implication of this picture which is of some importance for an understanding of the communal problem in India. I submit, against the grain of nationalist mythology about the common Indian past, that we must see the process of admission of alien groups into Indian society in a slightly altered way. For the standard nationalist picture of what happened, which normally goes under the name of a composite culture, is implicitly a self-congratulatory Hindu idea celebrating the great readiness of the Hindus (and later also of Muslims) to absorb outsiders after a few initial battles. In order to make my point, I shall use another theoretical distinction.

Using Tönnies's idea of *gemeinschaft*, I should like to suggest that the sense of the community can be of various types. I shall make a distinction here between what I shall call fuzzy and enumerated, or counted, communities. The traditional sense of community, I suggest, was fuzzy in two senses. It was fuzzy first in the sense that the construction of individual or collective identity depended very heavily on a sense of context. Belonging to varying layers of community was not seen as disreputable or unreasonable. Given different situations, a pre-modern person could have said that his community was either his religious or caste or occupational group, or his village or his region. He might find it difficult to render these varying communities, to all of which he belonged, into some unimpeachable hierarchy, either moral or political. But I do not think such a person could be accused of lack of precision in the use of social concepts: he would have fairly clear ideas about how to deal with unfamiliarity, or likeness and unlikeness, and be able to sort these things out for appropriate moves in social practice. The distinction I am drawing then is not between a precise and an imprecise way of thinking about the social world, but between precisions of different kinds. And of course very different types of social worlds could be constructed out of these different ways of thinking precisely about likeness and difference.

This implies an answer to the question that early nationalists inflicted on themselves: how could such a large entity as India be so easily colonized by the British? The short answer is that the question was wrong. The horizon of belongingness and consequently of conceivable social action was such that there was no India to conquer. Since the British inhabited a different discourse of social science and looked at historical and social reality quite differently, for them there was an externally given object—India—that was the target of their political control and conquest. But the Indian opposition they had to face did not reason through similar concepts. Thus, one princely ruler looked on with unruffled equanimity at the undoing of his immediate neighbour, perhaps his immediate predecessor in the British agenda of conquest, and deplored philosophically the changeability of the human condition, including those of small princes. Basically the fuzziness of their sense of community meant that it occurred to none of them to ask how many of them there were in the world, and what, if they agreed to bend their energies into a common action, they would be able to wreak upon the world to their common benefit. At one level it was of course a society like any other: people lived in groups, had wars, peace, conflicts, births, deaths, and diseases. But the great difference was that they suffered or enjoyed these constituents of their common fates more passively, without any idea of their magnitude or numbers.

Another result of this was the manner in which external groups were allowed into this society. Contrary to nationalist ideas and narratives, when new groups with hard, irreducibly different social attributes and markers entered into this society, they did not automatically create a new culture composed of elements of both; more likely, they would be allowed to enter into the circle of circles by forming a circle of their own. Initially, this would make the society's general architecture lose its shape a little, but it would generally adjust to their presence. But this circle—of Muslim culture and community—existed not in any open dialogic communication with the rest of society, but as a circle unto itself. It existed in a kind of back-to-back adjacency with the rest—by way of a very peculiar combination of absorption and rejection.

The Proposals of Colonial Modernity

Into such a society—a circle of circles, but each circle relatively unenumerated and incapable of acting as a collective group—colonial power brought a series of basic changes. Ironically, such changes could have been brought in only by an external power—external not merely in terms of coming from outside, but also in the sense of using a social conceptualization that was fundamentally alien to this arrangement. Even the Mughal state could not do it, because it would have accepted eminence at the price of the traditional marginality. It could be done only by a political apparatus which had totally different moral, political, and, most significantly, cognitive values.

Curiously, however, British colonial policy did not have a single, unhesitating answer to the question of what to do in this very unfamiliar society. Its political history shows that it went through two policy phases, or at least there were two strategies between which its policies actually oscillated, sometimes to its great advantage. At first, the new colonial apparatus exercised caution, and occupied India by a mix of military power and subtle diplomacy, the high ground in the middle of the circle of circles. This, however, pushed them into contradictions. For, whatever their sense of the strangeness of the country and the thinness of colonial presence, the British colonial state represented the great conquering discourse of Enlightenment rationalism, entering India precisely at the moment of its greatest unchecked arrogance. As inheritors and representatives of this discourse, which carried everything before it, this colonial state could hardly adopt for long such a self-denying attitude. It had restructured everything in Europe—the productive system, the political regimes, the moral and cognitive orders—and would do the same in India, particularly as some empirically inclined theorists of that generation considered the colonies a massive laboratory of utilitarian or other theoretical experiments. Consequently, the colonial state could not settle simply for eminence at the cost of its marginality; it began to take initiatives to introduce the logic of modernity into Indian society. But this modernity did not enter a passive society. Sometimes, its initiatives were resisted by pre-existing structural forms. At times, there was a more direct form of collective resistance. Therefore the map of continuity and discontinuity that this state left behind at the time of independence was rather complex and has to be traced with care.

Most significantly, of course, initiatives for what has come to be known as modernity came to assume an external character. The acceptance of modernity came to be connected, ineradicably, with subjection. This again points to two different problems, one theoretical, the other political. Theoretically, because modernity was externally introduced, it is explanatorily unhelpful to apply the logical format of the 'transition process' to this pattern of change. Such a logical format would be wrong on two counts. First, however subtly, it would imply that what was proposed to be built was something like European capitalism. (And, in any case, historians have forcefully argued that what it was to replace was not like feudalism, with or without modificatory adjectives.) But, more fundamentally, the logical structure of endogenous change does not apply here. Here transformation agendas attack as an external force. This externality is not something that can be casually mentioned and forgotten. It is inscribed on every move, every object, every proposal, every legislative act, each line of causality. It comes to be marked on the epoch itself. This repetitive emphasis on externality should not be seen as a nationalist initiative that is so well rehearsed in Indian social science. I use it for just the opposite reason—to reject and deconstruct some of the well-known nationalist arguments about Indian history.[4]

Quite apart from the externality of the entire historical proposal of modernity, some of its contents were remarkable. Institutional changes that colonial modernization sought to introduce into Indian society

---

[4] I use the word 'deconstruct' quite deliberately: for the critique of nationalism comes here as an internal critique, as the critique and rejection of those who, as Derrida would say, have been its inhabitants. Only then can it be called deconstruction.

could be broadly divided into three main types, two of which have been fairly well documented and analysed. Economic reforms, or rather alterations (because these changes were usually unaccompanied by the moral arguments that attend genuine reformist impulses), did not foreshadow the construction of a classical capitalist economy, with its necessary emphasis on extractive and transport sectors. What happened was the creation of a degenerate version of capitalism—what early dependency theorists called the 'development of underdevelopment'. Political changes that accompanied these initiatives were of a very peculiar sort, and have been, in my judgement, often misread. In fact it was clear from the early period of colonial rule that Britain could not, without infringing the fundamental logic of colonialism, introduce forms of political rule current in Europe. However, in order to make the economic part of the social world tractable and amenable to its control, the colonial regime brought in a set of fundamental legal identifications which were new and unprecedented in the Indian con-text. Although the political institutions of liberalism were not introduced, precisely because the political forms of liberalism were deeply intricated with the system of property rights, the colonial state gradually introduced a complete vocabulary of liberal rights in the economic and social fields. It brought in the idea of a state as an impersonal regime of relations, the idea of an individual subject (which was necessary particularly to introduce the new regime of property and the entire regime of taxes and other obligations), the equality of rights or rightlessness—in which the important thing was the constitution of the political-individual subject, rather than whether he enjoyed democracy or suffered subjection—and, finally, a state which (illegitimately under colonialism) pretended to represent the collective interest of society, and from whose legitimate interference nothing in society was morally immune.

Evidently this entire gamut of conceptual transformations formed a structure. These concepts could not exist and flourish separately, they were preconditionally linked and formed in their totality a new way of conceiving the political world. The major difference between its introduction in Europe and in India was of course that, while in Europe these were seen by the major part of society as a result of experiments in controlling and reducing irresponsible power and therefore as liberating, in India they seemed the reverse. The society had to be subject to them because of the irresistible power of the colonial rulers. This array of ideas, when seen in their totality, constituted the invention of a new political world, or a re-cognizing of the world, and of the position of the society and the state in their modern versions—society as a large complex of *gesellschaft* organizations, and the state as an impersonal apparatus of public power.

A final point must be made about this picture of colonialism and its imbrication with modernity. The colonial structure represented not only a set of new institutions, but also a set of discourses. And the connection between the practices, institutions, and discourses could never be underestimated by this generation of colonial rulers, bred on the idea of the strong relation between knowledge and power, and seeing Europe's conquest of India as a consequence of Europe's scientific advance. Clearly, the new institutions were operable and intelligible only if worked through the new discourses of society and power. Long inhabitance in India's society had taught the colonizers about deep differences in the structures of consciousness in this society. Traditional Indian discourse formed a structure, just as rationalist discourses did, and there was no simple incremental transition from one to the other. Since colonial authority could not be legitimized in terms of the constituted common sense of traditional Indian society, the proper course of action was to try to reconstitute this common sense. This is why the question of education, the instrumentality through which the common sense of a society is created, was of such central concern to British colonial authority.

In this field the British followed what could be called a Gramscian line. Their strategy seemed to be that if a leading section of Indian society could be made to reconstitute their common sense—through the channels of encouragement, emulation, pressure, control—the rest of society could also be expected to follow suit, at least in the fulness of time. Of course, this operation went out of control, and in time produced results which must have completely surprised them, and even their political successors. But it is interesting to see how these went. First, of course, the British colonial apparatus undertook an enormous and unprecedented enumeration of everything in Indian society. Thus, this imposed on social action a completely different picture of what the social world was really like. From fuzzy communities, people had to get used to the strains of living in enumerated ones—with very different consolations and highly abstract threats. Nationalists soon began to turn this counting to good use, and often began to comfort themselves with the eventual power of the numbers, particularly when their movement seemed to be in decline. The colonial authorities themselves would try, at a later stage, to turn this counting against them by enumerating Muslims against Hindus. This showed one implication of living in a society that was enumerated: it was not just a secular nation which could name itself in this way. If disgruntled, other communities, based on different principles, could emerge in this way. Whether they did so or not depended to a large extent on the cultural reproduction of the national community. These communities, as Benedict Anderson has argued forcefully,[5] have nothing objective about them. If not given grounds for continuing to imagine themselves in a particular way, they might rapidly decline and dissolve.

At another level, too, the initiatives of the colonial state were unsuccessful, or at least came up against peculiar limits. The British had expected to alter through their cultural initiatives the self-evidential view of the social world not only of the new elite, but also of the common people. The new elite, it was expected, would carry this new alphabet of social reasoning into the lower orders via a sort of Gramscian relay of ideology. But the structure of traditional culture reflected the same segmentation as its social structure, and so it was not easy to identify the site of such a common sense which could be replaced with a new one. But the cultural space of Indian society was also divided in a different way, between high and subaltern cultures. It is wrong to believe, as conventional sociology and cultural theory does, that the difference shown by dominant and lower-order ideas are merely 'failures' to copy correctly, that the lower-order versions of the epics, for instance, would merely be badly-thought-out versions of high literature. More often, as the work of subaltern historians seems to show, they arc different stories, in terms of structure, escaping censorship and punishment by keeping a tenuous formal semblance of identity. Structural readings of popular stagings of the Ramlila would often be significantly different from those of the great epic. Illiteracy implies not just the 'lack' or 'absence' of high discourse, but the presence of a very different one whose rules, codes, emphases, and ironies are entirely different. And just as the intricacies of the upper discourse are not gathered by the lower, the intricacies and inflections of the lower

[5] Anderson 1983.

discourse are unavailable to the literate culture. The culture of the lower orders, therefore, has potent means of not learning, or insulating out the cultural instruction coming from the top. It is not surprising that the noisy political discourse of a garrulous, ambitious, self-regarding new middle class would not by itself be able to enter into the confidentiality of the discourse of the lower orders and reorder their alphabet. It failed to create a single circle of publicity for political ideas, as the British and the Indian elite had expected. This resulted in my judgement in the most significant cultural fact of modern Indian political life. There were two ways of dividing Indian society—in terms of discourses and in terms of political ideology—and the two divisions would be asymmetric.

This will become clearer if we relate it to the history of Indian nationalism. How does it relate to the spread of nationalist ideology? Does drawing this distinction do something to the major distinctions of nationalist politics, or does it make us displace in some way our analysis of the national state?

The introduction of this new discourse—limited, imperfect, thin as it was—also produced other unintended consequences. The modern elite in Indian society of course began to inhabit this new social conceptual world with relative ease. But very soon they turned the political point of this discourse against colonial authority itself, earning (not entirely unjustifiably) notoriety for their ingratitude. They came to nurture internal dissatisfactions, which arose out of figuring the political world out in the modernist-rationalist way. Indian nationalism, at least the form in which it came to be enshrined in the Congress, was primarily a product of this discourse, a complex of dissatisfactions worked out by the modernist-rationalistic elite. It is necessary to analyse the internal logic of this body of ideas more carefully.

The Syllogistic Structure of Nationalism

The first item in this ideology was of course the double complaint about the economics of colonialism. Contrary to the justificatory argument given in favour of imperialism, it seemed to impoverish the colony to enrich the metropolis. Politically, the rationalist conception of the world strongly emphasized autonomy and self-determination, and it was inconsistent to promote the autonomy of the individual and

On State, Society, and Discourse in India 21

discourage it for collective entities like the nation. This was particularly so because a connection between the economic and political arguments of this rationalist liberalism seemed natural and politically inviting. To the early nationalist elite this connection was so clear as to be put into a nearly syllogistic form.

1. The proposal of rationalistic modernity was rationally acceptable, and indeed deeply desirable. It was rational to wish to live in a civilization structured according to rationalist principles. And the picture of this civilization was one that emerged in Europe. The new elite looked covetously at that part of European history.
2. Originally, colonialism may have seemed an ally in this process, through its support for social reform. But as its logic unfolded, colonialism seemed to be a more complex and sinister process, incompatible with its declared ideology. Instead of helping, it hindered politico-economic development in the direction of capitalism, liberalism, modernity. Instead of creating a worldwide commonwealth of societies moving in parallel, if somewhat unequal, motion towards this rationalist, liberal modernity, it exploited colonies and made it difficult for them to embark on such a path.
3. The rationalist argument itself suggested a different course. Liberal democracy, based on individual and collective self-determination, was rationally the best form of government. Collective self-determination implied a movement to end colonial rule in India, to take national destiny into 'our own' hands. Once colonialism was removed, all these ideals could be realized. The political form would naturally be some sort of universal suffrage democracy, and what this sovereign state would try to achieve would of course be what had already been accomplished in the West, in other words a re-enactment. Although startling in some ways, this shows how strong the relations are between the positions advocated by earlier nationalists like Naoroji,[6] and later, far more radical ones, like Nehru, if seen in terms not of political ideology but of the discourse about history. Of course, the differences are fundamental and obvious: Naoroji expected the colonial power to accomplish this re-enactment (Or did he? Was he really pretending to be trapped inside their ideology in order to stretch it to its limits, bring it to a crisis, and reveal itself?). Nehru had no such illusions. Re-enactment for

---

[6] The most celebrated work by Dadabhai Naoroji, which illustrates my point. See Naoroji 1901.

Naoroji would have meant the happy replication in India of the desirable society of nineteenth-century *laissez faire* capitalism of England—liberal, property-oriented, unequal. By Nehru's time what was to be re-enacted had altered in several ways. The ideal model itself had been restructured by the internal critiques of Western political reason, through socialism, to issue forth a more redistributivist model of democracy. But a re-enactment it remained. The historical task for the movement of Indian nationalism, led by its modernist middle class, was not to invent an ideal adequate to the structure, pressure, or logic of Indian history, that is, the structure and discursive possibilities of their own society and history. It was to follow tasks, models, ideals, and historical paths that were universal, but enacted earlier only in Europe, through discourses that were equally universal.

This point should be made with some care. Nothing is simpler than a sort of anachronistic criticism of nationalist leaders, accusing them of not seeing things that were revealed only by later history. As nationalists they were intensely conscious of the peculiarity and specificity of their own history. What they made appears to be not a political but a cognitive mistake, along with their generation of social scientists. They acted on an uncomplex and overrationalistic theory of social change. First of all, they considered all 'forward' transformations irreversible, because they assumed that, given the basic rationality of all men, there could be no two opinions about their progressiveness. It will be seen that the picture I have drawn is similar to the one offered in recent years by observers like Kothari, Nandy, and Madan.[7]

This kind of theory is unlikely to be valid or universally popular, but it could create difficulties in a different direction, in the internal compatibility of principles. If much of Indian society did not agree with a single rationality or its single, dominant construction, given an adult suffrage democracy, it could lead to paradoxes. Democracy works, alas, on a sociological theory of truth. It allows to members of the largest number the right to act upon the political world, assuming that their beliefs about how it was were the true ones. And they can go on

---

[7] Kothari 1988; Nandy 1986; Nandy 1988; Madan 1987. There are some serious differences which will become clear as we proceed. I have considerable sympathy with what they say has been happening in India, but not with their views about why it is happening, and what should be done about it, and finally about how *we* relate to the relevant discursive structures.

building the political world for the relevant period of the 'truthfulness' of their views. This brings us to the elite–mass relation in the last phase of the nationalist movement, because after freedom that would be written as the state–society relation. The elite's view of the truth of the political world would become the state's view—though there are various serious internal limits to this, because a state as vast as modern India's is deeply stratified, and the lower elements of the bureaucracy would hardly share the rationality of the elites at the commanding heights. There could be subtle and subterranean resistance from some layers of society. For although the masses in times of great political movements follow their elites, they do not surrender the confidentiality of their political world. From the analytical point of view, however, it may be difficult to produce maps of these ideas or plot their cognitive terrain, because unlike the ideas of the elite and the state which are constantly broadcast, propagated, repeated, theirs are less structured. But precisely for that reason they might be excellent as defensive weapons.

The colonial period saw the appearance of two types of divisions in Indian society: the discursive division between those who made the world they inhabited intelligible via modernist discourse, and those who did not. This division ran decisively between the Indian elite and the lower orders. On top of it, however, nationalism put in place a political division between colonialism and the Indian nation. I consider Gandhi's discourse, or rather his discursive position, to be of crucial importance. This is not because he created a discourse of inexhaustible originality, as some argue; but his kind of discourse managed to bridge the gulf between the two sides, and keep the values, objectives, and conceptions of the world of the two sides intelligible to each other.

The Indian national movement did not produce an inevitable Nehruvian result. The way in which Nehru was able to shape the ideals of the Indian state after Independence was partly a result of some fortuitous circumstances. No logic of the previous movements, no wave, made it necessary for the Nehruvian elite to come to power, but there was something deeper which went in favour of this modernist dominance at the time of Independence. He enjoyed a silent but subtle and massively significant cultural approval among the modern elite. Members of this class, dispersed thinly but crucially throughout the governmental and modern sectors, approved spontaneously the assumption of power by a rationalist 'philosopher king'—though some of them knew that he might incline towards a statist radicalism common in the 1940s and 1950s. However, this did not represent a serious discontinuity at the level of discourse. Entrepreneurial groups and politicians favouring the propertied classes knew that they would have differences with Nehru on socialism, the state sector, redistribution, foreign policy, land reforms, the state's power to take away property, and so on. But these were comprehensible differences, differences of political ideology among those who inhabited the same social discourse. Political disagreement is of course a form of successful communication.

A paradox of mobilization made this early period of political construction in India relatively easy. If the divergent types of political discourse, with what they considered to be politically rational, their incommensurable ideals, had simultaneously found utterance in Indian political life, it might have been exceedingly difficult to carry on institutional formation. But the backwash of mobilization of the national movement ensured an implicit trust within the masses in the initiatives of their leaders. Thus these various conflicting discourses were not brought immediately into dialogue on equal terms. During the nationalist struggle there had occasionally been distinct initiatives from the lower orders when political space was opened up within the national movement. But recent historical research has also shown how quickly the main Congress leadership was able to shut off such space, or bring their movements under control. Thus the support that the Congress leadership received was not of the kind that the bourgeoisie in classical bourgeois revolutions of the West created for themselves, by reconstituting through a process of prior cultural movement a hegemony and directive pre-eminence for themselves. Ordinary people were mobilized in the Indian national movement in tremendous numbers, but not by creating hegemony of this kind. At the same time, as the failure of the communist moves towards insurgency indicated, subaltern groups were not ready to break with the bourgeois nationalist leadership and prepared to take large world-constructing actions on their own.

This led to several consequences. First, of course, the setting up of political institutions passed off relatively peacefully; the Constituent Assembly, though strangely unrepresentative, still represented a sufficient consensus of the organized groups to bring off a constitution which was not seriously contested. At the same time, internal realignments within the Congress led to serious political decisions.

The systematic exodus of the socialist left from the Congress weakened Nehru considerably inside the party that he formally commanded, but the death of Patel also left his own personal eminence uncontested. He was therefore free to pursue a set of policies about which his party colleagues were not wholly enthusiastic. The construction he placed on secularism, for instance, was clearly resented by a section of Congress leaders. His drive for redistributive policies of land reforms met with serious, if undeclared, hostility from his own party's lower-level leadership. Most Congress leaders were more lukewarm than Nehru about developing friendly relations with the Soviet Union. Few understood in a clear theoretical form the logic of the massive heavy industrialization drive that he pursued through the second Five Year Plan. This shows in a sense a miraculous contingency of some of the central segments of the fairly impressive institutional structure that Congress under Nehru built up. But precisely because of his relative isolation within his own party, Nehru undertook another initiative which has seemed over the long run to overshadow other parts of his institutional strategy.

Nehru began to create a base, an alternative apparatus, in the bureaucracy. Planning, on a large scale from 1956 onwards, made for a great extension of an economic bureaucracy inside government. As the rhetoric of social justice and redistribution increased, this bureaucracy expanded rapidly. This differed from classical European bourgeois revolutions, where capitalism first emerged in initiatives and in institutions within civil society, and the state was later used as an instrument to correct its spontaneous production of inequality. In India there was no developed civil society and many of capitalism's classical initiatives within civil society were undertaken by the state.[8] The most serious consequence of this, of course, was that the state became omnipresent, since it was performing functions left to the institutions of civil society, and it was impossible to abjure transactions with this state. At the same time, it could work only through the techniques of an unreconstructed colonialist bureaucratic style, wholly monological, criminally wasteful, utterly irresponsible and unresponsive to public sensitivity. Its history had made it ill equipped to be civil or solicitous, or to explain itself. And naturally its manner, rather than its policies, was bound to create a scramble. Those after power would want to

---

[8] I have advanced an argument of this kind. See Kaviraj 1989b.

get into its seats, completely screened as they appeared to be from accountability, and those who could not get into them would become increasingly alienated.

The manner and structure of capitalist growth accentuated such differences. Instead of reducing regional inequalities, capitalism intensified them and tended to concentrate opportunities and resources in centres of political power. The cultural consequences of this process have not been analysed carefully until recently. Over the long term, the strategy of development in India, precisely through its relative successes, has tended to reopen the deep division of discourse in Indian society between a homogenizing elite-speaking English, the Esperanto of the upper orders, and a vast lower-order population looking and speaking with an intense vernacular hostility against some of the consequences of this form of capitalist development.

The Nature of Indian Nationalism

From this point of view it appears justified to say with Rajni Kothari that the first phase of Indian politics was built on a kind of consensus.[9] But Kothari seems to have misjudged the nature of the consensus he identified, and its possibilities. It was of course an elite consensus, which passed uncontested because of its nearness to the mobilization of the national movement, and the relation of implicit trust between its leadership and the masses. It was a consensus of discourse, rather than of ideological positions. The institutional pattern that Nehru wished to put in place came up against serious ideological criticism from the left, especially the socialists and the communists. But there *was* still a commonality at a different level: they had very different things to say about the political world, its structure, purposes, and ideals, but they shared a common way of arguing about these things. This seemed to create real divisions among them, which was what they primarily saw. But it also created underlying unities among them when looked at from outside this discourse, which is what must have impressed the other classes and groups in Indian society. The constitutional frame that was adopted, though it was exhaustingly detailed (and therefore a lawyers' constitution rather than a citizens'), still was silent and vague on various questions. And although the ideological

[9] Kothari 1970.

conflicts in the Constituent Assembly went in favour of a more conservative reading of the Congress programme, the Nehru regime took significant steps immediately afterwards to counteract this in actual policy. The Planning Commission, soon to become the actual centre of economic policy-making, remained outside the formal constitutional framework. Initially the federal structure worked through the federalism inside the Congress Party rather than constitutional channels. The regime of rights, centred on the individual subject, made legal concessions to minority rights which could be enjoyed by people only as members of communities, rather than as bourgeois individuals. But despite these underlying problems, which took some time to break out into the open, the achievements of the Nehru regime were massive by any standards. True, some of this was fortuitous, and caused by the fortunate overdetermination at the time of freedom. But one can clearly see that, given a slightly different turn of events, India could have had a very different set of foundational policies, and these most likely would have been relatively retrograde.

It is in the economic sphere that Nehru's policies have enjoyed the greatest long-term success, though at the start his government often seemed on the point of being overwhelmed by financial and resource difficulties. By the time he became prime minister, Nehru had moved away from his 'scientific socialist' beliefs, though importantly he would still have characterized his beliefs as scientific; from his point of view he had moved away from socialist doctrine because it was not scientific. He had given up that construction of socialism, but he had not given up science. Still, his commitment to a British Labour version of social democracy made him interfere with what others would have considered the more 'natural' course of capitalist growth. Indeed, Nehru's certainties were shaped by and shared with the emerging discourses of social theory, soon to be inscribed on the whole world in the form of reformist Keynesian economism in all sectors of public policy. The economic growth of society was predicated on the building of the industrial sector. In this, heavy capital goods industries took precedence, and since these could not be built by private capital, this led to the steady growth of a large public sector with strong links to ministerial bureaucracies.[10] In this milieu, it was subtly misleading to speak in

---

[10] For a detailed historical argument, rich in empirical detail, see Frankel 1977.

the language of the interventionist state, and to transfer, implicitly, a whole set of expectations from the European case; because that was a language on which the history of European capitalism was inscribed quite clearly. In Europe, the state did 'intervene' in a society whose basic structures had earlier been formed by civil society, and the existence of a strong civil society made the state act in responsible ways. In India, where there was no prior civil society, one could hardly talk of an interventionist state since many of those institutions were brought into existence by the state. Therefore, in a subtle but significant way, the direction of the descriptive language and justificatory rhetoric was wrong.

Some of the problems with this kind of economic planning have been noted for a long time. Even economists who favour the state sector and its leading role agree that the planning models probably neglected the question of agriculture. Not surprisingly, the Nehru regime faced both economic and political difficulties arising out of food shortages during the late 1950s. The theoretical fault in all this was that the regime worked, along with all others thinking about development at the time (irrespective of ideological positions), with a heavily reductive economistic theory of social change. Economic arguments tended to be aggressively ahistorical. Everything else was turned into problems for which economic policies had the solutions. The sequence in which the sectors had emerged, their specific institutional forms, how the historical sequence of their emergence could have affected their institutional logic—such questions were seldom asked. There is a minor irony in this, since much of this discussion was analysed by Marxism, and Marxism at least in its classical form, is deeply sensitive to sequences and trajectories.

Second, the irresistible bureaucratization of social life, in the absence of the structures of civil society, created difficulties. But the effects of this politics on the discursive map of Indian society were interesting, and these have not been carefully analysed. The structure of Nehruvian democracy was raised on an anomalous base. It did represent, as some of its admirers put it lyrically, the greatest experiment with democracy in the history of the world, but that was possible partly because the large masses on whom these rights were conferred found them too unfamiliar at first to use them immediately. Planning was aimed not only at the construction of a wide industrial base, but also at the reduction of some of the gross inequalities in incomes. Nehru certainly saw the alleviation of poverty as a condition for genuine democracy, but it depended increasingly on the monologic instruments of the state and its bureaucracy rather than dialogical, movement-like forms. The falling apart of the Gandhian language in Indian politics, which had reduced for a time the hostile unfamiliarity between elite and subaltern political semiotics, contributed to this widening gap, accentuating this ironical divergence between populist government policies and popular consciousness. And the discourse of the elite tended to turn increasingly inwards, in two senses. First, the debates were directed at intelligibility and justifiability in terms of the political stances of the high discourse, leaving the task of formation of a vernacular, popular discourse around these questions to an unmindful educational policy. Second, there was a further tendency in later years to withdraw issues of development from public arenas of discussion and to surrender them to so-called expert groups, creating a sort of elite confidentiality around vital decisions about politics and society.

It must be acknowledged that Nehru personally was conscious of this withdrawal and sought to continue to publicize the development debate. But it was not a matter so much of the personal predilections of leaders, but a tendency of the structure of development strategy. Indian democracy remained vibrant, with occasional mass movements being able to register their demands on the state, as with the regional autonomy movements of the 1950s and the food movements some years later. So the enormous extension of the state was not coercive but remained external. The elite around Nehru were sensitive about retaining democratic forms and pursuing, within what they considered to be reasonable limits, the reformist aspirations of the state. But they did not see the problem of its externality. In retrospect, its basic failure seems to have been the near-total neglect of the question of the cultural reproduction of society. It did not try deliberately to create or reconstitute popular common sense about the political world, taking the new conceptual vocabulary of rights, institutions, and impersonal power into the vernacular everyday discourses of rural or small-town Indian society. It neglected the creation of a common thicker we-ness (something that was a deeper sense of community than merely the common opposition to the British) and the creation of a single political language for the entire polity.

Thus, unnoticed by the bustling technocracy of the modern sector, the transient links across the political and discursive divide tended to give way. The independent Indian state followed a programme of modernity which was not sought to be grounded in the political vocabulary of the nation, or at least of its major part. As a result, precisely those ideals—of a modern nationalism, industrial modernity, secular state, democracy and minority rights—came in the long run to appear not as institutions won by a common national movement but as ideals intelligible to and pursued by the modern elite which inherited power from the British. More than that: subtle and interesting things began to happen to this logic of 'modernization' which have gone unnoticed in the works of its supporters and opponents. Precisely because the state continued to expand, precisely because it went in a frenetic search of alibis to control ever larger areas of social life, it had to find its personnel, especially at lower levels, from groups who did not inhabit the modernist discourse. Thus it is wrong to believe that the Indian state or its massive bureaucracy is a huge Weberian organization binding a relaxed, fuzzy, slow-moving society in its iron structure. What has actually been happening is more complex. By overstretching, the state has been forced to recruit personnel from groups that speak and interpret the world in terms of the other discourse. Since major government policies have their final point of implementation very low down in the bureaucracy, they are reinterpreted beyond recognition.

As a result of its uncontrolled growth, the policies of the state have also lost some of their cohesion. If one does not have a purely romantic view of the Indian past, one can see the direction this reinterpretation of government policies, this utilization of internal space for lower-level initiative, would take. It is not surprising that arguments of social justice are often used as an unanswerable justification for the encouragement of nepotism and corruption. Indeed, there is very little corruption in India that is not practised in the name of high moral principles. The actual conduct of those in authority has also tended in recent years to slide backwards towards a more historically 'familiar' style of irresponsible power, with the withdrawal of significant decisions, under various excuses, from the arenas of public criticism and responsibility. It must be seen, while debating the effects and justifications of modernity, that these trends come straight out of India's glorious past.

However, the point here is not to tell the story of Indian politics, or to present a convincing periodization. In the accepted ways of standard social science, the story has been told many times over. Indeed, my point is that despite those familiar narratives of the achievements and failures of Indian democratic institutions, there appears to be another story to be told. This seems to be sketchily glimpsed by many recent observers of Indian politics, but no one seems to know what it is a story of. I am quite clear that this ambiguity is reflected in the curious way I have just presented the problem. I think it can be sorted out in a preliminary way by using the distinction between political ideology and structures of discourse, and acknowledging that the classifications that can be produced by their different criteria look quite different. I should like to look at some of these diagnoses of the recent problems of the Indian state, and move our discussion towards some theoretical conclusions.

Political Diagnoses

One of the punctuations generally observed in Indian politics is the spectacular difference between the Nehru period, which ended in 1964, and the later one. There is a further division: the electoral instability of governments in the period after the fourth general elections in 1967 has since been changed into a more serious and frightening uncertainty about the state form itself. On the one side the political behaviour of party leaders and managers seems to discredit the institutions of democracy; on the other, sometimes popular anger against such political games has assumed a form in which it seems that it might pass into a vote of no confidence on the state form itself.

What has been the historical record of this complex of institutions? This question has been discussed so often that only some of its implications need to be assessed. But we must also keep in view the standard and fairly reasonable defence by Nehru's followers (in ideas, not in party affiliation: indeed, the Congress Party under later leaders has been the main destroyer of the institutional logic that Nehru sought to make safe) that forty years is too short a span for institutions to take root or to adapt them to a very different historical milieu. But even in the short term, its achievements are not negligible. Unlike in most other Third World states, a formal democratic constitution was not initially adopted, to be dropped soon after in favour of dictatorial authority. In fact, the way the Emergency ended in India showed the great ideological depth of the democratic idea. Mrs Gandhi believed that even the record of the Emergency regime had to be electorally justified. Often, however, other achievements of the Nehruvian model are clouded in a discussion either of pure economic growth, in which dictatorial regimes accepting subordinate productive roles in the international capitalist system are shown to be remarkably superior to India's record in growth rates, or of radical theories based on strategic ignorance which show the distributive advantages of a communist economy. But industrialization in India, though wasteful in many ways, has a wide base. And the institutional form of the economy has ensured that its political sovereignty has not been renegotiated through extreme economic pressure. All these relative achievements are undeniable, but this shows the present predicament of the Indian state in a curious light. For the state is not threatened by forces from outside. On the contrary, most powers acknowledge its resilience and regional dominance. It appears threatened from inside. Its difficulties arise not because its performance was bad, but rather from what its rulers would no doubt consider among its modest achievements. And, most remarkably, the institutional forms that the early nationalist leadership created for the benefit and well being of the common people seem to have come under greater pressure as more and more common people have entered into the spectacle of party politics.

This then is the basic form of the paradox of democracy in India. It is undoubtedly true that some of Indira Gandhi's electoral moves and the rhetoric used consistently by all political parties—of popular participation, the realization of rights, the eradication of poverty—have led to a greater political articulateness among ordinary people. To that extent high politics, even in the spectacular arenas, which were earlier the preserves of a modernist elite, are coming under pressure from the alphabet of the lower discourse. It seems, however, that the more the ordinary people have written their minds into the format of politics, the greater the pressure or threat has been on democratic structures—as generally understood in terms of Western precedents. There seems to be some incompatibility between the institutional logic of democratic forms and the logic of popular mobilization. The more one part of the democratic ideal is realized, the more the other part is undermined. The paradox, to put it in the way in which T.N. Madan has done,[11] is that if Indian politics becomes

[11] Madan 1987.

genuinely democratic in the sense of coming into line with what the majority of ordinary Indians would consider reasonable, it will become less democratic in the sense of conforming to the principles of a secular, democratic state acceptable to the early nationalist elite. What seems to have begun in Indian politics is a conflict over intelligibility, a writing of the political world that is more fundamental than traditional ideological disputes. It appears that the difference between the two discourses is reappearing, now that the lower discourse is asserting itself and making itself heard precisely through the opportunities created by the upper one. The way it rewrites the political world might not be liked by the ruling modernist elites, but it is too late to disenfranchise them.

This is an interesting and challenging line of thought, and very different from earlier diagnoses of political difficulties in India. Earlier, social scientists usually began by expressing solidarity with the project of introducing modernity, equating modernity with a re-enactment of the European drama. (Indeed, there was no Asian drama to stage at all. What occurred in India was merely the Asian premier of the European narrative, luckily with an appropriately cultivated cast.) They expressed irritation or puzzlement at the obduracy with which the society seemed to resist it, and such resistance was generally accounted for by a simple, malignant form of direct political agency—corruption, lack of political will, and so on. The explanation that I am proposing seeks a less agency-oriented answer to the difficulties; it is prepared to be puzzled by deeper questions and is ready to turn the questions around towards social science itself. From this perspective, the equation is to be arranged not between a rational programme prepared by the elite and carried out by an instrumentally viewed state on the one hand, and a resisting, irrational society on the other—but the other way around. Indian politicians of the Nehru type made a mistake very similar to the one that has now been, a trifle theatrically, traced through the entire history of social science. Western social theory moved from a sort of high orientalism practised by Marx and Weber to a very inadequate theory of modernization worked out by Parsonian developmentalists, a move often celebrated as from philosophy to science, but in fact from tragedy to farce.

Nothing is more disorienting than when our fundamental taxonomies are turned around and we blink within a world in which things occupy entirely unaccustomed places. This argument tries something like this about development thinking in India. Clearly, many Indian social scientists carried on their earlier debates within a world which was firmly held by the solid homogenizing taxonomies established by nationalist beliefs. Most political argument was internal to these boundaries. The emergence of such arguments in serious social theory shows that the pervasiveness, the self-evidentiality of the nationalist construction of the world is gradually fraying and disappearing. It has been argued forcefully in recent years, by social scientists like Chatterjee, Nandy, and Madan,[12] that the state and the ruling elite uncritically adopted an orientalist, externalist construction of their society and its destiny reflected in the wonderful and tragic symbolism of 'the discovery of India'. Its initiatives were bound to be one-sided. To the world of India's lower orders, it simply refused or merely forgot to explain itself. Indeed to some it would have seemed that the Indian elite was more concerned about justifying its initiatives to external audiences than to its own. Historically, its absentmindedness about cultural unity has driven apart the political diglossia of the national movement, held together in a sense by the easy bilingualism of its political leaders and cultural intelligentsia. Today, that cultural terrain is increasingly broken into a unilingual English-speaking elite, and equally monolingual conglomerate of regional groups which are losing a dialogical relation not only with the upper strata but between languages as well, leading to greater friction and hostility across regions.

The implications of this critique must be seen clearly. It has brought into question the cognitive, the political, and the moral legitimacy of the whole institutional regime constructed after Independence. Of the whole lot—the impersonal nature of public power, the rule of law, the democratic order, the idea of a complex and composite nation, a secular polity—it asks whether it is legitimate for a relatively small elite to impose their ideals on others who do not necessarily share them. It also asks if this political form, because of its unintelligibility, can be worked by this people. It must be seen that it moves from moral to cognitive questions to radicalize its critique. It must also be clear that these questions are addressed not only to the Indian political or modernist ruling elite, but also to social theory in equal measure—because they can be

[12] See Chatterjee 1986; Madan 1987; Nandy 1988.

logically so directed, and also because it is these theories—which the elite believed—that gave them the intellectual justification to do what they had undertaken.

But some of the more general, abstract, epistemic implications of this kind of argument should be noted. In a sense, this sort of theoretical discomfort tries to break from the vulgar pretensions of being a policy science (which posited too direct a relation between social science and government policy) and seeks to return to a more classical conception of political theory, as a kind of historical self-reflection of society. It assumes that one of the tests of good social theory is whether it can relevantly comment on what is happening in society, and contribute to a general management of social destiny. It rules out a distancing, reflective attitude to social and political questions. Its own performance must be as subject to this criterion of success as that of the previous theory that it rejects.

The approach which I am proposing offers more promise than do reassessments either of Gandhian ideas or of traditional Indian or Hindu thought. Gandhi did not seek an answer to the problems of the modern condition. He shrewdly refused to deal in modernity's terms. His answer was not about how modern conditions can be brought under cognitive and moral control, but that modernity as a condition should be abjured. In a sense he embraced a deliberate obsolescence. His critique of modernity is of course powerful and lucid, but too radical, for he offers not an alternative solution to modernity's problems, but to modernity itself. I do not therefore seriously expect help from the side of Gandhian theory, though as a student of the history of ideas I can see that there can be a great deal of good theory which flies the Gandhian flag; that a lot of good, interesting theory could be done by illegitimately using Gandhi's name.

It appears that one of the curious things about the Indian, or at least the Hindu, tradition is that although it has a high history of philosophical reflection, and though the political organization of society was highly pronounced, it lacks for some reason any strong tradition of applying this apparatus to the analysis and justification of political (it is perhaps possible to say social) phenomena. If language gives a kind of condensed history of a culture, this is reflected in the constant trouble over translating basic conceptual terms like society and state into the Indian languages. Thus, to find an indigenous vocabulary for making sense of the political world, going back to the indigenous tradition might not be very fruitful.

Even if there is a vocabulary, even if we pretend that it is interregionally sufficiently common, it will be a language that was adequate to state–society relations of the pre-modern form. The modern state cannot go back to the high ground in the middle of the circle of communities. The circles themselves cannot be made fuzzy again. There is certainly a great deal of humanity in the pre-modern languages of social living. Its sentiments are valuable, but its conceptual apparatus cannot work out solutions to modern calamities.

Theoretical Questions

It should be clear that the failures that we have examined here offer a potentially rich field for political theory to analyse. When even massive coercion fails to modernize or democratize nations, it is likely that these efforts are up against an intangible barrier, like the problem of conceptually reinventing a political world. That is why it seems necessary to return to the problem of theory for this whole field. This has been analysed so carelessly that it is still in a sense unnamed. For the 'Third World' is really the absence of a name. We must ask if this aggregation is defensible and look into its conceptual archaeology. It remains a negative and residual description, indicating the West's 'other'. And a negative otherness is particularly hard to theorize, because we are required to theorize what these societies are not.

Much of the blame for the blundering inadequacies of modern American development theory has been wrongly laid at the door of the Western tradition of high historical theory. This misreads the relationship between American social theory of the 1950s and its nineteenth-century European ancestry. It is to accept the past that American theory has given itself, shopping around in the earlier traditions of European social reflection. There were also critical self-limiting moves within European social theory which have not been studied with an equal seriousness in the eagerness to construct a paradigm. John Dunn has sought to revive, in a more radical fashion, some of these self-limiting moves of Western theory.[13] He engages Western theory in an unaccustomed task—of finding its limits, something which in the last

---

[13] See Dunn 1979.

century at least it had become unused to doing. In India, Partha Chatterjee has offered the interesting and powerful hypothesis that nationalists accepted the Orientalist construction of Indian society and the limitedness of social reconstruction, and the present difficulties of the state begin from there. This is not a cultural complement or a version of the dependency thesis, for this line of argument is far more self-critical and modest. Dependency theory believes that most third world states do what is wrong, but it has no doubt about what it means to do right. The new line of criticism is more radical: it appears to suggest that colonialism ruptures the self-relation of a society through time in such a fundamental way that it becomes difficult to imagine what would be right. It shows the task to be one of inventing right and wrong—the true function, according to one definition, of political philosophy.[14]

Dunn's book speaks in the cultured, civilized tone of withdrawing into Europe as a region in history. But the withdrawal of Europe is not going to be such a simple affair. Others would object to its withdrawal; because that would amount to withdrawing not a familiar theory, but the assurance of a familiar world which made this theory relevant. Others have named their *lebenswelt* through these ideas and have started inhabiting them. This of course alters them unrecognizably, as happens with European languages which others have made their own. Dunn thus takes a rather narrow view of the responsibilities of Western theory. In much of the world, it faces the future of others.

References

Anderson, Benedict. 1983. *Imagined Communities*. London: Verso.
Chatterjee, Partha. 1986. *Nationalist Thought and the Colonial World: A Derivative Discourse?* Delhi: Oxford University Press.
Dunn, John. 1979. *Western Political Theory in the Face of its Future*. Cambridge: Cambridge University Press.
Frankel, Francine. 1977. *India's Political Economy*. Princeton: Princeton University Press.

---

[14] T. Smith 1985 offers an understanding and wide-ranging critique of this whole field; but his criticisms of dependency are weaker and less pointed than they could have been. It seems that now it is time to do something like what Foucault would call an 'archaeology' of third world studies, or to provide something like an in-depth narrative of its epistemic and methodological structures.

Kaviraj, Sudipta. 1989a. On the Construction of Colonial Power. Paper presented at a seminar in Berlin on the Foundations of Colonial Hegemony, German Historical Institute, London.

———. 1989b. A Critique of the Passive Revolution. *Economic and Political Weekly*. Annual Number. March.

Kothari, Rajni. 1970. *Politics in India*. New Delhi: Orient Longman.

———. 1988. *The State Against Democracy*. Delhi.

Madan, T.N. 1987. Secularism in Its Place. *Journal of Asian Studies* 46 (4). November.

Nandy, Ashis. 1986. *The Intimate Enemy*. Delhi: Oxford University Press.

———. 1988. *Traditions, Tyranny, and Utopias*. Delhi: Oxford University Press.

Naoroji, Dadabhai. 1901. *Poverty and Un-British Rule in India*. London.

Skinner, Quentin. 1989. The State. In T. Ball, J. Farr, and R.L. Hanson, eds. *Political Innovation and Conceptual Change*. Cambridge: Cambridge University Press.

Smith, T. 1985. Requiem or New Agenda for Third World Studies? *World Politics*. July.

2

On the Construction of Colonial Power: Structure, Discourse, Hegemony

The ideas in this essay are a preliminary sketch towards a more theoretically informed model of the relation between power and discourse in colonial society in India. The language itself indicates the provisional nature of the arguments and the enterprise undertaken. But it is not enough to simply call it provisional; in order to know how to move towards more complete theoretical arguments one must clearly indicate the nature and grounds of this provisionality. Part of this tentativeness arises from my own professional limitation as a student of social theory. I have been asked to rush in where historians, the most well-informed group about colonial societies, fear to tread. Because of this strength, all study of colonialism must necessarily be compiled around the discipline of history. Yet a study of more abstract questions, such as the nature and structure of colonial power, cannot be produced by the unreconstructed discipline of history. Nor can it be produced by an unreconstructed state theory out of its own internal, purely conceptual, resources. The historical discipline, cautious and measured about facts, has to become more hospitable to more risky theoretical generalizations.[1] Colonial power or the state is not one of

First published in *Contesting Colonial Hegemony: State and Society in India and Africa*, eds D. Engels and S. Marks (London: Published for the British Academic Press and German Historical Institute by I.B. Tauris, 1994), pp. 19–54.

[1] Although historians have produced a rich and diverse literature of empirical material, they have rarely tried to gather the results of their collective research by asking a second-order question of this kind.

the classically constituted objects of either political theory or colonial history; it has to be constituted as an object at the frontier.[2] A proper object of historical sociology, it cannot be addressed until the two disciplines enter into a cognitive dialogue.

Colonialism is both a set of institutions, and also, emphatically, a set of discourses. Both these sets—of structures and discourses—change in their constitution over the long history of the colonial period. Yet while there is a general awareness of the historicity of such objects (would it not be curious if historians were not conscious of the historicity of their objects of analysis?), the kind of difficulty that this historicity introduces is not often appreciated. When we say any object in history presents an epistemic difficulty, we indicate by this the methodological necessity of differentiating between objects which are structurally different but genetically linked. These are usually problems of anachronism. But anachronism can be of two kinds. One of these is the danger of conflating a new kind of process or object with a class of things which belong to an earlier historical period, although historians are usually exceptionally sensitive to this danger.[3] Conventionally, however, the historiography of Indian nationalism has shown less acute awareness of a different type of anachronism due to the inextricability of the objects we seek to understand from the discourses which constitute them. These discourses are often shaped and determined by those processes themselves. In much of modern Indian history the object of analysis is nationalism, yet the categories, distinctions, and periodizations through which the historian approaches it are constituted by nationalism itself. To understand nationalism (or colonialism) objectively it is important to stand outside its history; and if that means standing outside its consequences, that is clearly impossible. This would mean, if the argument were taken to an extreme form, that to study history satisfactorily one must stand outside history. Clearly, this

---

[2] Political scientists have usually neglected this direction of research because of the curious but widely prevalent idea that events since 1947 constitute the present, and everything before is past and therefore appropriate material for the historian's enquiry. No less surprising is the fact that though the history of colonialism is such an obviously rich field for studying what a European-style state can and cannot do to societies, state theorists have paid little attention to colonial regimes as a specific state form.

[3] Of the kind discussed by Quentin Skinner in Skinner 1988.

raises in hard and distressingly unclear forms the familiar difficulties of Husserlian bracketing. Paradoxically, we cannot understand these objects properly if we do not in a way stand clear of their self-descriptions, i.e. the concepts or discourses which went with them. At the same time, we cannot stand outside so easily because our own discourse, by means of which we identify and argue, is sometimes derived, sometimes developed in dialogic relation with those discourses. The trouble is manifested in the unacceptability of an archimedian point, and the unacceptability of the evidence of purely internal descriptions.

Any attempt to understand the structures of the field of power under colonialism must contend with three interconnected things. At the first level are the political power relations, which present no mean difficulty of theoretical description, because in the early period they constitute a very irregular structure without the focus of a regime at the centre. As colonialism in India becomes more powerful, and extends over the whole subcontinent, these congeal into the peculiar forms of the colonial state. To understand this regime, however, it has to be placed in the context of two networks of temporal and conceptual relations: that is, within the tangled complex of memories and structural legacies of earlier regimes;[4] and in the space allowed it by the pre-existing structure of social relations. And these cannot be theorized or even described through the resources of conventional state theory with its traditional focus on linear transitions.

This state, secondly, is peculiarly dependent on and inextricable from certain discursive structures; its history must be written as part of the discourse of the Enlightenment, in terms of the rhythms, ruptures, and punctuations of that different history. Its power is believed to be derived, by both its functionaries and its critics, from the grand discourses of European rationalism—its theories, self-definitions,

---

[4] In India the ancestry of the colonial and post-colonial states has been analysed with markedly different emphases in Saberwal 1986, especially ch. 2, and Ravinder Kumar 1989: 27–49. While Saberwal's account emphasizes the segmentary nature of traditional Indian society, Ravinder Kumar's argument brings out, nonetheless, the reality of a long-term, united, cultural sensibility. The insights which form the core of both these arguments could perhaps be extended and brought together if something like a *Begriffsgeschichte* of fundamental concepts of Indian social life could be attempted. For methodological problems relating to this, see Koselleck 1985.

narratives, delusions, and strategies. It uses that discourse to define and describe itself, to negotiate and bring under control the alien social world it has entered. Others in this social world who have to deal with it, as enemies, friends, applicants for its favour, also see the centrality of this discourse to understanding its institutions and their logic of functioning. They pursue a great variety of strategies in order to do so. They were, after all, entering a myth-structure of Western invincibility and respected the indivisibility of myths. Some sought to master its occult powers[5]—by acquiring Western education and culture with an amazing, often ridiculous, thoroughness,[6] not neglecting table manners, and toilet styles. Others tried heroic translations, making figures of Hindu mythology speak flawlessly the language of English utilitarianism.[7] Still others tried to avoid its mesmerizing and polluting contact by turning inwards into indigenous discourse.[8] All produced interesting and complex unintended consequences. Conventions and concepts

---

[5] Occultness is of course a relative term. Just as some beliefs and acts of the natives appeared occult to Europeans, so the technology and social practices of the latter must have appeared magical to the natives: though I do not deny the possibility of an asymmetric explanation of the surprises in the two sides.

[6] Societies arrange their self-reflection quite often not through standard modern devices like history or academic sociology, but through creative writing and literature. It is true that in nineteenth-century Bengal imitations of European cultural practices were attempted with a rare thoroughness. Sociology—seen as scientific and empirical understanding of Bengali society—and historical analysis—attempting self-reflection on a larger scale—was not uncommon. But some of the best critical comments could be found in creative literature, a field in which long-standing skills were available. On the curricular construction of the intellectual soul, one of the best comments can be found in Tagore's early poem 'Bangaveer', in Tagore 1946.

[7] A striking example is the reconstructed Krishna in Bankimchandra Chattopadhyay's 'Krishnacharitra', in Vandyopadhyay and Das 1946–50.

[8] To take examples from Bengal (simply because I am more familiar with that literature), one could mention two contemporaries of Bankim—Bhudev Mukhopadhyay arguing his complex traditionalist case; and Ramakrishna Paramhansa who, accepting a traditional theory of the wastefulness of doctrinal disputations among religious paths, consequently spurned learned theological debates but crafted out a highly original combination of middle-class and folkish motifs in religious discourse. His advice to mistrust woman (allegedly to be blamed unilaterally for the ills of sexuality) and money matters enjoyed a not easily explicable success among the *bhadralok* élite of

of rationalist discourse, if not high theory, surrounded this state on every side, mediating crucially its relations with the three dissimilar and largely unrelated publics between which it stood, carrying on three discrepant dialogues, trying to render them into some coherence. In its dialogue with British public opinion it adopted a tone of reasonableness; with the indigenous middle class it carried on a dialogue through education and legislation; while *vis-à-vis* the sullenly distant popular masses it adopted primarily a monologue of force.[9]

Finally, all these structures and their constructions are to be captured in and through the conceptual discourses of colonial historiography within which we are all located. It would be wrong to forget that the discourse of colonial rationalism and the predominant discourse of modern social science have a common source, in the admittedly distant and complex philosophical discourse of modernity. I use the term 'construction' in my title with the full force of its ambiguity, for there are *two* constructions in this process: the discourse of colonialism tries to construct a state, and it is the discourses of present-day historiography which try to construct accounts of that construction. It will be interesting to determine what each historiographical trend sees in that discourse and what it leaves out, and what sorts of problems these varying constructs of the same historical object create for the gaining of historical truth. I shall in the present essay leave out the discussion of historiography, however. The term 'construction' implies at least two things: the processes of state-forming and historical description are both contingent processes, though once they occur they take on a semblance of necessity and self-evidence. By implication, their significance has to be assessed by setting them in a causal field of usually *inus* conditions,[10] and often by means of counterfactuals. Secondly, construction

---

Calcutta, who could hardly have achieved their professional success had they been naïve about monetary questions.

[9] It must be noticed that this relation between force and compliance assumed various forms over the different periods of colonial rule. It oscillated between a glum acquiescence to increasing rent burdens in times of peace, and dramatic violence at times when the peasantry decided to attempt defiance.

[10] J.L. Mackie has tried to move away from the criteria of necessity and sufficiency in the discussion of the everyday idea of causality, and suggested that we replace them by the much weaker notion of 'insufficient but necessary

implies a choice between alternative strategies of description and explanation in which, precisely because we choose one in preference to other possible candidates, we must give grounds why we do so.

The Structure of Society and the Space for the State

Colonialism is much written about, but there is great internal unevenness in the historical literature. Colonialism is, if anything, a political subject—at least from the nationalist and the imperialist points of view. Ironically, however, it is this political field which has received least theoretical attention. This can be illustrated by a discrepancy—which appears to me quite significant—between the economic and political treatments of the phenomenon of imperialism. Economic arguments about colonialism conventionally run along two different, but related, planes. There is of course a great wealth of purely descriptive accounts of the economic transactions central to the colonial experience. But, equally, these are often given a redescription through theoretical considerations of the nature of the colonial system, its central dynamics or laws of motion. Occasionally, such discussions reach an unhelpful level of theoretical generality, like the speculations—of uncertain cognitive value—about the colonial mode of production.[11] One is struck by the absence of comparable suggestions about the state or the field of power. Marxists have not (except on rare occasions) been willing to advance theses about different modes of domination or power because of widely prevalent reductionist beliefs.[12] It is singular that the great annals of the political history of colonialism have not been given a similar theoretical redescription through an enquiry into the nature and form of the colonial state.

Any argument about the state is parasitic upon the empirical evidence historians have provided about viceroyalties and administrations;

---

and unnecessary but sufficient' (*inus*) conditions. I think that this is the notion of causality most appropriate to historical discussions. See Mackie 1975: 15–38.

[11] See Alavi 1975: 160–97.

[12] In India the clear exception is the attempt by Partha Chatterjee: see Chatterjee 1985. Others, including a few belonging to the Subaltern Studies group, have gingerly made approaches in that direction.

and a case for a separate study of the colonial state can be made only if the new theoretically informed redescription is significantly different. What then goes into this suggested redescription, or what kind of question are we reproving the historians for not asking?

The historical literature on British imperialism in India is vast, but even detailed descriptive accounts do not ask some general and abstract questions. For instance, the success or failure of individual policies through which the British sought to gain control over the society they had conquered depended on their feeling their way into the structural map of this society; but historical accounts are usually reluctant to enter into large sociological questions about the structure of the earlier social form. Fairly detailed administrative histories do exist, but they rarely ask what kind of state colonialism put in place through its series of administrative and legislative measures. Similarly, there are accounts of popular disturbances, disapprovingly or lovingly told, but they did not, until recently, try to get at the structure of popular discourse.[13] Of course, these accounts contribute towards a study of the colonial state, or of popular discourses, but they cannot directly constitute it. A historian of the colonial state has to study the accounts of Curzon's viceroyalty attentively, but when he uses that account it undergoes a crucial transformation, because he is studying an object of a different class. In a manner of speaking he is studying other happenings through the happenings of the period, and the difference between these two orders of happenings is not just a matter of *scale*. To write a history of the state has to be distinguishable from a history of politics written over very long rhythms. If this is true, then to try to address these questions in the same idiom would be to commit a category mistake.

It would be wrong, however, to stress only this analytic difference. The internal logic of historical evidence impels its enquiry to turn, to alter its nature, to transform the axial question it addresses. All the stories about conquest or administration or dissent told in straightforward historical narratives, with such scrupulous sense of limits, evidence and boundary, are, in a commonsensical way, at least implicitly seen

---

[13] In the case of the history of popular politics, these two stages of enquiry seem to be condensed into a single one. Subaltern Studies historians are having to do both—compile detailed historical accounts of popular resistance, and, at the same time, delineate the structure of popular discourse.

as part of the narrative of colonial rule in India, as the descriptively unnarratable story of the British empire. Of course, a story of the British empire can also be narratively told, and has indeed been told by many historians. But to tell that story there are choices to be made at every turn about what is to be told, what deserves a place; and the larger and more inclusive the story the more crucial such choices. These choices are theoretical; or perhaps, as the more scrupulous would say, narrative decisions have to be made which are only theoretically defensible. When confronted with an infinite object, like the British empire in India, the first cognitive strategy, or cognitive step, must be theoretical. It can be a Hegelian sum of all such different and to some measure discordant stories; and therefore it cannot be a story of the same kind. In such cases the narrative of governments and administration would already have begun to turn into a theoretical narrative of the colonial state. This turn is caused by both internal and external logic, the internal evidence of the historical material as well as the attempt to provide theoretical constructs.

Thus the sceptical objection—is such an enterprise necessary or worth the effort?—can be given a preliminary answer. There is no choice. The accumulation of evidence, both in its infinity and its internal variance, forces us towards a theoretical solution of the difficulties. Besides, it can be argued that there is a necessary relation of sequence between the historical and theoretical discourses, of the type Hegel suggests in his *Phenomenology* of the stages by which knowledge emerges.[14]

Yet it must be said that the history of the colonial state has not begun to be written. The reason for this can be found in part in the immense cognitive indebtedness of Indian nationalist history to the academic conventions of British empiricist historiography. Clearly, despite its great ideological disagreements with much of British historiography, it implicitly accepted the epistemological programme of British empiricist social science, and British philosophy has been hostile to what it considered—in my judgement falsely—metaphysical questions like the state, basing its arguments on a logical positivist realism which

[14] What I mean by this is that without descriptive histories, and without the questions posed by their intractable internal complexity, a second-order enquiry is really not possible.

mistrusted these as false questions.[15] Justifiably mistrustful of large, sonorous and analytically elusive abstractions which stood in unhelpful majesty across the path of sober historical investigation, it has often closed off the possibilities of generalizations arising out of its own teeming discourse. Yet the interest in the idea of the construction of a hegemonic process around the colonial regime, which is inextricable from the ideas of the state or a field of power, shows a movement towards sociological theory, and opens up the prospect of interesting interdisciplinary constructions which might eventually change the whole way of doing history.

I consider the concept of hegemony to be inseparable from the question of the state. All the theoretical connections they indicate run in the same direction. There are at least two obvious similarities. They operate on the same level of generality or abstraction; and both of the concepts are relational: they do not indicate or refer to entities with clear boundaries, but fields with fuzzy edges. In them one must see the whole of the colonial world reflected in the grain of a term. The quality of both concepts does not lie in their large coverage of the political world but in their specific manner of describing political things, providing us with a conceptual node to which all significant lines of relationship must run. Once the colonial state gets built up it becomes the controlling structure through which all proposals of power and dissent are mediated. But control can mean, as it does in this case, not interference in basic processes of production and everyday life-forms, but rather the judicious exercise of a veto.

Following Wittgenstein and some recent deconstructive theorists one can say that concepts carry a metaphorical charge: they carry along with them some intuitive and sharply perceptible 'pictures', and it is these which determine our choice and preference about them rather than their purely rational explanatory force. The intuitive picture that goes with the state is that of a 'power field', a *champs* in Bourdieu's terms, rather than the strongly bounded, vertical picture of an administration. The effectiveness of a structure of power depends quite often on the precise balance of formal and informal relations within and

---

[15] A good example is T.D. Weldon's famous stricture against using any aggregative or collective entity which cannot in principle be found in the telephone directory. See Weldon 1953: 36–7.

around these structures themselves. After all, most states function within legitimating discourses of their making and sanctioning, but these often contain indispensable implements of control which are impossible to bring into the open universe of discourse.

There are some operations which wielders of power consider both vital and unmentionable. Purely administrative histories find it difficult to name such things. Formal implements of governance quite often depend on informal mechanisms which cannot by their very nature be part of the declared world of political language; and formal histories, while being scrupulously correct about their own self-described sphere, may lead us away from the truth by their inability to pronounce about these regions of shadow and guilt. Power and state, being relational concepts, help us bring out the hidden resources and levels of domination, if not by spelling them out directly, at least by acknowledging them through their consequences.

Hegemony is a similarly relational idea; for it is a condition which cannot be described without inscribing in every part of the equation of subordination and dominance. The nature of the superordination of the dominant groups also contains the description of the mode of subalternity of the masses. The two-sidedness is conceptual, and not descriptive. Its use does not mean that at every stage both sides of this world have to be portrayed; it is a manner of portraying in which from a description of one side the condition of the other can be inferred, in however underdetermined a way. On one reading, hegemony is a term which is an antonym, or a continuum, opposite to repression. Thus it immediately brings into analytic focus the existence of cultural, discursive conditions for formal power. In the colonial setting, hegemony refers to the conventional modes of arranging compliance to constituted authority, and this authority's search for a *langue* which makes such compliance assured and habitual.

Before we begin the more concrete argument about the processes of legitimation of the colonial regime (because I take the idea of 'imperial hegemony' as a translation for this problem), it is necessary to state that compliance, as opposed to hegemony in the narrow sense, can be arranged in two different ways, requiring different analytical and conceptual strategies for their explanation. Political compliance can be induced by structural reasons, peculiar configurations of social institutions which make it unusually difficult for the lower orders in society to identify and attack structures of dominance. This compliance may have little to do with the second source of compliance, the political–moral hegemony of the ruling elite. I need to state this because the argument I advance about the arrangement of compliance in colonial India uses both types of ideas. Secondly, it is perhaps better to state some mild criticism of a tendency towards an over-rationalistic conception of political control in some of Gramsci's writings. Occasionally, it appears that he overstates the extent to which compliant political action of the lower orders must be based in reasons in a circle of common sense, which requires in turn a wholly porous boundary between the discourses of the hegemonic and subaltern classes. This model of the discursive field may not leave room for the techniques of secrecy and confidentiality that are discussed for instance in Bakhtin's analysis of lower-order discourse.[16]

When constructing the picture of a political field, the usual, almost reflex move of political theorists is to do so around the central concept of the state, to place it in our taxonomies of the state. Here it is worth alluding briefly to the debate about the connection between the concept of the state and the idea of publicity. The argument advanced by some theorists is that the state is not a name for any arrangement of power, but one that requires a certain publicity of its power arrangements. This affiliates the 'stateness' of regimes to modernity in a way that raises powerful and I think interesting questions, for in both imperial and nationalist arguments about the nature of the colonial regime there were considerations about the impersonal and public quality of political power. It had to be central to that debate because publicity is of course vitally linked to democracy and, strange though it is, both sides sought to use arguments from democratic theory to support their very different political claims about what was good for the country.

---

[16] It is notoriously difficult to judge when subaltern groups are really persuaded of the 'justice' of the initiatives of hegemonic classes, and acquiesce in them, and when they merely pretend to do so, surrounding their actual beliefs by a wall of mockery and travesty-obedience. Both are possible strategies, and ought to be part of the standard arsenal of historians interested in their role in history. Bakhtin's work on travesty, though formally part of literary theory, has much to offer to the historian of subaltern groups. See Bakhtin 1984.

It is valid to introduce the notion of publicity in the discussion of colonial political discourse, for it also serves to indicate the internal distances, disconnections, and complexities with which rulers and their more voluble subjects had to contend. Power under colonialism was public in the sense of being at least a formal and impersonal set of laws and institutions, however iniquitous.[17] In trying to define its own institutions in the 'public sphere'—a European institution perstition brought, some thought gratuitously, into a colonial society—the imperial regime also provided a discursive space on which nationalist ideas could eventually be formed. However, publicity of power also has a Gramscian connotation, and hints at it being rooted in a public and generally accepted discourse, in which the upper echelons reached into high political theory and the lower into a living, amorphous and ubiquitous structure of common sense. This in turn implies that although all classes and groups in society do not share the same picture of the world (which would be a travesty of Gramsci's conception of common sense), their different pictures, reinforced by their life experience, are made according to the same rules of drawing. It is hardly conceptually possible to use the idea of hegemony without its complement—the commonsensical self-evidentiality of a certain way of constructing pictures of the social world. But can one speak of a relay of common sense such as this, stretching from the ruling elite to the lower orders?[18] To answer this question it becomes necessary to discuss the form of society

---

[17] This relates to a recurrent problem in nationalist historiography. It is common for nationalist historians to claim, paradoxically, that British rule introduced the rule of law in Indian society. Though it is puzzling how nationalists could make an assertion so injurious to their ideological case, it could not be so persistent had there been no point to it. This seems to be related to a conceptual ambiguity about the idea of a rule of law; it means constitutionalism and lack of arbitrariness; but it could also mean rule by laws which were made and promulgated by a procedure more impersonal than those followed under previous regimes.

[18] I have used the concept of common sense here uncritically, putting in abeyance some of the really interesting questions—what is really common in common sense, and what are the mechanisms by means of which it stays common. A particularly interesting question here is the one of language, the medium that connects and divides. Such questions cannot be raised in the context of this essay.

in pre-colonial India,[19] and the way it arranged a distribution of common sense discourse between its various segments.

In India, the colonial state underwent a process of construction in the most literal sense. It did not emerge out of the internal logic of evolution of earlier Indian society, and had little by way of internal relation to do with the state it came to succeed in India. As a corollary, I feel that the change it represents in Indian history cannot be fitted easily into the model of a transition process drawn from the model of European history; it is an excessively 'economic' picture of this change which confers plausibility on that approach.[20] But, clearly, the spread of British power from early insecure footholds in trading zones to large parts of the subcontinent was linked to the spacing of social institutions, and the determinate ways in which the earlier political forms (or state) were related to society.

Although both imperial and nationalist histories in their popular forms agree in seeing the battle of Plassey or the conquest of Bengal as the date of India's loss of independence, this is obviously anachronistic. The actual translation of commercial privileges into imperial power was a slower, considerably more complex, affair. Although it is easier to understand long-term transitions in social history by starting with an account of its productive arrangements, it does not follow that economic forms have the same constitutive power in all societies. In the contact between British imperial power and traditional Indian society there was also a contact between two very different principles of construction of society and state. Since these principles and constructs mediated their images of each other, and influenced their socio-political initiatives, this point needs to be made a little more fully. Ambitious merchants of the Company would probably have interpreted the world they were slowly coming to influence and control through the

---

[19] The significant problem here is the one of form or morphology of pre-colonial Indian society, and not the empirical extent of trade connections, or cash and commodity flows. Traditional history and social anthropology may have underestimated the extent of such connections, but that does not significantly alter the argument about social form, and the place of the state in social relations.

[20] Those who advocated the idea of a colonial mode of production did appreciate the difficulty but attempted to solve it in a manner I consider unpromising.

apparatus of rationalist social ideas and the bourgeois belief in the primacy of commerce and economic control. Yet in traditional Indian practical social thinking, commerce and the economic were treated as insignificant both in theory and in practical political arrangements. Local rulers considered merchants politically insignificant, because they apparently did not work as a collective (or a class); rulers never expected a threat to their political power to come from that direction. To Indian rulers, accustomed to conceptualizing the social world in the traditional manner, a challenge to the political order by a commercial enterprise was as much a conceptual anomaly as it was an insufferable political interference. The Company, for its part, in stretching its reach towards the state was proposing not only a shift in the locus of political authority, but a change in the fundamental map of social relations.

In arguing this case, I would merely extend the point generally made by sociologists and historians about the segmentary nature of traditional Indian society. Capitalist societies are structurally similar, but each type of pre-capitalist society is traditional in its own way.[21] Traditional Hindu society appears to have been decentred in a peculiar way (though that does not make it less repressive), and it had a determinate way of arranging its social space which has important implications for the relation between state and society. It did not have a clear hierarchy of classes presided over by a strong and fairly 'thick' state (in terms of the size of its bureaucracy and their functions) with the right, given to it by the predominant discourse, to interfere in and work around patterns of authority and economic benefits. The hierarchy was what can be called asymmetrical, in the following sense: if we imagine a society of four groups, *a*, *b*, *c*, and *d*, a symmetrical hierarchy would mean that if we disaggregate the hierarchy in terms of three criteria, say, of political control, economic power, and status, the distribution would tend to be symmetrical, i.e. those with a high rank in one would tend to enjoy a high rank in the others as well. Traditional Hindu society tended to work on a formal theory of asymmetry, in which the three criteria would yield wholly different orders, and there were ritual prohibitions to prevent large-scale infringements of this basic map.

Secondly, traditional society seemed to work on a practical arrangement of a thin, rent-receiving, partly marginal state. The structure

---

[21] See Mukhia and Byres 1985.

of the society, despite its obvious hierarchies, is less integrated in terms of its ordering discourses, and, misusing a Hegelian trope, can be likened to a circle of circles of caste and regional communities, with the state sitting at the centre. Of course the state impinges on these communities economically: but its right of economic extraction is more by 'squeezing' a sector than by restructuring it. In this scheme, the rulers were given a deep obeisance at the cost of a certain marginality, i.e. on condition, not legally but structurally enforced, that they did not intrude into the everyday life processes of the communities, and did not take upon themselves the right to legislate a fundamental restructuring of relations as long as their appetite for a 'reasonable' rent was satisfied. Hindu social ontology was based on this internal balance between a dispersed, permanent, and practically unalterable social order and the impermanence of political power at which society looked with perfect composure and indifference. As long as political regimes respected these ground rules of rent reception and non-interference, it mattered little which dynasty or set of rulers was actually transacting the political business. As long as the undoubted incremental alterations in social life did not threaten to alter its basic map of dispositions, and the state did not arrogate to itself the right to restructure relations, Hindu society could deplore with poetic detachment the tragic rise and fall of all eminence, including the political.[22]

Given this relationship between state and society, the entry of Muslim rulers carrying a different religious doctrine, but not a fundamentally different cognitive apparatus, does not seem to have altered the structure in any basic way. Although Islamic religious tenets were more egalitarian than Hinduism, the incursion was not in large enough numbers, nor were the conversions numerous enough to threaten the basic frame. The mechanism of distancing and marginalization allowed Hindu society and rulers to look upon the destruction of their principalities as a part of the necessary mutability of political fortunes,

---

[22] The rise and fall of states could be covered by the Gita's advice to regard with an imperturbable calm and philosophic indifference life's inevitable cyclical changes—*sarve kshyayanta nichayah patananta samucchrayah/samyoga viprayoganta maranantancha jivitam*. It was advice effortlessly practised when it pertained to the rise and fall of others, but required rather more self-control when these concerned the self.

rather than as a civilizational threat to be collectively resisted. More importantly, the arrangement of a circle of circles could cope with such intrusions, allowing the entrants their own circle, at the expense of making the system a little more ragged and shapeless. This response was a strange combination of acceptance and rejection. Thus the Hindu and Muslim rulers who confronted the British at the stage of their passage from commerce to imperial power were singularly handicapped in dealing with them. This historical phenomenon was unprecedented in their political experience, and unrecognizable in terms of their dictionary of social identification. In dealing with the threat of the British, Indian rulers were not merely politically inept: at a more fundamental level, they were conceptually unprepared.

This conceptual mistranslation of what they saw was not confined only to the Indians. The British, equally, tried to make sense of an unfamiliar social ontology in terms of the familiar conventions through which rationalist modern Europe had learnt to map its social space. My constant emphasis on conceptual grids is not meant to advocate an 'idealistic' theory of colonial power. I do not ascribe mystically sufficient causal powers to discourses alone. Of course there were other causal fields—more properly political, strategic, economic, international, etc. But the conceptual element in all these has to be emphasized because the constitutive significance of discourses has not been recognized in so-called hard-headed analyses of political power. Political actors, both individual and collective, do not react to discursively neutral 'objective' situations, but to threats and possibilities fashioned by their perceptions of the political world. Discourses also sometimes provide the vital connections between the various causalities through patterns of beliefs held by actors, which help us identify their intentions. This is a particularly fertile field for misunderstandings between contending forms of rationality.

What the British eventually did, or at least tried to do, to this asymmetric and dispersed traditional structure can be understood not only in terms of their power compulsions in a brute data sense, but through the discourse they brought with them. No history of British rule can be complete until it is seen as part of the history of rationalist modernity, as distinct from the spread of extractive capitalism. On the British side, the entire grand business of colonization is affiliated to the grand structure of rationalist discourse. Groups of early colonizers, small enclaves within vast Indian society, claimed invincibility in the name of the rationalist programme—a view of the world that is clear, precise, instrumentalist, technical, scientific, effective, true, and above all beneficial to all who come in contact with it, both rulers and subjects. This is central to the self-image of the early colonizers, the white man with his burden, a gun in his hand and God on his side. Indeed, each of those adjectives flowed out of some central principle of rationalist discourse about society, unmodified at the time by hermeneutic scepticism. In particular, the early adventurers' belief in their invincibility and in the possibility of controlling a society of such enormous size was a product of their insertion into the mainstream discourse of rationalism—not its intellectual discourse, which was often full of self-doubt and criticism, but the popular mythic discourse—unselfcritical, arrogant, aggressive. Thus, interestingly, both sides in the colonial transaction make sense of their historical experience in terms of large, necessary forces or powers: the British see their success not as a result of individual acumen or bravery, but as a function of a large, impersonal, invincible discourse of rationality of which they were products and 'bearers'. Indians, uninitiated in the intricacies of this cognitive apparatus, see in British power evidence of supernatural accreditation or the visitation of suffering for collective karmic sins. This was, if ever there was one, a theatre of Winchian incommensurable rationalities.

Early nationalist writers often wondered how a large society like 'India' could be colonized and held by such a small group of British people. They puzzled in a direction that was, in my view, crucial in understanding colonial power; but the form in which they asked their question involved a basic anachronistic error. The simple answer to the puzzle (which is why the way they formulated their question was wrong) was that of course there was no pre-existing India which was conquered by British rule. India in that political sense was the result of comparable and increasingly coalescing indignities of colonial rule, and in this coalescing, which was conceptual and again not objective, ideas of rationalist discourse played a major part. It was clearly the product of conceptualizing political possibilities introduced by the discursive bestowals of colonial rationalism. This leads in turn to an interesting question as to how the process of cognitive identification of communities changed as a result of colonial rule and the incursion of Western education.

If we accept the meaning of the term 'imaginary' in Castoriadis's sense[23]—as the internally accepted boundaries of a constituted social form—the principle of community construction in traditional India was different from the modern nationalist one. I have elsewhere suggested a distinction between a fuzzy and enumerated community, which I would like to use for the present argument.[24] The main difference between traditional communities and the modern community of the nation is not in their size, but in their internal constructive principles, of which size was a function. Earlier, people belonged to communities which did not make claims on their identity and strategies of self-description of the type modern states would make. Communities were fuzzy in two senses.[25] Rarely, if ever, would people belong to a community which would claim to represent or exhaust all the layers of their complex selfhood. Individuals on suitable occasions could describe themselves as Vaisnavas, Bengalis, or more probably Rarhis, Kayasthas, villagers, and so on; and clearly although all these could on appropriate occasions be called their *samaj* (they were Bengalis), their boundaries would not coincide.[26] The complex sum of these identities, now anachronistically termed 'selves', would be fuzzy in the first sense.[27] More significantly, it would be fuzzy in a second sense as well.

To say their community is fuzzy is not to say it is imprecise. On the appropriate occasion, every individual would use his cognitive apparatus to classify any single person he interacted with and place him quite exactly, to decide whether he could eat with him, go on a journey with him, or arrange a marriage into his family. It was therefore practically precise, and adequate to the scale of social interaction. It would not, however, occur to an individual to ask how many of them there were in the world, and what they could wreak upon the world if they

---

[23] See Castoriadis 1987.

[24] In a study of Bankimchandra and the formation of Indian nationalist discourse.

[25] I have tried to develop these ideas more fully in Kaviraj 1992.

[26] Only the boundary of the village could be said to have relatively clear spatial delineation.

[27] These would be partly competing identities. The occasion would decide which particular one would be invoked by an individual to identify himself. Finally, these would not display any clear ordering.

decided to act in concert. In other words they did not inhabit a conceptual world which could contemplate collective transformative actions on a large, universalist scale because all the crucial terms were absent from their vocabulary.[28] They would not represent themselves as a large universalist collective group—i.e. every Vaisnava, for the very fact of being one, being involved in some action: they would rarely contemplate action instrumentally to alter the balance of social advantages in their favour, because there would not be a sufficiently common register of social benefits. And it was at least partly because of this many-layered sense of community that those who were attacked severally, and destroyed by the colonial political regime, failed to make common cause. It was not lack of rationality in some transcendent political sense which failed them when dealing with the British, but precisely the operation of a rationality which had hitherto proved adequate. Thus, the revolt of 1857, which was undoubtedly anti-British, but equally certainly not 'Indian', represented an anti-colonial protest still trapped within the fuzzy and unenumerated community.

Into this carefully constructed equilibrium of the decentred totality held together by its internal distancing, the back-to-back spacing of groups, dispersal, and countervailing power, the British brought a highly symmetrical, centralized, technologically effective apparatus of control. The earlier social form may have been technologically ineffective, but it was very stable and exceptionally difficult to reform; it is not entirely accidental that it was after an integrated structure was set up by the British, not before, that we find an increasing incidence of rebellious action by the popular masses.[29] The system of social action that the British brought and gradually entrenched in urban India and its hinterland was instrumentally extremely effective. Yet because

---

[28] Universalist in the sense of every member of a social group being a putative participant in such actions, like every Indian's putative participation in the national movement. These actions are collective in a rather peculiar sense, entailing an idea of an abstract, non-optional, and non-intentional membership, which needs to be further analysed.

[29] I suspect that the relative lack of chronicling of popular protests in India may not have been because these events occurred yet remained unreported by upper-class chroniclers, but rather because they might indeed have occurred less frequently. Such infrequency must have something to do with the basic principles of social organization.

of its high salience and centralization—because it presented a clear and unambiguous institutional target—it could be challenged, and was vulnerable, as nationalists found out later, to pressures of collective action of its own type. Mature nationalists would turn the rationalist apparatus itself against the colonial state.

Once colonialism establishes itself in state or proto-state form, it faces the problem of constructing a 'hegemonic' discourse in its favour. Although I am generally unwilling to use the term 'hegemony' in colonial conditions, I agree that some conceptual surrogate is necessary to explain the fact that, though defiance and repression happened in dramatic episodes throughout colonial history, acquiescence was the rule rather than the exception. The question is how this acquiescence was arranged, its concepts constructed.

But before we enter into that discussion it seems necessary to ask how the terrain was structured upon which this question of legitimacy (or hegemony) was to be contested; the question is clearly related to the earlier one we noted of the publicity of power.[30] The regime had to contend with the demands of publicity in several directions at once;

---

[30] Evidently, the idea of publicity—of something being a public place (like offices), institution (like the state), or process (like judicial proceedings)—is quite central to the enterprise of modernity. At the same time it is a rather elusive concept, because it seems to order and influence other social practices which are more visible, definable, and codifiable. This concept is central to the republican tradition which demands that the state and its decision-making institutions be regarded as fiduciary powers, and to the democratic one which emphasizes the publicness of state processes of various types, such as elections. However, the concept of the public is not confined only to political life. Art and literature historians are interested in tracing the genesis of a reading 'public' for the emergent literary form of the novel. Thus the underlying presence of the idea of a 'public realm' stretches from judicial processes on one side to the consumption of the novel on the other, clearly an idea of great significance, though it is difficult to find systematic explorations of its historical development. Non-European intellectuals could not be attracted to the general project of modernity without feeling the attraction of this central idea. At the same time the idea of a public realm, with its accompaniment of a clear definition of what is private, could not have an easy entry into the conceptual vocabulary of Indian social life. Nor would its career here, once it does make an ambivalent entry, parallel its European career. Still, a history of ideas of

and it was in terms of intelligibility and 'reasonableness' (which were different in each of these) that it had to present its policies. First, the colonial state was of course a subordinate arm of the state or regime in England. It was subject therefore to two kinds of pressure from that direction. It had to keep India a marginal subject and not allow problems arising out of the colonial entanglement to intrude too deeply or frequently into the agenda of domestic politics and demand an unreasonable share of attention. The less these questions were aired the greater the possibility of maintaining a low-level consensus on the colonial question. At the same time, the discourse of politics could not be fragmented and fractured beyond a point. Although it was possible to invite British public opinion to remain indulgently indifferent towards details of imperial politics in India while passively enjoying its material benefits and imperial glory, significant issues in Indian politics were still bound to be judged by the criteria of justice, effectiveness, and honour that were current in internal politics in Britain. Imperial policy in India had therefore to remain legitimate in the internal terms of British political discourse.[31]

The way this discourse was shaped historically displayed the plurality of possibilities contained within the alphabet of rationalist theory. Rationalism in politics was not a singular or entirely monolithic affair. Undoubtedly, the radical demands for the extension of democracy, the enfranchisement of the poor, and for social justice were as much historical products of the rationalist project as the empowering discourse of technical knowledge, power, conquest, and invincibility. However,

---

colonial India cannot be written without some attention to the troubled history of this concept, the intelligentsia's fascination for it, and their half-successful attempt to introduce it into political discourse.

[31] The political requirement that administrative policies must remain intelligible to contemporary British opinion while being effective in India's wholly different climate of politics made life difficult for colonial officials, who complained bitterly about such translation problems. Abstract principles of rationalist humanism demanded that Indians be treated on a footing of equality with the British; the logic of colonial rule made it impossible to follow such high-minded principles. Colonial policies led to an uneasy existence between conservative charges of excessive leniency and reformist criticism on grounds of excessive harshness.

it is important to note the odd fact that, though British public opinion was commonsensically imperialist, and in general the popular forces were too absorbed in their domestic struggles to notice symmetries of aspiration with distant subject peoples, there were internal elements within this discourse which placed real limits on the extent and manner of the use of force in colonial society. Avowal or implementation of such principles was far from straightforward or consistent. In the enlightened pages of John Stuart Mill,[32] or even Robert Owen,[33] this is displayed as disquiet and bad conscience, rather than as an acceptance of the rights of, or equal treatment for, colonial peoples. But there were real, if occasional, consequences of the doctrine of power's public character, and the fiduciary nature of public office. The discursive formation which provided Clive and Hastings with the crucial arguments of invincibility also, unfortunately for them, contained a puritanical side that condemned illegal gratification. Some important officials therefore had to pay the price for an inconsistent and self-servingly one-sided reading of what rationalist politics enjoined. Unsatisfactory and inadequate as these incidents may have appeared to the colonial peoples who suffered at their hands, this discourse had a reality in terms of a social ontology, and was forceful enough to claim occasional victims.

This was the first paradox of the colonial regime. Because it was in fact far more powerful (in the sense of the sanctioned or possible use of force in having its way) than the state in the mother country, it was entirely uncircumscribed by the democratic rules and demands which inconveniently restricted elite politics in the metropolis. It was an external, in a sense suspended, state which was not the product, or the terrain, of social conflict (as bourgeois states are) in the society over which it ruled. Compulsions arising out of publicity in England, only too real for its officials, were in large measure incomprehensible to its Indian subjects until quite late. Precisely because of its dual context, some of its domestic supporters also misunderstood the compulsions arising out of the fact that it was, after all, the *Indian* state, and had to respond in intelligible ways also to the pressures and the social logic of

---

[32] See Mill 1861. Mill confers high praise on British India government as one of the best contemporary mixtures of popular consent and aristocratic quality in Mill 1835: 180.

[33] See Owen 1858: 215.

the country over which it sat with such imperial majesty. Its double publicity— the two publics it had to make itself comprehensible to— made it a possible area of misunderstandings.

Officials who were entrusted with the task of ruling India, however, were quick to realize the sharp difference between the dominant discourse they brought with them and that of the society they were to enter and hoped to hold in permanent, and preferably peaceable, control. And their ideas of the nature and limits of cognition, of social knowledge—its arguments of justification of political authority, its picture of society and the moral consequences of the division of social functions, even the levels of the social totality—were entirely different. Lively rationalist curiosity, driven by self-related prejudices into the familiar forms of early ethnology, made the British compile records about this society and its intellectual discourse (though often misleadingly classified). In a very short time early civilians had attempted, assisted by the more esoteric labours of the Asiatic Society, to produce a reliable map of the social relations and modes of reasoning in this culture. Indeed, some of these early researchers affiliated themselves doctrinally to counter-Enlightenment tendencies in European culture like romanticism and came to the verge of questioning the comfortable civilizational hierarchies of rationalist thinking.

Under these circumstances two broad strategies of legitimation were possible. Since legitimation meant that political forms and strategies had to find the structures of self-evidence on their side, it could be accomplished by fitting the patterns of the new political regime into the existing justificatory discourse, or at least appearing to do so. Alternatively, the discourses of Indian society could be remodelled by a serious and missionary spread of Western education, so that the activities of the colonial state would appear justified through the new structure of self-evidence acquired by the rationalist intelligentsia. In actual fact, the colonial regime followed a complex combination of the two strategies—to its immediate advantage and with some unintended long-term results.

Construction of Colonial Discourse

What we are calling hegemony is after all the matter of creating legitimacy for the new apparatus of political control which was seeking to integrate Indian society vertically, and which was giving it, without deliberate design, a symmetric form from an asymmetric structure.[34] (This is a description from the point of view of social design of what is more familiarly referred to as the transition to capitalism.) Legitimacy—the constitution of a fit between acts, policies, and forms of the political regime and the conceptions of self-evidence about what was right, appropriate, just, honourable, defensible within a society's constituted discourse—immediately implied a choice of techniques. To create legitimacy the colonial state had a choice between two mutually exclusive strategies, poised as it was between two civilizations with powerful discourses about the political world. Yet the colonial state failed to make a clear choice between the two strategies—to its great advantage, as it turned out. It followed variants of both in different periods, sometimes shifting emphasis with dramatic rapidity between two viceregal administrations.

Of course, above all, the colonial state was the product of the discourse of the Enlightenment.[35] That discourse stressed the possibility of Cartesian conceptions of knowledge in preference to asymptotic Aristotelian ideas and asserted as part of its cognitive programme the ready translatability of all knowledge into technical control over the world thus known. Enlightenment theories were proto-positivist (i.e. positivist before the recognition of a positivist position), and extended such general beliefs about the nature, means, and consequences of knowledge from nature into the historical world. Another, equally significant, part of Enlightenment theory was not only its belief in the possibility of precise, incontrovertible knowledge, but also the impossibility of all men attaining it in equal measure. Externally affiliated to the doctrine of the rational equality of all men, this theory immediately resulted in a hierarchy of people as attainers of knowledge and

[34] It could be objected that this is simply a reference in somewhat different language to what was earlier standardly described as the colonial transition to capitalism. I still prefer to retain this particular description because it points more sharply to the arrangement of social hierarchy rather than making an inattentive gesture towards it as an inevitable part of an economic transformation process.

[35] For an excellent account of how Enlightenment discourse is related to sociology, see Hawthorn 1976. Enlightenment thinking left a deep imprint on the Bengali intellectual consciousness of this period, but less in the form of philosophical reflection, more in the form of sociological analysis.

users of technology. Moreover, apart from there being a possible exhaustive rank order of individuals on this cognitive scale (and Locke showed more clearly than any other social theorist the incalculable significance of this theory of an order of rationality for the justification of early capitalism),[36] societies also could be placed in a rank order, using an implicit but ubiquitous premise of methodological individualism. This structure of reasoning, turned around, provided the principal frame of explanation and justification of Western imperial rule.

In the initial period, perhaps naturally, officials of the Company accepted traditional nomenclatures like the *dewani*, and generally tried to translate their own political existence into the earlier cultural and symbolic order. Historians have recorded in detail how self-consciously early and even later colonialists modelled themselves on the cultural and institutional legacy of the Mughal empire.[37] The basic function of the Company's official structure was, of course, the extraction of rent and related revenue, and the classificatory schemes for rent and tenurial system were taken over from Mughal administration.[38] But obviously the imitation of the Mughals could only proceed up to a point, and led to contradictions, for the civilizational discourse of bourgeois imperialism was incommensurate with Mughal social forms and cultural idioms. Although the Mughal system was more successful and long-standing than previous empires, it was still constructed on the traditional dualistic principle—a stable village social structure on the ground, based on caste rules, and on top a superordinate empire, which nevertheless left the business of social and cultural reproduction alone. The discourse of European rationalism did not allow such a policy of majestic aloofness for long. Once their political control was secure, the colonial administration went for a strategy which decisively infringed this dualism. It was no longer content to limit its majesty to the narrow space in the middle of the circle of circles. This was naturally related to the second strategy of legitimation. Western education, now extended with vigour, was calculated to produce a social group which would ensure an ideological relay of this language

[36] See Macpherson 1964.
[37] See Cohn 1987: 632–82.
[38] See Bhattacharyya 1971.

and structure of self-evidence—an expectation that was, ironically, both fulfilled and frustrated.

These British moves can be interpreted, in part at least, in terms of a Gramscian theory of common sense. In the early period, when its control was confined to greater Bengal and it did not see itself capable of taking on the task of restructuring social relations, the regime followed the earlier strategy. But there was a price to pay, quite apart from the unconvincing pretence that the British were a small infeudatory power to the pitifully declining Mughal order. The price was that by accepting the logic of the traditional marginalization of the state they abandoned their rationalist right to restructure society in their own image through enforced reform. It meant, moreover, adopting a sentimental feudal language which made it impossible to advance a Burkean traditionalist argument to justify their authority over Indian society. The early regime therefore spoke both languages—an idiom of reasonableness shown in its willingness to tolerate indigenous practices, a sort of conservative Winchianism, and also an idiom of rationality committing it to reform and an ideology of progress against domestic reaction. This curious incompatibility of 'reasonableness' and 'rationality' is reflected in the successive viceroyalties as late as Lytton and his successor, as Seal has shown.[39]

Despite the vestigial existence of the traditional language of authority, by the mid-nineteenth century the colonial state had begun to speak in a more authoritative, rationalist, liberal voice. This stiffening of its tone could be attributed to several things. On the Indian side, by this time, colonial power was far more securely entrenched and began to entertain the normal illusions of untroubled permanence. The experience of the 1857 uprising (in which the Indian political coalition was between disgruntled elements of the old ruling classes and some elements of the peasantry in the form of the ordinary soldiery) made the British realize the vulnerability of their earlier line of non-interference and winning princes over by diplomacy and pressure. In short, the gradual entrenchment of the British destroyed the mutuality of interest between them and traditional rulers. By contrast, the new middle classes, particularly in rationalist Calcutta, showed exemplary loyalty, siding decisively with the forces of reason against the forces of freedom.

---

[39] See Seal 1978.

They appeared a better candidate for political and pecuniary investment than the traditional ruling orders.

Significant changes occurred in the climate of ideas in the West as well. Edward Said's work has popularized an exaggerated construction of Western rationalist orientalism, stressing the linearity in the rationalist discourse of otherness.[40] The actual structure and arrangement of ideas was more internally differentiated and varied. Indeed, contrary to Said's claims, in the early discourse of the Enlightenment the Orient fills the logical position of an other which in fact saves the sense of diversity of life-forms in the world and prevents a rash Eurocentric doctrine of superiority. To take only two well-known examples, Montesquieu,[41] and then Voltaire,[42] central intellectual figures of the Enlightenment, use a fuzzy and partly romantic conception of the Orient to set up imaginary archimedian points to tell the truth about European history.

This is a type of intellectual argument and comparison quite different from the confidently Eurocentric visions of the world unsurpassably classified, not only horizontally, but also vertically. The priorities and preoccupations of colonial administrators could not be unaffected by the shift in climate of opinion. This made the colonial regime more confidently interventionist. It remained dependent on rent, but it intervened in major ways to restructure the economy, the relation between state and society, and in the cultural constitution of social relations through its moves for social reform. It was not a state which could be treated in the old terms.

This is not to say that the earlier strategy of legitimation entirely disappeared. Indeed, as Bernard Cohn has tried to show, the attempt to incorporate the older symbolic order continued, and the more stable and expansive empire now deliberately sought to appropriate

---

[40] See Said 1978. Partha Chatterjee has made a very perceptive use of Said's argument in his study of nationalist discourse, though at times his treatment of Said seems a trifle uncritical.

[41] In Montesquieu 1760.

[42] In Voltaire 1971; also in Voltaire 1966 and Voltaire 1978. These two stories require a joint and parallel reading as they show the journey through the same inhospitable world of two individuals—one armed with the rationalist conception of knowledge, the other with an oriental version of wisdom.

the whole train of symbolic memory of earlier empires.[43] But the new state required a new kind of legitimating discourse; and its earlier, more unsystematic initiatives in spreading Western education had created conditions for this shift. Earlier, legitimacy was really not the question; the major point was to produce a strategy which would prevent the rise of an overwhelming adversary coalition of political forces. From the mid-nineteenth century that was no longer relevant, and the colonial regime required legitimacy of a deeper kind. It sought to create that at three different levels in the field of discourse, and it is to these to which we must turn.

Hegemony and History: The Politics of the Past

It would be presumptuous even to try to give an account of the field of colonial discourse and the internal transformations brought in by politics over its major terms.[44] After some general remarks I would like to pursue my point by attending to the career of one idea which came to acquire extraordinary political significance in colonial culture—the idea of history.

But first it is necessary to understand how the terrain itself (to use a Gramscian phrase) was structured. This appears to be something like a quadrilateral of discourse, with the ruling British administration speaking to the natives at three discursive levels constituted by the beliefs, symbols, media, and tropes of the traditional upper classes, of the new urban Western-educated middle classes, and of the predominantly voiceless masses of the people below. (Voiceless does not mean they had no discourse of their own; but their discourses were not always communicative with those of the others, and because academic history is itself a part of these other discourses, we know much less about this intellectual field than the others.) It would be wrong to

---

[43] Cohn 1987.

[44] Unfortunately, while there is a wealth of research on the cultural history of the colonial period, little has been done by way of writing histories of fundamental concepts embedded in social practices, something like a *Begriffsgeschichte,* to use Koselleck's term. One of the rare attempts in the field of legal and administrative practices is Washbrook 1981.

say that there was no distinctiveness to popular discourse, or that the thickness of internal communication was less than the noisy newspaper exchanges between groups of the babu culture. Nevertheless, their culture was primarily inner-directed, and not particularly transactive towards the other three elements, protected as it was from interference by their wordy superiors because of the boundaries of literacy, the deep entrenchment of a popular-traditional symbolic order (e.g. the *Ramayana* of the Ramlila and of Valmiki are very different narratives, and the first is not just an inept translation of the more hallowed text), and their reliance on non-linguistic aspects of the semiotic range. As the labours of the Subaltern Studies historians have shown, popular culture is the most interesting but, with the tools of literate history, the most difficult to enter.[45] My own remarks about this quadrilateral of discourse would therefore perforce be most uneven; I am going to confine myself to the relation of reciprocal self-respect between 'master and slave', read in this context as the British rationalist intellectual tradition and its babu pupils, in relation to history.

We find two forms of thinking about the problem of history—theoretical and narrative. Of course, theory and narrative are often inextricable, but what is interesting in this cultural context is how from one point of view the inextricability is sought to be maintained, and, from the other, sought to be riven apart. It is important to remember that the rationalist culture that students at Hindu College imbibed was likely to be more monolithic than the considerably more inflected and critically engaged form in Europe. Critical trends, like romanticism, or reco-ordinations like German idealism, were less familiar to Indian pupils,[46] though Derozio apparently did a review of Kant's First Critique. But the curricula of Western education contained not only theoretical tools, resources, and techniques which could be applied to

---

[45] The successive volumes of *Subaltern Studies* contain a wealth of material in this field: see esp. Guha 1983: ch. 2.

[46] German idealism later found some influential adherents among professional philosophers, though their interest was mediated by the transient dominance of British idealism. Mainstream utilitarianism, however, had serious critics, and they, in looking for counter-arguments in English social theory, often turned to the works of Carlyle, Green, and Bradley.

historical material critically to appraise and control them; they also contained and pressed upon their students a narrative of universal history, assigning values and places to civilizations. The whole story appeared very close to showing how human history was a preparation for the present Western colonial dominance. Rationalist thinking of course influenced the discourse of the Indian middle classes through both its theoretical apparatus and its narrative configurations.[47] Soon, however, it was the narrative which came particularly to concern the Indian intelligentsia. The reasons are not far to seek. It was the legitimating discourse of imperialism which made the question of the past so political. In order to justify its claims imperialist discourse, often assisted by missionary writing, had to advance a picture of the Indian past as one of indifferent civilizational achievements. On that depended the credibility of its claim that colonialism was the bestowal of the benefits of modern civilization by a distant and not wholly self-interested people. A favourable view of the accounts of British rule by the Indian intelligentsia depended on the acceptance of this picture of their past by the new elite, and their carrying it down by a relay of ideological common sense to the lower social orders.

This rationalist-colonial narrative advanced two essentialisms, and it is interesting to see that history writing is not by definition anti-essentialist.[48] Particularly central to this view is the essentialist dichotomy between the self and the other. All dichotomies of this type are asymmetric: the self is portrayed as historical, determinate, laden with actual attributes, capable of the radical reformation of its structures, and the other is seen as empty, abstract, a repository of negative characteristics—negative not always in the sense of bad, but *non-x*.[49] It follows that the self would have a much thicker historical representation than the other. After all, one purpose of the picture of the other is not simply to be true to its object, but to facilitate what its constructors wish to believe about the self. The thinness of the description of the other in turn reinforces essentialist thinking. Excessive historical details are apt to disturb the beautiful symmetries of negative belief. A whole line of discourse theorists has shown the construction of the Orient to follow this format.

[47] Tagore's poem on history learning, mentioned above, note 6.
[48] For a discussion of the essentialism, see Chatterjee 1985.
[49] I have tried to argue this case more fully in Kaviraj 1988.

Essentialism can assume various forms. One common form denies the privilege of history to social formations in this place of otherness, simply because the rhythms and forms of their historical evolution are different from those prevalent in Europe. A second and more refined form does not deny history in that elementary sense but argues that historical change occurred through a stable, almost transcendent structure of national characteristics which history can give form to, and refigurate, but cannot really alter. Historiography of this kind produced two essentialist narratives—a narrative of European reason moving conveniently from ancient Greece and Rome, unmindfully through the 'dark ages' into a linear connection with the post-Renaissance history of Western Europe; and a narrative of India, which, in its most charitable forms, showed an early efflorescence followed by a linear decline down to the pre-colonial times of modern darkness. The European narrative, as some Bengalis pointed out, infringed some of the elementary rules of stability of narration and fixity of subject.[50] Though there was some sense in this construction of a cultural tradition, Bengali authors pointed out sardonically the peculiarity of modern Englishmen choosing as their ancestors ancient inhabitants of Greece rather than the less philosophically engaged people of the British Isles. Above all, this seemed to show that historical narration was a political act, and provided one with a pleasurable freedom in choosing one's cultural ancestors. Bengali writers showed how well they had learnt these history lessons when they revealed their own deep conviction that they were incontrovertible descendants of the writers of the Vedas. Imperial historiography constantly emphasized the rationalist character of its constructions. History not only uses critical tools of analysis, but, precisely because it does so, can provide a place from which fond fables about the past can be criticized and rejected. History was the best cure of cultural chauvinism. The proximate result of this history teaching was, in the first few generations of students at least, what was broadly expected. Later, however, it began to produce unintended and surprising results.

Two other elements in the legitimizing discourse of imperial power are worth mentioning—for both had serious consequences in the not-too-distant future. First, as practical students of the Enlightenment theory of knowledge, the British imperial elite began its massive and

[50] Bankimchandra Chattopadhyay did this with particularly mordant irony.

unprecedented project of enumeration and classification—a procedure enjoined by the rationalist connection between precise knowledge and effective control. To control a society it was essential to locate it in taxonomic systems. The British administration accordingly inaugurated the great process of counting—through censuses, maps, and statistics, familiarizing the inhabitants of their empire with their great numbers, and offering them clearer pictures of their own land and peoples. Nationalists would quickly learn to count equally well and equally politically. Instead of seeing these as entities divided by the final lines on the census tables, they began to consider what they would look like, and what would happen, if they combined.

Secondly, another element of rationalist thought gradually removed the basis of the impossibility of collective action. As Indian society traditionally was a circle of circles it was unfamiliar with the processes of what Gellner has called social entropy.[51] This ruled out any possibility of conceiving Kantian, attributeless individuals who could, driven by self-interest, freely enter into *gesellschaft*-like associations. Even a rhetorical disruption of the boundaries of those circles, turning them from a number of fuzzy communities into a single enumerated one—to be called, after European models, a nation—was now a logically possible step. Finally, the rhetoric of rationalism attracted Western-educated intellectuals so powerfully because of its principle of an abstract universality of reason; it offered them the possibility of taking the slogan of all men being rational in quite a literal sense, ignoring the fine print introduced by constitutions and liberal theory. It was so inviting and irresistible because its theory, in a pure form, seemed to make all human beings eligible for entry into the rational condition. It was subject only to some cognitive accomplishments which no student of Hindu College and similar institutions considered beyond his reach. Rationalist education had provided these intellectuals with critical implements by which they rejected their society's traditions and its past. To be consistent, it had then to acknowledge their right to enter into the great narrative of reason, as reasonably respected if not equal participants. Babus in Calcutta particularly affected such inclusion, and very soon most of them knew in extraordinary detail events in European history at the cost of a condescending ignorance about the Indian past. But this was not just a matter of ignorance; rather, it was

[51] Gellner 1983.

a strategy for the constitution of the self. Historically, this was the hegemonic moment of imperial rationalist discourse.

But this hegemony was limited and unstable. Those babus who were convinced of their right to inclusion in this illumined side of humanity were bound to be deeply disenchanted and resentful when confronted with the arbitrary barriers of race and subalternity. The imperial narrativization of European history, and the colonial civilizing mission rhetoric, had held out a promise of the diffusion or re-enactment of the great narrative of reason on alien soil. Some colonial intellectuals came to envy Europeans and literally covet their history. If the colonial regime's policies systematically obstructed and belied such possibilities, this was bound to cause disillusionment. Thus, all these effects of structural and discursive change, after initially seeming to offer a secure base for hegemonic control, came to have contrary results. By integrating society, introducing symmetric trends of social hierarchy, enumerating society, familiarizing Indians with the theory of public power and democracy, placing before them the universality of reason and the great narratives of European nation-formation and introducing the skills of forming associations, this imperial discourse also taught Indians how rationalism could be turned against the European colonizers themselves. The lessons of rationalism were learnt unfortunately too well.

Some of these great changes were reflected in the contest around the idea of history. History came to be a central idea—a concept, a trope, a slogan, a metaphor. It came to be the obsession of a whole generation of nineteenth-century Bengalis, and this absorption did not weaken or disappear until India attained freedom. Its culmination can be seen in the great narratives of Nehru, in their classical rationalist design of composition, their three interconnected narratives of the world, the nation, and the self,[52] arranged as circles within circles. The average colonial intellectual from the mid-nineteenth century lived in an intellectual world full of narratives and of choices about how to relate to them, and it is obviously impossible to tell with any detail the story of all these stories. We can only remark some of its primary forms.

The use of history took two contradictory forms. One section of the colonial intelligentsia, strangely enough, accepted a version of essentialism. If there was a relation of Gramscian hegemony—a productive

[52] Nehru 1934; Nehru 1936; Nehru 1946.

connection between two social groups in which the lower one accepted the worldview, apparatus of knowledge, criteria of judgement, narratives, and blindnesses of the dominant class which made their ideology its common sense—this was the social relation between imperial rulers and the middle-class intelligentsia, particularly up until the mid-nineteenth century. This constitution of common sense went so deep that this intelligentsia and their social class repudiated the massive protests of 1857 and offered their rulers a touching if servile loyalty. One paradigmatic argument particularly cemented the common sense of the rulers and the ruled. The form it was given by Max Müller was particularly suited to this hegemonic consensus. Indian history, according to this view, showed the superiority of its civilization in spiritual matters, a heart-warming compensation for colonial self-respect, in exchange for control over vital political and economic matters—fields in which the rational superiority of the British was, it implied, equally evident. A surprisingly large number of authors, until surprisingly late, cheerfully accepted this offer of cultural equivalence. Among its adherents one finds men like Vivekananda and Tagore. As long as Indians were satisfied with this concession of mystical superiority they were not likely to be active in political dissent.

Other trends, however, emerged in colonial culture. Those with a more critical historical curiosity began to reject the essentialisms of both the aggressive and the patronizing variety, for they realized that though some of its forms might be good for self-respect, they had a common ground. The only way out of such essentialism was a discourse of actual history, an argument which showed structural transformations to have been possible and which showed the contingency of all happenings that constitute history. This destroyed the essentialist notion that subjection was inevitable by showing how close some things that did not take place in history came to actually happening. Much of the point of this historical contestation was of course political—deploying the prestige of rationalist historiography in favour of the right kinds of prejudices, imperialist or national. Of course there was academic history as well, but it also tended to be absorbed into the large ideological structures. Jadunath Sarkar wrote approving introductions asserting the credibility of Bankimchandra's historical novels. History, thus, did not mean present curiosity about the society's past. It signified much more an interest in the structure and implications of, and the techniques of constructing, these highly political narratives.

The question was not to find out exactly what happened in the past, but what kind of past to have, how to construct the best possible past, one which could suit most effectively the interests, aspirations, and conceits of the present.

It was commonly held that British, or more generally European, narratives of Indian history obstructed the path to the past so elected. The past thus became most political, the nodal point, the terrain, the prize of the ideological contest between imperialism and nationalism. Indian authors, using the rationalist apparatus itself, complained increasingly that Western education offered a history of India that was a complex combination of the factual and the imaginary. With the heightened sensitivity of the insulted they pointed out the constructivist, narrative elements in these accounts. Anticipating modern arguments, more radical writers like Bankimchandra pointed out that it was not only the history of the other, but also of the European self, which contained large elements of the imaginary. The rationalist history of Europe was about as trustworthy as the European history of India.[53] There was a connection between the two narratives: in order to believe what it wished to think about itself Enlightemnent Europe required negative beliefs about its others.

Bankimchandra pointed to the asymmetry between Europeans and Indians on the question of history. 'If Europeans go duck-shooting, histories are duly composed of the affair, but a whole nation of Bengalis do not have a history to themselves.' And further: 'The Bengalis must have a history; or else, they would never become human beings.'[54] Remarkably, Bengalis need history not because they are assailed by irresistible curiosity about their past, about how much tax burden, for example, fell on the peasantry in the Mughal age. They can exist in reasonable well being without such empirical knowledge. They require history in order to become human beings in their present. It is not history in the ontological sense that they lack; what they lack is an account, mortifying and uplifting, of their collective self.

I have suggested elsewhere that there is a surprising degree of tentativeness in early modern Bengali writing about this collective self: they argue on behalf of a 'we', but they are very unclear about who this

---

[53] I have tried to present a more systematic argument elsewhere: see Kaviraj 1989.

[54] See Chattopadhyay 1965: 336.

'we' is. Bankim himself tried three different proposals for a politically viable self—nominating first the *bhadralok,* then the Bengali 'nation' (*jati*), and then the Hindus for this noble and crucial role, before he discovered the advantages of being an Indian.[55] There is also an interesting inversion in this presentation of the self—the India whose history they were collectively engaged in writing was not in the past, but still somewhere in the future. An Indian nation is assumed to pre-exist its history; in fact, it is this narrativization which brings the imagined community into existence. Bhudev Mukhopadhyay, a contemporary of Bankim, even wrote a history of India received in dream—*Swapnalabdha Bharatvarsher Itihas.*[56] Contrary to what Bhudev meant, it is not the history that is created by a political imagination, but also India, the object of his dream.

History is thus seen as a peculiarly empowering discourse. It brought this sense of power to its possessor precisely because it could produce a gigantic anachronism in popular consciousness, making all previous periods of a nation's history appear a preparation for what it was carrying out at the present time. But this faced these Indian intellectuals with a paradox: the imperial glory of the British Isles was reflected backwards into earlier episodes of British, and, when convenient, European history. By the logic of the same simple anachronism, Indian history would appear grim indeed, a teleological construction showing the inevitability and long 'preparation' for current servitudes. Several strategies were tried out against such depressing conclusions, of which I shall briefly mention three.

The obvious first move was to enquire into the actual historical past of the communities that were owned, in search of episodes of defiance which could be narrativized and turned into a metaphor for the future. No wonder the intelligentsia entered into the business of compiling histories on a very large scale. But *history*, this empowering narrative, was pursued in two *very* different forms. Oddly, alongside this *history*—scrupulous and critical about facts and objectivity—they pursued a parallel discourse of what can only be called imaginary history, the title Bhudev gave to his unconvincing fiction. These 'imaginary histories' sought empirically underdetermined episodes in the Indian

---

[55] Ibid.: 241.
[56] Mukhopadhyay 1895.

past, counterfactualizing them (as in Bhudev's *Swapnalabdha Itihas*) or extending them, filling their interstices with narratives of defiance and patriotism (as in Bankim's *Rajsinha*).

Oddly enough, although rationalism made such a strong distinction between fact and fiction, many authors pursued both routes of factual and imaginary history. An ideal reader of R.C. Dutt, for instance, would see him as the utterer of a complex but single discourse distributed, because of a political *decalage*, between on the one hand the *Economic History*,[57] and on the other his historical novels *Rajput Jivan Sandhya*,[58] and *Maharashtra Jivan Prabhat*.[59] It was the second kind of discourse—of historical novels, not perhaps impressive in their internal architecture but given great respect because they were affiliated to the great emergence of vernacular literary cultures and because of their political point—which contributed most to the creation of the first stratum of anti-colonial, and proto-national, discourse. (I prefer to call these anti-colonial, because of the embarrassment of calling them by the name nationalist, a discourse which has not yet chosen its nation.[60])

Interestingly, there was a parallel process in literature to the one in social reflection. Just as rationalist theories restructured social reflection, contact with European literatures, when the novel form and lyrical poetry predominated, restructured the canons of literary creation. Since much of the persuasion for the nationalist idea was done by a narrative rather than a theoretical discourse, historical novels which played out plots of patriotism in a transparently metaphorical past figured very significantly in the nationalist reading lists. Through these, the colonial intelligentsia were able finally to disrupt and pre-empt the tight unity of the discourse that rationalism offered to them, in which the offer of the theory was conditional on an acceptance of the narrative. By dividing off the narrative from the theory, by making it

[57] Dutt 1906.
[58] Dutt 1960: 250–326.
[59] Dutt 1940.
[60] This may appear a cryptic and puzzling assertion. What I mean is that intellectuals first decided that British power must be opposed; only subsequently did they make up their mind about whom this 'nation' would consist of. The idea of a territorial Indian nation gained currency later than is normally assumed.

possible to accept and absorb the theory while sharply rejecting the narrative of European reason, they opened up the space for all kinds of new configurations of political thought. Through its great impact on colonial discourse, this highly political literature about the past accomplished a fundamental transformation of the map of relations in the present. Earlier, the indigenous Westernized intellectual had assumed he belonged along with Europeans on the right side of a line of rationality drawn across humanity. By their intervention, these narratives and ironies of literature showed that the map was drawn very differently and that the Bengali babu and his counterparts were decisively of that part of humanity which was on the wrong side of the line between domination and subalternity. Often, this was the difference between a politics of collaborative reform and one of nationalist defiance.

There was, however, also a third strategy adumbrated by nationalists of the late nineteenth century, which continued down to Jawaharlal Nehru. If all narratives were constructions and were in that sense ideological, it followed that the choice of a narrative in which to include one's collective and individual self was a political act. Arguments taught by the imperial rationalists themselves created conditions for some very different solutions to the ones they perhaps expected. In early imperial and nationalist thinking there was some kind of sanctity to space, and discourses were seen as culture- and space-bound. Colonialism was seen as a cultural invasion of space, to be ended and neutralized and rolled back when the time came, a necessary corollary of essentialism. By the infusion of a new kind of social theory, these would be seen less as culture-space entities which were indissoluble and had some transcendent existence; rather, they were seen as processes which could be distinguished from their individual and collective 'bearers'. Rationalism could then be seen as a diffusionist process,[61] rather than an ineradicably European attribute, and its acceptance and control could then be seen as progress rather than Europeanization. Bengali babus in the mid-nineteenth century affected a cultural Europeanization, claiming to include themselves in the rationalist

---

[61] Diffusionism, popular in early sociology, was a two-sided idea. It asserted the superiority of a culture that was imitated by others; but it also implicitly conceded the historical contingency of such dominance, because others could also become proficient in those skills. In this sense diffusionism could provide counter-arguments against conventional forms of essentialism.

narrative, though accepting a place on its underside, drawing sarcasm from someone as phlegmatic as Tagore.

The position that Nehru represented was not identical, and was far more plausible: it did not accept the essential connection between Europe and rationality and apply to be included in it. It claimed to have a right to that narrative precisely because in its view treating that narrative as European was wrong. In this form, this choice and this assertion of a right to be included in that illuminating narrative of progress gradually came to dominate the minds of the Indian intelligentsia, permeating the national movement despite the strategic significance of Gandhi. Politically, Gandhi remained indispensable and central. But the discourse of nationalism moved away from his stance of cultural intransigence against the West, and his non-cooperation with the great rationalist narrative, and the allure of its re-enactment.

Though this cannot be the place to enter into that separate and large question, Nehru's choice indicates, to my mind, a much deeper difficulty. Partha Chatterjee has given us an excellent analysis of the discourse of nationalism, using Bankim, Gandhi, and Nehru as its three historical moments. Underlying this series, there lies a fundamental question of the 'transfer' of social theory.[62] Bankim, midway in his career, apparently decided quite deliberately to move away from Western social theory and find resources from Indian tradition to do that work for him.[63] I do not think this project entirely succeeds. Nor does Gandhi's project, not in his own terms, but in the perceptions of the most effective, well-organized, and vocal segment of his countrymen who inherited the state from the British. And there could be two reasons for this lack of success. First, despite a long and high tradition of philosophical and theoretical thinking, the Hindu tradition, at least, failed to form serious curiosity about society and the state. Its reflections about the world around it seem to be stretched upon three levels: of the ascending unities of the self *(atman)*, the world *(jagat)*, and the infinite *(brahman)*. In this arrangement, the level of society does not, for some reason, get clearly spelt out.[64] In addition to this, it was clear

---

[62] Chatterjee 1985.
[63] Raychaudhuri 1989.
[64] Any reading of a text like the *Arthashastra* in search of a social and political theory in this sense is unproductive, and medieval texts by Muslim authors are not very different. Note, for instance, the remarkable similarity in the

by the early twentieth century that Indian nationalism was marked by a deep attraction for modernity, and saw independence as a condition for achieving it, unhindered by the inconsistent, disingenuous, and contradictory process brought in by the imperial power. The choice of narrative by Nehru is thus not just a personal decision; it showed deeper, more fundamental difficulties about thinking through modernity by means of indigenous discourses.

Nehru showed very clearly the tensions of accepting the two narratives he had chosen and tried to render compatible. Every history is narrated from a position of the self, in order to define the self. *Glimpses of World History* includes the self of the Indian nationalist in the rationalist narrative which earlier he had feared to call his own. Acceptance of that large frame did some violence to, and created some difficulties for, the other line of historical causality and construction of selfhood presented with eloquence in *The Discovery of India*. Nationalist modernism has always had problems in choosing its own self-constructing causal line, whether to see itself as the product of modernity or of Indianness. It could see that in a way it was entangled in both without recourse. Attempts to reconcile these two 'heritages', to produce a common new language out of the political diglossia of the national movement, have not been entirely successful after Independence.[65] The consciousness produced by the 'hegemony' of colonial discourse has remained an unhappy consciousness. It is irresistibly attracted to the historical proposal of modernity, but even accepting its division between two contending social forms, it also sees this modernity as being inextricably linked to the West. It retains the image of the West as an enemy 'to vanquish whom is really to suffer defeat'.[66]

Let us return briefly to the theoretical question about hegemony. Can the history of colonialism be written as a history of hegemonic strategies and their historic fate? I have used the term in this essay within ellipses of a sort, suspending the question of whether it is entirely justified to use it about colonial society in India. But concepts can be

---

arrangements in two widely different texts on statecraft coming from very different periods, the *Arthashastra*, and the *Ain-i-Akbari* of Abul Fazl.

[65] I have argued this elsewhere: Kaviraj 1990.

[66] A phrase from Hegel 1931 in the discussion on the unhappy consciousness.

used heuristically in two ways: some concepts of this kind can give us an intuitive picture of the facts of the social world, and, as we go along, this picture gets confirmed and more deeply etched, as it were. It is possible, however, to learn from concepts the other way round: by using a familiar concept, and by carefully observing the processes and reasons for its disconfirmation, we can begin to inflect or change the concept, or see that in its *logical* place we need some other concept, not the one we have used. By this I mean a conviction that at that logical space of analysis we require a concept; it must be a concept of the relevantly similar class; but it may not be the one we used. The problem we face in applying the concept of hegemony (in Gramsci's sense) to Indian colonial society is I think of this kind.

Thus, I am still unwilling to use the concept of hegemony in an explanatory capacity, though I admit that it may have some usefulness in two ways: (1) it helps us to set the question, and feel our way about its real form; and (2) it assists us to look for an answer to our problem in the realms of culture, common sense, and discourse, instead of the purely structural directions in which such answers have been sought before.[67]

Some of the difficulty in using the term can arise from insufficient attention to the subtly different meanings it can be given, and to Gramsci's specific construction of the concept. Gradually, the idea of hegemony has become so influential that it has tended to move away from Gramsci's specific use. Some of its present difficulties arise from the conceit of mirroring a whole world in the contrast between two terms.[68] Hegemony is often used as a limit term in an abstract and universal typology of political forms, irrespective of their historical location, in which hegemony represents one extreme form, 'pure' repression (whatever that means) being the other. This clearly obliges us to characterize any political state of affairs not marked by intense and explicit repression as being hegemonic in some sense. Gramsci's term,

---

[67] Curiously, both the dominant trends in colonial historiography have been governed by different forms of interest theories—group or class interest in the case of nationalists and Marxists, and a Namierite individual or factional interest in the case of the early works of the Cambridge School.

[68] That is, hegemonic/coercive—which leads to the ironical result that any period that is not blood-spattered comes to be regarded as hegemonic.

however, was not meant to be used this way, as an ahistorical taxonomic device; indeed, one can argue that developing terms like that is not possible within the logic of concept-generation in Gramsci's philosophic position. At any rate, this concept seems to me to be deeply historically indexed, housed inside the problematic of a theory of high capitalism and the role culture plays in its reproduction.

If Gramsci's concept is firmly housed within a theory of capitalism, it must be resistant to an easy shift to an explanation of imperial hegemony, except in some limited and specific ways. Some of its internal conditions of application are not satisfied. First, capitalism gradually integrates discourse by means of literary, non-formal, or religious instruction into a single culture, in a sense which is not available in colonial society. Traditional Indian society—at least its Hindu part—it can be argued, is held together by a common 'theory', but it does not work with a single-order common sense. Its common sense is fractured between the different social circles, precisely because it lacks a theory of the abstract individual, formal rights, and social attributes as 'possessions' of human beings. Attributes of individuals are integral rather than possessed. Therefore, it lacks a first-order *common* common sense, though it certainly has a 'theory' or a 'mechanism' of a 'second order' which shows such differential common senses related to each other in a complex unity. Secondly, the state–society relation is different from the Gramscian one. Sense of community, though intense, is fuzzy. But far more significant from our point of view, the state, instead of sitting on top of and constituting an integral part of the social hierarchy and its everyday reproduction, occupies an exalted but distanced space in the circle of circles. True, the colonial regime eventually broke this down through its economic and social initiatives. But its forcible integration of the segmentary productive regimes of rural India into an integrated economy did not find a cultural counterpart.

The imperial order did, however, propose a hegemonic arrangement, for that was how, in the nineteenth century, the bourgeois political order in Europe was formed, and officials, like other men, were condemned to the hermeneutic rule of understanding the unfamiliar in terms of the familiar. To a limited extent this hegemonic strategy worked. The stratum of the new middle class related itself to imperial authority in a way reminiscent of the typical hegemonic construction. But it singularly failed in carrying this ideological relay down towards the people. It was nowhere able to break down the state of 'neighbourly uncommunication' between the spheres of middle-class and subaltern-class discourse. Subaltern cultures protected their frontiers by a defensive use of illiteracy and strategic incomprehension. Certainly, during the last phase of the nationalist movement, popular forces strategically gave their support to a movement led by a coalition of propertied classes. But it can be emphatically argued that subaltern cultures retained their conceptual distinctness and privacy, and, despite their wordiness and impressive argumentative apparatus, middle-class discourse was not able to break down these techniques of confidentiality and reconstitute their historical common sense. This is a part of any explanation of the difficulties of the present Indian state. While I find some historians' use of hegemony as a term to explain colonial peace intelligible (i.e. I think I grasp the conceptual or argumentative occasion), I am not persuaded that its use is particularly apt. Even the nationalist Indian state is not hegemonic.

Hegemony refers to a dialogic connection between contending classes. If such dialogic relations existed in the colonial world, they held between the imperial rulers and the new elite, a class they had created. Its members were also the greatest indigenous beneficiaries of the colonial restructuring of Indian society, and politically the least grateful. Rationalist discourse, brought in by the imperial rulers to convince both Indians and the rulers themselves of the rational justifiability of British rule, provided intellectuals after an initial period with the cultural weapons with which they would undermine imperial dominance. The new elite, however, could not create its own hegemony, or create a dialogic relation with the subaltern classes. The spread of rationalism therefore reworked the cultural structure of Indian society in deep and long-term ways; and its effects are far from exhausted. In its historical role, rationalism in the colonial world was both a success and a failure. It failed in its political objective of gaining permanent compliance. The alphabet it presented to the colonial society was broken apart, parcellized, turned around to spell dissent. But in a different sense of course that was precisely the mark of its success. Even those who ended colonial rule and inherited their country used this alphabet, now neither wholly alien nor wholly familiar, as the means to their liberation and to construct their own social order. This shows the causal irreducibility of culture. Neither those who introduce an alphabet nor those who are its most effective users can know all it will do to the world. This of course is a fundamental Gramscian principle.

References

Alavi, H. 1975. India and the Colonial Mode of Production. In R. Miliband and J. Saville. Eds. *Socialist Register*, xii. London.

Bakhtin, M. 1984. *Rabelais and His World.* Bloomington, Indiana: Indiana University Press.

Bhattacharyya, S. 1971. *The Financial Foundations of the British Raj.* Simla: Indian Institute of Advanced Study.

Castoriadis, C. 1987. *The Imaginary Institution of Society.* Cambridge: MIT Press.

Chatterjee, Partha. 1985. *Nationalist Thought and the Colonial World: A Derivative Discourse?* Delhi: Oxford University Press.

Chattopadhyay, B.C. 1965. *Bankim Rachanavali.* Calcutta.

Cohn, Bernard S. 1987. Representing Authority in Victorian India. In idem, *An Anthropologist among the Historians and Other Essays.* Delhi: Oxford University Press.

Dutt, R.C. 1906. *Economic History of India,* 2 vols. London: 1st edn.

———. 1940. *Maharashtra Jivan Prabhat.* Calcutta.

———. 1960 rpnt. *Rajput Jivan Sandhya.* In idem, *Ramesa Rachanaval: His Collected Novels in Bengali.* Ed. with an introduction by Y.C. Bagal. Calcutta.

Gellner, E. 1983. *Nations and Nationalism.* Oxford: Blackwell.

Guha, Ranajit. 1983. *Elementary Aspects of Peasant Insurgency in Colonial India.* Delhi: Oxford University Press.

Hawthorn, G. 1976. *Enlightenment and Despair: A History of Sociology.* Cambridge: Cambridge University Press.

Hegel, G.W.F. 1931 rpnt. *The Phenomenology of Mind.* Trans. with an introduction and notes by J.B. Baillie. London.

Kaviraj, S. 1988. Construction of Otherness in Marx and Weber. *Occasional Paper* no. liii. Delhi: Nehru Memorial Museum and Library.

———. 1989. Imaginary History. Occasional Paper no. vii, 2nd Series. Delhi: Nehru Memorial Museum and Library.

———. 1990. Why Do We Lack Common Sense? Paper presented at a seminar on the Future of Indian Democracy. Delhi: Centre for the Study of Developing Societies, 2–4 March.

———. 1992. The Imaginary Institution of India. In P. Chatterjee and G. Pandey. Eds. *Subaltern Studies VII*. Delhi: Oxford University Press.

Koselleck, R. 1985. Begriffsgeschichte and Social History. In R. Koselleck. *Futures Past*. Cambridge, Mass.: Harvard University Press.

Kumar, Ravinder. 1989. The Past and Present: An Indian Dialogue. *Daedalus*: cxviii, 27–49.

Mackie, J.L. 1975. Causes and Conditions. In E. Sosa, ed. *Causation and Conditionals*. London.

Macpherson, C.B. 1964. *The Political Theory of Possessive Individualism*. London.

Mill, J.S. 1835. Democracy and Government. In G. Williams. Ed. *John Stuart Mill on Politics and Society*. Glasgow.

———. 1861. Considerations on Representative Government. Ch. 18 in J.S. Mill, *Collected Works*, xix, ed. J.M. Robson. Toronto: University of Toronto Press.

Montesquieu, C.S. 1760. *Persian Letters*. Trans. from the French. Glasgow.

Mukhia, H. and T. Byres. Eds. 1985. *Feudalism and Non-European Societies*. London: Frank Cass.

Mukhopadhyay, B. 1895. *Swapnalabdha Bharatvarsher Itihas*. Calcutta.

Nehru, J. 1934. *Glimpses of World History*. Rpnt. London: Bodley Head, 1959.

———. 1936. *An Autobiography*. London. Rpnt. London: Allen Lane, 1971.

———. 1966. *The Discovery of India*. Rpnt. Calcutta: Signet Press.

Owen, R. 1858. A Plan for India. In A.L. Morton, *The Life and Ideas of Robert Owen*. New York: International Publishers, 1962.

Raychaudhuri, T. 1989. *Europe Reconsidered*. Delhi: Oxford University Press.

Saberwal, S. 1986. *India: The Roots of Crisis*. Delhi: Oxford University Press.

Said, Edward. 1978. *Orientalism*. London and New York: Vintage.

Seal, A. 1978. *The Emergence of Indian Nationalism*. Cambridge: Cambridge University Press.

Skinner, Quentin. 1988 Meaning and Understanding in the History of Ideas. In J. Tully, ed. *Meaning and Context*. Cambridge: Cambridge University Press.

Tagore, Rabindranath. 1946. *Manasi*. Calcutta: Viswabharati.

Vandyopadhyay, V.N. and S.K. Das. Ed. 1946–50. *Collection of Bengali Essays: Bankim Centenary Edition*. Calcutta.

Voltaire. 1966 rpnt. *Candide, or Optimism: A New Translation, Backgrounds, Criticism*. New York.

——. 1971 rpnt. *Philosophical Dictionary.* Ed. and trans. T. Besterman. Harmondsworth: Penguin.

——. 1978 rpnt. *Zadig*; [*and*] *L'ingénu.* Trans. with an introduction by John Butt. Harmondsworth: Penguin.

Washbrook, D. 1981. Law, State and Agrarian Society in Colonial India. *Modern Asian Studies*, xv, 649–721.

Weldon, T.D. 1953. *The Vocabulary of Politics.* Harmondsworth: Penguin.

3
On the Structure of Nationalist Discourse

What is implied by putting the term 'discourse' in the title, the very initial statement of our problem? Does this mean simply a casually fashionable way of indicating nationalist ideas? Or do we, by the use of this term, indicate that our inquiry would be of some particular type, or attend to some special aspect of nationalist thinking? Terminological questions should be sorted out first.

What is Discourse? What Kind of Discourse?

The term discourse can be used in a general way, but I intend to use it to emphasize the *structure* of nationalist discourse (Sathyamurthy 1989). A simply general way of using the term might jeopardize what we can eventually get out of our exercise if it is carried out systematically. Does discourse mean all that is said by people in the actual political world—the mere totality of words, ideas, concepts, and more complex combinations of these, like speeches, dispositions, programmes, rhetoric, ideologies, official documents—all of this without some discernible internal order; a totality that is as pointless as it is unencompassable? Politics is of course a world of words, but which words, which parts of these words and things made out of them are we trying to study in the analysis of discourse? Is it this totality? Is it an inner structure buried in it? Is it a conceptual grid which holds them together and sets limits to what can be thought and done through them?

First published in T.V. Sathyamurthy, ed., *Social Change and Political Discourse in India, vol. 1: State and Nation in the Context of Social Change* (Delhi: Oxford University Press, 1994), pp. 298–335.

Studies of discourse can turn to two different traditions of rigorous thinking about these questions. But the curiosities of these traditions go in distinctly different directions. The first of these is the tradition of structuralism of various types, starting from structural linguistics, which tries to separate out the differences between living speech, its effervescence, its contingency, its quick, dramatic life and death, and deeper underlying ordering forms which govern our ability to undertake such episodic speech through grammars ordinarily unavailable to common thinking.

These are deeper regularities—forms, constraints, limits—which make speaking, writing, thinking what they are without being interchangeable. Speakers implicitly obey constraints of grammar without being able to formulate its formal rules and exact restrictions. These rules form a structure, latent, constraining, unavailable to the ordinary user of language, and consequently recoverable by deliberate strategies of research. Foucault extended the existence of such grammars from natural language to conceptual and theoretical languages and would identify deep structural networks of exclusion, silence, various forms of unutterability constituting the vital frontier between what can be said inside a discourse and what cannot (Foucault 1972: especially 46ff.).

Of equal distinction is a second tradition in which the study of discourse represents an object with just the opposite characteristics. To Volosinov (Bakhtin), equally interested in what can be done to the world through words and the subtle politics of representations, study of discourse means precisely living speech, the performance, the enactment with its circumstances and conditions, not the deep configurations which make them possible. In his work, the silent constraining existence of these deep configurations is not denied, but he is primarily interested in understanding how their classical lines are being constantly wrenched in different directions, and how the contingent but insistent demands of social life alter them historically. For Volosinov, Saussurian structures can never fully explain or clarify why what is said is said. It can indicate what kinds of things in principle can be uttered under some structural conditions. It never shows how a particular speech came to be chosen out of those that are all structurally equally possible. Structure, in this sense, cannot explain history; though structuralists would answer—I think justifiably—that structures do not aim at explaining history in this sense. On this view, discourse study must try to capture precisely the irruption of linguistic phenomena, the individuality of living speech, expressions of experience, or poetically, the breath of life (Volosinov 1986).

Schematically, we can isolate three ways in which the term discourse is used in political analysis: the first is a general use of the term which indicates that a body of ideas has a certain internal coherence both due to their linguistic meaning and external association with political events so that they are grouped together in history. These two ways of imparting coherence to ideas can loosely be called internal and external; the first a coherence imparted to them by their conceptual meanings, and the second by their act-meanings (or force, to use Austin's language). Both these aspects have to be gathered up in a Marxist conception of ideology.

Vulgar conceptions of ideology, using a simple dichotomy between a correct and a false consciousness, may not be able to incorporate such inflections, but a more sophisticated rendering of the argument extending Volosinov's distinction between theme and meaning must move in that direction. Indeed, the purpose of the theory of ideology is precisely to insist that use-meanings and act-meanings go together in historical analysis. Inside this kind of a theory of ideology, we can then take recourse, when necessary, to the more rigorous distinctions made by the two types of discourse analysis.

In the analysis of nationalist discourse, it seems a more promising approach to search for simple versions of false consciousness. If there is any field about which nationalist thought establishes plausible but misleading narratives, it is about the society it tries to bring under its political control and its historical self-representation. But this narrative emerges in several distinct stages: it acquires a particular outline through its first skirmishes with colonialist ideology, and this narrative of the self bears a strong historical relation with the early growth of nationalist politics. After some time it has clearly crossed the threshold, and the initial narrative about the self is restructured in the Gandhian phase of Indian nationalism. Finally, there is a third stage, post-Independence, in which this narrative undergoes some significant changes associated with the demands of serving as an ideology of a new nation state. In this essay I shall try to present a brief account of this process of historical re-formation of the nationalist narrative.

If we take nationalism seriously as an ideological discourse, it is not adequate merely to say that it is a configuration of false but plausible beliefs. Each ideology arranges its falsity and plausibility in its own particular way. Thus, it becomes vacuous merely to assert its falsity. Its peculiar structure and form must be unravelled. Ideologies appear to have an intimate connection with history and its narrative construction, the persuasiveness with which historical constructions enable people to make sense of the complexities of the modern world. The power of modern ideologies depends often on its self-portrayal, its rendering of its own history.

The first step in developing the critique of any ideological discourse then must be to disbelieve its autobiography, the history it gives to itself (Chatterjee 1986: 51). While dealing with Indian nationalism, Marxists often fail to make this primary move. It is more common to take for granted the history that nationalism has traditionally made familiar, only to contest its ideological evaluation at some crucial points. Thus, it is usual to agree that the Gandhi–Irwin pact was a crucial stage in the history of the nationalist movement, but see it as a 'sellout' to imperialism rather than an 'astute step of temporary retreat' (Dutt 1970).[1] Similarly, it is usual to write the story of the Congress in terms of the division between Moderates and Extremists, but see the Moderates as social progressives (Roy 1971). I am far from suggesting that these arguments and evaluations are wrong. But in order to understand nationalism better, we must transcend these descriptions internal to nationalist history and attend to other things which have, for various reasons, not found a significant place in this history—other regularities, other structures, other resemblances.

Two questions are central to this enterprise: what is the discourse of nationalism? Secondly, what is the right way of going about understanding it? I assume that nationalist discourse refers to the intellectual process through which the conception of an Indian nation is gradually

---

[1] R.P. Dutt's *India Today* (1940) is a representative example of such alternative history. I think it is wrong to deny that this constituted an alternative historiography, but at the same time this is not the only way or only valuable or sensible way of writing one. Indeed, any idea of a single alternative history which would replace all the evils, errors, biases, and blindnesses of others is a suspect ideal, based on a simplistic understanding of the historicity of history writing.

formed, the discourse that forms it, is in favour of it, and gives it historical shape. I shall try to indicate some major stages by which this imagining of the nation happens, treating it as contingent and historical, rupturing the absentminded and long-practised continuities through which we customarily think about this. The right way of understanding it, it seems, is not to follow its own telling, but to surround it with other relatively neglected cultural processes which provide it with its historic preconditions (Guha 1982–91).[2]

Initial Responses

To modern students of colonialism, the early reception of ambitious European merchants in Indian society may appear puzzlingly positive. Indians who saw Europeans take the first steps towards colonial power did not respond with strong resentment; for reasons which are easily found. Traditional ruling groups, consisting of rajas and nawabs and their effete quarrelsome nobilities, could not conceive of an eventual British capture of their continental country. They saw them as transient enemies or allies, depending on how their loyalties were ranged, and since the British made it amply clear that their loyalty to Indian rulers was far from unchangeable, even present enemies realized the possible future usefulness of these potentially powerful allies in what was bound to continue, in their view, to be a predominantly domestic scramble for political ascendancy.

Surely, they were not the only social group whose destiny was to be affected by colonialism. Lower orders of society were customarily far-removed from turmoil at the upper stratum of political authority, and looked at the rise and fall in the fortunes of their distant lords with indifference. Some other, primarily intermediary, groups responded to the European presence more positively, as it provided unforeseen avenues of advancement. To their intellectuals it provided, or seemed to promise, a historical opportunity of subjecting a traditional social order to criticism. For these groups the attraction was very strong indeed, precisely because it occasioned the happy merger of moral and material interests.

---

[2] The work of the Subaltern Studies group is significant because they have undertaken a task of this kind.

Early responses to European entry into India were, interestingly, dominated by political and cultural considerations, rather than basic economic ones. Much of the early thinking of Indians about colonialism centred less on the hard economics of exploitation and more on the cultural 'meaning' of Europe. Europe meant different things to different generations of Indians who came into contact with its impressive power and glamorous modernity.

This was again due to two reasons. Europe was going through a period of unprecedented rapid change in its economy, political institutions, and culture; and kept offering a different countenance to the world which observed this new kind of society with wonder. Europe, before and after the Cromwellian revolution, before and after the French revolution, before and after Napoleon, before and after 1848, before and after the coming of socialism, before and after the unification of Germany, before and after the World War, and before and after Nazism could not either materially or symbolically appear the same.

These events appeared disorientating enough to those who experienced them in Europe, but they at least carried with them the consolation of historical immediacy. To Indians, wildly enthusiastic or denunciatory about that history, but less informed, unacquainted with the culture or politics which supplied these events with their internal causal logic, it must have appeared a bewildering illustration of de Tocqueville's dictum about modernity: a time when living is strenuous because 'the past had ceased to throw light upon the future' (de Tocqueville 1974: 396–7).

But Indian reaction was limited or constrained not only because of its relative lack of information; Europe came to India predominantly through powerful rationalist narratives. Successful civilizations always construct myths about themselves. The European intellectuals' feeling that the meaning of modernity was still unclear, its processes still unmastered, its riddle not unravelled, did not stand in the way of the creation of ideological myths and their persuasive narratives. Ideological narratives simplify historical complexities of the growth of a civilization and force it into an accessible group of cliches. The first encounter of Indian intellectuals with Europe's history was through a mythical narrative of this kind—the great story of reason—conveyed to them through the curricula used in the institutions of new Western education. In time, greater acquaintance with Europe's history served to destroy this classical ideological theory. The idea of Europe came to acquire much greater complexity and the narrative of European reason lost some of its stifling dominance.

In later nationalist thought it was realized that trajectories of modernity differed from one part of Europe to another, and even after the stabilization of distinctly similar forms of modern social life all over Europe serious dissimilarities persisted. French and British political institutions were recognizably different even at this distance, and gave rise to constantly renewed polemics between conservative and radical sections of European liberal opinion. Ideologically, Europe did not present a homogeneous picture either, contrary to the mythology of reason—a narrative which attempted to demonstrate the triumph of European rationality starting from ancient Greece, through Rome, down through the southern and northern renaissance into a generalized modern rational life evenly shared by the inhabitants of this enlightened continent.

In the later discourse of Indian nationalism, this internal diversity of Europe, the several voices with which Europe spoke in history, was utilized to great polemic effect. Dissenting intellectual trends within European modernity, sometimes trends which dissented from modernity itself despairingly—especially romanticism, idealism and, later, socialism—found their way straight and easily into the nationalist's heart because of their different yet related contributions to a critique of the crystallizing discourse of bourgeois modernity. In his/her search for foundations and support, the nationalist, in a gesture of implicit internationalism, often turned to them.

Colonialism entered Indian society initially in stealthy steps, through misunderstandings and misconstruals. Indeed, before it took firm political root, the British were more concerned to conceal the extent of their success than to make a display of it, for fear of putting into effect a desperate and overwhelming opposition against the power of alien intruders. However, once it became stable, the colonial state came to acquire not only a particular economic structure and form but was also inextricably linked to some cultural processes.

Acts of the colonial establishment in India were poised between three different publics at the same time. Its actions had to make sense to a public at home exulting in the achievements of rationalistic modernity, including its military adventures in faraway foreign lands. Due to its demands, colonial administrations slowly had to change their policies of a minimal cultural strategy, keeping away from troublesome entanglements in processes of reform. Demands from a section of the native elite, which played on the distant but more compelling expectations of British public opinion, made such indifference untenable. It became, through a slow but irreversible process, an apparatus which set out on a large 'civilizing' process—of altering, restructuring, conquering the most difficult terrain of all—the culture of Indian society, the realm of the mind (Deuskar 1970).[3]

When administrators from one culture face another, strange and incomprehensible, there is an understandable inclination to start from a presumption of similarity, and gradually, through experience, work in perceptions of difference. This movement from similarity to difference remains always an imperfect and unconcluded process. Always, some part of this project of defamiliarization remains unachieved or uncomprehended. Colonial rulers, when they undertook reform, worked with a picture of the cultural structure of Indian society that was surreptitiously similar to the one in bourgeois Europe—a culture that was highly integrated after the success of bourgeois revolutions, which had a common core of moral, cognitive, and social beliefs at their centre constituting a general, social 'common sense'. This stock of beliefs mirrored the structure of society, and holding them made the business of undertaking social actions more internally consistent and practically successful.

This core of beliefs was articulated and re-coordinated to contingent historical needs by a specialized intelligentsia, often by means of social theory. Evidently, the cultural organization of traditional Indian society was not like this in all respects, but colonial policy-makers assumed that it was. The colonial order followed what could be called a strategy of 'Gramscianism', assuming that if the structure of common sense beliefs of the directive classes in Indian society was altered, this would gradually lead to an alteration of the core common sense of society as a whole.

---

[3] Some early nationalists saw the cultural process as vital. Sakharam Ganesh Deuskar, writing in Bengali, presented a popular version of the drain theory; but added to it a trenchant critique of colonial ideology and culture that was his own.

Historically most remarkable was the mixture of success and failure encountered by this cultural strategy of colonialism, and its long-term unintended consequences. Eventually, the colonial establishment was able to alter the entire conceptual apparatus of a significant crust of the Indian elite, especially the new elite that had come into being through the colonial process itself. Given the model of unified European societies, through the general laicization of knowledge, these groups, by virtue of constituting the intellectual elite, should have performed the function of being the creators, shapers, repositories, and communicators of its common sense.

However, the unqualified successes of the colonial educational process made this impossible. It created a new elite without much historical continuity with traditional social groups which had earlier performed these functions. Indeed, their cultural transformation was so drastic and complete that it turned around what may be called, in Dilthey's (1974: 171 and 231) well-known phrase, the 'historical *a priori*' of their thinking about society and history, and the basic register of identification of social objects themselves.

A most vital part of this cultural transformation consisted of the alteration of their historical aspirations; in other words, given their new way of thinking, the new elite came to be covetous of the history of the West, along with its prosperity, technical control, and political power. However, the very success of the colonial enterprise made the fulfilment of its other, related objective less likely. The more British cultural policy was successful in transforming the conceptual alphabet of this group, the further it was removed from its deeper historical objective of fashioning a new common sense for the entire Indian society through their intermediation. The more the British persuaded them, the less their collective ability to persuade the rest of Indian society. This frustrated the plan of making the Indian people, through their intellectual dominance, see the social world in a manner that would make colonialism appear largely as a benign institution—an altruistic enterprise in the spread of enlightenment.

The acquisition of this alphabet of thought made this class gradually share its language, common presuppositions, theories, prejudices, and inclinations with the Western intelligentsia and colonial administrators; but it also broke off, in the course of a single century, any links it may have had with their own society's popular discourse. The consequence of this direction in Indian culture is immediately reflected in the history of protests against British rule.

The insurrection of 1857, despite its traditional elite leadership, contained ideological motifs, organizational principles, social norms, and political slogans that were more genuinely common between different social groups. It could thus create, however temporarily, a bond between traditional elites and the rebellious peasant–soldiery of the Company. Afterwards, grievances against British rule certainly did not disappear, but the discontent of the upper and lower orders lost a common language, forcing middle-class discontent to turn into the mendicant constitutionalism of the early Congress, and the resentfulness of the subaltern classes into occasional, blind, local outbursts. Both types of disorder were much easier for British authorities to contend with, all serious threat having to wait until their reconnection after the arrival of Gandhi.

Early Anti-colonialism

The entry of colonialism not only introduced a set of unfamiliar new institutions into Indian society, but also a set of discourses on which the functioning of these institutions depended. Although the new middle class had enthusiastically accepted its alphabet, it would be wrong to argue that these altered only *their* social world. The social world was decisively restructured for *all* groups and social classes, irrespective of whether they accepted it, liked it, or underwent a training in using this discourse of colonial rationalism. Even those left out of this crucial education, or those who sought to resist its advent, were obliged to live in a world which was transformed in fundamental ways.

There is a strong temptation to think theoretically about this transition through the distinction between *gemeinschaft* and *gesellschaft* which Tönnies used to analyse the rise of European modernity. What happened in India does not seem to fit easily into the Tönnies framework.[4] The transition appears to have been from one type of community

---

[4] In much of the discussion about modernizing initiatives and consequences of colonialism, the dichotomy between traditional and modern is automatically joined to the opposition between *gemeinschaft* and *gesellschaft* derived from Tönnies.

to another, rather than to an unqualified form of *gesellschaft*. In traditional society, people did have a strong sense of living in *gemeinschaft* organizations. But the colonial drive towards a truncated and distorted modernity does not force people to change their life into unambiguously *gesellschaft*-like associations. They move from a fuzzy conception of community to one of an enumerated kind.[5]

The lived world of society was traditionally marked by the sense of community, an unexplicated, pre-reflexive sense of belonging to collectivities which produced the individuals who lived in them, unlike the modernist conception of pre-existing individuals producing collective entities. This traditional community sense was fuzzy in two ways. First, because, in a variety of instances of social exchange, persons would have chosen different types of senses of belonging in order to give themselves a social face. An individual, when asked to define who s/he was, could have mentioned his/her village, his/her region, religious denomination, caste. There was also the territorial boundary of the kingdom, though these must have been the least determinate because so heavily prone to fluctuation.

Among these identities some are territorial (village, kingdom, region), though territoriality could be of different sorts (Fox 1977). Others are clearly non-territorial. What is central in this configuration of identities available is that a traditional person would not have been under such pressure to clarify the identity-structure in terms of which s/he lived. They would not accord to these identities a clear hierarchy: these would be ranged in a line out of which s/he would pick out the right one, as the occasion demanded. The arrangement of identities is fuzzy in the sense of being indeterminate in rank order; though, paradoxically, this allows for greater precision and flexibility in the social identification of persons, and is more complex than the modern unidimensional assertion of a national tag.[6]

There is a second sense in which communities are fuzzy. Some of these communities do not have clear territorial boundaries, or a map

---

[5] The following section restates a distinction I have used in Kaviraj 1992.

[6] My use of the term 'fuzzy' is not meant to indicate imprecision, only a different way of being precise. Although the argument is quite different from my own, see Bose (1989) for an analysis of the complexity of identity ordering in India.

in the way modern societies must have. It is a world of a much finer, graded, and more complex organization of difference, much like the way one tone of colour would shade off into another in a spectrum. The best illustration of this can be that of the history of formation of linguistic communities, one of the identities with which the identity of the nation must later compete for loyalty and space.

Indian society had traditionally, due to the caste system, known a dual system of high and low language. The structure of its speech communities would have had something like the form in Figure 1.[7]

It will be noticed that such a structure is not extraordinary: it is, indeed, exactly similar to the structure of agrarian societies outlined in Gellner's studies. A small, spatially dispersed but more tightly knit and self-recognizing élite can keep under its control the horizontally

Fig. 1

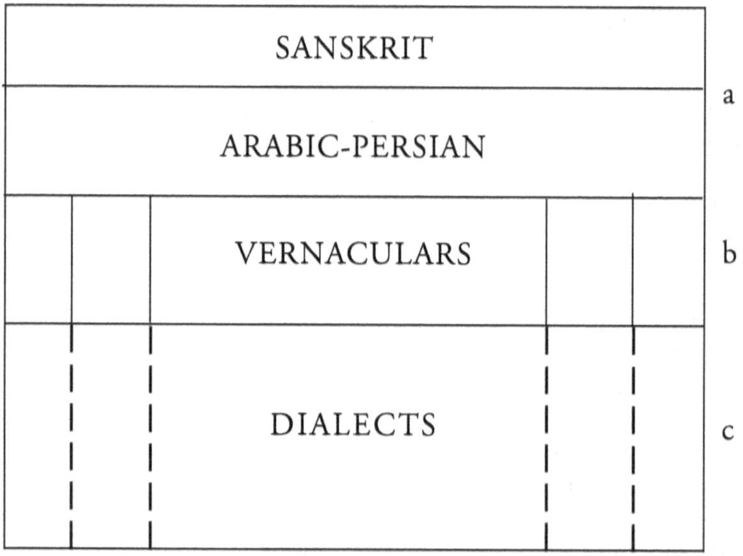

SANSKRIT	
	a
ARABIC-PERSIAN	
VERNACULARS	b
DIALECTS	c

(*Note:* While those who had *c* had only *c*, users of *b* could use *bc*; and correspondingly, users of *a* had *abc*, though, obviously, those who knew Sanskrit did not necessarily know Arabic–Persian and vice versa.)

---

[7] The diagram in its basic design is based on an argument similar to the argument about agrarian societies in Gellner (1983).

segmented masses of the ordinary people. This was certainly true of the superior caste-for-itself character of the Brahmins, as opposed to the other more deeply segmented castes.

Thus we have to modify the usual segmentation thesis about Indian society; though all parts of society were segmented, they were not segmented in the same way, to the same extent, or with the same consequences. This principle of differential segmentation was reflected still more intensely at the level of spoken language, where language shows its universality. At the lowest level, then, language communities were speech communities of dialects confined to small areas, and heightened a feeling of a pre-critical identity among its native speakers. To fit this picture of difference between neighbouring dialects into a modern map would be difficult. Modern maps would require clear boundaries and thresholds. In this picture one dialect would gently and imperceptibly shade off into the next. Thus, even though the region now called Bengal might speak dialects belonging to a single family, and thus related to each other, at the edges of this region, in Medinipur or Mithila, the dialect would not be demonstrably different from the neighbouring speech of Orissa or Bihar.

Into this world of gradual difference, new forces were released by the entry of colonialism. The emergence of dominant economic and social elites, which enjoyed the circumstantial gift of the colonizers' partiality, created 'natural' norm-setting communities in particular regions. The dialect spoken around the once unknown hamlet of Calcutta, formerly without any particular claim to literary eminence or aural melody, suddenly emerges as the indispensable vehicle of a high Bengali literary culture.[8] As the power of this elite became more entrenched along with their colonial patrons, and the coming of the printing press, its preeminence was soon inscribed on the language, through the general acceptance by regional Bengali elites of its grammatical and syntactical foibles and subsequently through imitation of pronunciation. The local elites of outlying regions, and Orissa and Bihar on the borders of Bengal, would start copying this language, initially for formal communication and writing, and later for oral exchange, in order to underline their membership of the elite grouping, not only economically but also in terms of its styles of cultural self-identification.

[8] This process is sketched in somewhat greater detail in Kaviraj 1992.

This is particularly attractive for the new *bhadralok* elite, because it provides them with a constantly used social signifier which marks them off from the slovenly lower orders. Their claim to distinction cannot be mistaken the moment they open their mouths, and this process of linguistic refinement is carried to such excessive lengths that it would not be far wrong to say that the Bengalis are a people held together by the differences in their language. Through such processes of élite homogenization, it becomes possible, after about a century, to draw a modern linear boundary between regions, because similar processes are also at work on the other side.[9] While, in the sixteenth century, it might be impossible to tell the difference in dialect between neighbouring villages, by the mid-nineteenth century it becomes possible to say that two villages belong to two different speech communities, and that this determines their political, economic, and cultural demands, rights, and aspirations. It must be recognized, however, that at lower levels of the social order the earlier system of spectrum-like difference might still survive, and remain effective in everyday life.

What is the relation between this story, if credible, and the story of nationalist discourse? There are two significant connections. First, nationalist discourse is crucially connected with the political use of languages, and the relation between English and the vernaculars; mature mass nationalism invariably has to await the emergence of cultures of vernacular assertiveness. Second, there is also the vital question of what exactly should be the relation between the two strata of identities—the national (which in India does not have a linguistic marker) and the regional (which does): in one view, the absence of a spontaneous community with those speaking the same language, a major source of strength of nationalism in the European context, becomes a source of weakness in the Indian subcontinent.

The first implication emerging from this specificity in relation to India is that an idea often adopted by nationalists influenced by modernization theory has to be rejected. The conventional dichotomy between a recent, constructed, occasionally even rational, identity of the nation and the primordial and pre-existing identity of the region is undermined. It must be recognized that although in many parts of India vernacular languages may have originated as early as the tenth

---

[9] For a discussion of the Oriya case, see Mohanty 1982.

century, regional *political* identity centred on a language is a relatively recent phenomenon, derived largely from the same historical forces. To decide between the claims of the region and the nation is not to choose between a modern and a relatively ancient identity, but two configurations thrown up by the same historical process.[10]

Into the earlier world of fuzzy identities colonialism, especially its rationalist cognitive apparatus working most strikingly in administration and education, brings in an entirely new way of making sense of and acting practically in the world. The census, initially planned in 1862, eventually carried through in 1872 (Barrier 1981), is part of a process of immense and irreversible enumeration of the social world; it creates a new world of maps, boundary lines, divisions, numbers and statistics, and a new technique of living in terms of these. Once this social ontology is firmly grounded in the main social practices of the state and dominant groups, its logic sinks into the everyday consciousness of the lower orders as well.

A second aspect of this change in social ontology also needs to be mentioned. Certainly, all these new definitions require a certain cognitive apparatus disseminated by special educational and intellectual processes. The majority of Indian people remained unlettered, and therefore distant from this formidable apparatus. Yet it would be fallacious to believe that, because they had no secure control over these skills, their world remained unaffected by its consequences. Not to be able to count does not mean that people can remain immune from the processes of this fateful counting. To be illiterate does not mean remaining unaffected by new boundaries drawn upon the world by literate politics. Gramsci's theory points out graphically how illiteracy is a form of political resourcelessness, how, precisely because they are culturally deprived, poorer people are powerless against hegemonic processes and respond blindly to agendas set by others.[11]

Today, an unlettered Muslim might not know exactly how many per cent of India's population belong to his/her community, but s/he

---

[10] The forms of religious identity commonly termed communalism in India are modern identities of religion, and, therefore, products of the modern instead of the traditional world.

[11] I read Gramsci's conception of subalternity as indicating this complex mixture of a proneness to dissent and an inability to set agendas.

surely knows s/he is a member of a minority group and how to behave in accord with that knowledge, and what implications this has for his/her political rights. One implication of this modern world in which boundaries are clear, distances are measured, and populations are enumerated—a world grasped in numbers in every sense—is often missed in nationalist thought.[12] It is now not only the national community which is counted and feels invigorated by this statistic; so do all other potential communities—religions, castes, sects, languages.

All these identities, which can be candidates for political mobilization when associated with a sense of disadvantage and distress, can now mobilize their knowledge of numbers, territorial distribution, social award of benefits, and make politically adroit uses of the display of the power of helplessness. There is no historical necessity which ensures that the nation wins out, the historical pronunciation of a certain identity—that of the nation—among all others is entirely dependent on the process of politico-cultural persuasion. Politics decides which arguments win and lose in the increasingly open and crowded marketplace of ideas about identities.

It is thus not a matter of inner necessity, but political contingencies and some luck, that it was eventually a largely, vaguely, idealistically, and optimistically secular identity which came to represent the identity of the Indian nation. It was a fragile achievement, fortunate for some. But this was not the end result of a linear and simple process. However, there are two current narratives through which nationalism presents itself to its adherents.

The first, which is both simple and linear, works with a minimal definition of nationalism (based on the ideas of those who opposed the British) and assimilates the most diverse strands of thought and activity into this concept. Tipu Sultan, Nana Fadnavis, the Rani of Jhansi, Mir Kasim, and Gandhi and Nehru are treated together as coming under the same broad trend of anti-imperialism. Incongruously, this would also include figures such as Raja Ram Mohun Roy—who never wished the British empire ill—to form an impressive but also misleading pageant.[13]

---

[12] Cohn 1987 contains a pioneering analysis of the social consequences of the census.

[13] Joshi (1975) contains some early contributions to a revisionist history of nationalism . See especially Sarkar 1975 and Sen 1975.

More recently, a second narrative has gained currency which would simply deploy a criterion of the Nehru brand of nationalism and exclude from the title 'nationalist' all those who failed to fulfil its retrospective demands (e.g. Chandra *et al.* 1988). A surprisingly large number of nationalist figures would fail the test if it were to be stringently administered; besides, it would also produce a misleadingly benevolent picture of what Indian nationalism in reality was. Its drawbacks are twofold. First, this view romanticizes Indian nationalism by neglecting the power of strong religious, occasionally communal, sentiments that often worked in its favour, even within the Congress. Second, it gives us a false picture of the past, and would have us believe that all forces of nationalism were in favour of a secular state (Chatterjee 1965).[14] This will grossly underestimate the difficulties in the way of secularization of the state in modern India.[15]

To understand nationalism it is essential to break away from these narrative structures, but that is not easy, because we have ourselves lived inside them, and they have, in large part, helped us constitute ourselves.

The Formation of an Anti-colonial Consciousness

Of necessity, colonial ideology in its early phase underplayed the enormity of the political change taking place in India. This may or may not have been due to deliberate design or cunning. The process of establishment of British dominion over India was very uneven, and initially shaky, It depended vitally on preventing the cementing of an overwhelming coalition against itself. A voluble ideology of colonialism under these circumstances would have been injurious to British interest.

The first steps taken by this colonial power were not accompanied by an overarching ideology of social reconstruction or historical

---

[14] The political intent behind this move is clear: this would take away any legitimacy that communal forces in present-day India can claim as inheritors of the Indian nationalist tradition.

[15] Bankimchandra's political essays furnish good examples on both these counts; he was much concerned with a critique of utilitarian ideas which he called 'the philosophy of the belly', and yet he agonized over the rights of indigenous tyrants, and foreign reformers (Chatterjee 1965: 54ff).

'improvement'; rather, British agents sought to create a misleading feeling of the everydayness of their efforts, so that they were seen as one unremarkable party among many others contending to advance their material interest in a fluid political situation. To the extent rationalist ideas played any part at this stage, it appears to have been limited merely to accentuating a sense of invincibility of British arms.

In deep isolation in such a varied and alien land, without hope of quick reinforcements, they liked to picture themselves, entirely understandably, as invincible warriors with guns in their hands and reason on their side. It was important to convince not only themselves but also their Indian adversaries and fickle friends. Even this attenuated version of occidental presence introduced a militarily conceived notion of superior modernist rationality. Several of the more successful Indian rulers, Tipu Sultan in the South and Ranjit Singh in the North, showed their acceptance of this idea by enlisting the skills of European gunnery, sometimes by employing European mercenaries despite their reputation for notorious undependability.

The theatres of war in early colonial India were at the same time theatres of ideological conflict, a constantly renewed and repeatedly lost battle against European reason in military uniform. The eventual failure of all opposition by native powers against British rule posed a basic historical question to thinking Indians: how does one explain this failure—its persistence and finality?—since, clearly, this was not a failure of individuals, but of an entire civilization. Was it to be consigned to an extraordinary series of military accidents? Or to some underlying historical necessity? In any case, how did Indians cope with the forces of modernity that Europe represented?

The answer came in two directly opposite forms. The first acknowledged the superiority of European arms, but extended this to the related superiority of principles of *social* organization. But, interestingly, adherents of this view refused to accept any racialist or historical essentialism which often went with this belief; in other words, there was something in the social character of Europeans which made such feats possible but barred these to mere Indians.

The 'Young Bengal' movement, which saw such rationalist symbolism in food and dress, and found in forbidden meat not only good food but also evidence of philosophic rationalism, was one illustration of this line of thought. But Bengal also witnessed an understandably conservative reaction which wished to deploy against the British the strategy which, they believed, had worked against Muslim rulers of Hindu society—of secreting the operation of the basic social processes by raising barriers of orthodoxy. By intricate interdictions and prohibitions, they would draw their social practices away from the inchoately emerging arena of public law and open debate. The convention of open public discussion of the rationality of religious practices appeared to them a particularly threatening device exclusively meant to bring ridicule upon indigenous religion and to subvert them.

As colonialism grew more stable and the administration grew less anxious about the durability of the empire, the nature of the argument from the colonial side underwent rapid transformation. Colonial modernity was now pictured as an advanced social form, internally consistent, though occasionally flawed because of the hesitation and cowardliness of colonial policies of social reform. Gradually, the justification of British power in India was taken over by arguments of distinctly utilitarian provenance.

Utilitarianism exercised a powerful appeal on the collaborative Indian intelligentsia for two related reasons. First, it offered in a schematic form the outline of a general rationalist theory of history; it allowed Indians and the British to have a common and discursive picture of historical evolution and a common language to dispute its intermediate hypotheses. It made collaboration easier, and at the same time made it appear not as collaboration. Within its rational frame, some answer could be sought to the great puzzle of Indian experience—what was happening in Indian history, going beyond the purely parochial accounts of glory or misfortunes of single dynasties or regions.

Utilitarianism offered a simple theory of transition. It saw the current historical process as progress, a unilinear, largely teleological movement of all societies towards technological modernity and attendant forms of social organization represented by nineteenth-century Europe. Civilization was the common fate of all humanity; only some societies were able to devise these processes endogenously and others would have to undertake this enlightening journey under the tutelage of the pioneers. Utilitarian theory thus perfectly fitted the colonial setting.

Just as it undermined earlier prescriptivist theories in Europe, it undermined the traditional title to rule of indigenous claimants to political power. Utilitarianism taught people to judge all such claims consequentially. The right to rule simply should accrue to those who would provide more of the benefits of modern civilization to larger numbers. By this logic, the claim of the British to political authority in India after providing it with stability, administrative unification, rational legal systems, modern education, and other material benefits of modern civilization, was clearly incontestable. No wonder some early nationalist thinkers spent a good deal of time disputing whether the right to rule of an enlightened foreign ruler was weaker than those of malignant indigenous tyrants. Many of them had to admit that the claim of simple indigenism was sentimental and unacceptable (Chatterjee 1986).

By the 1880s the hitherto unproblematic dominance of utilitarian theory began to be challenged. Indeed, the original forms in which challenge was mounted were to be of indelible significance to the ways in which nationalist Indians, since then, have tried to come to terms with their history. This critique was mounted first by writers who are conventionally, unjustifiably in my view, characterized as conservatives.

To question the ideological conceits of British imperial authority against the tide of the times was hardly an unproblematically conservative attitude. Partly, of course, this is a problem of interpretive classification: this tendency to regard thinkers as conservatives, liberals, and radicals derives from the unthinking imitativeness of both nationalist and some Marxist historiography. The practitioners of both these tendencies believed that they performed their classificatory obligations by finding the most perfunctory similarity between Indian and European currents of thought.

Since utilitarianism justified modernity, the critical argument maintained that it was possible to contest the moral validity of the claims to modernity's superiority over tradition, or of the organization of modern European over other social principles. This was not merely the other side of rationalism, as European romanticism was, which shared a great deal of the deep structural elements of rationalist thought. It signified a deeper rejection—a combination of misunderstanding, apprehension, and rejection out of conviction, and in the late nineteenth century it required great intellectual courage to take this line against the easy triumphalism of colonial ideology, and the still flimsier rationalism of job-seeking babus.

Without doubt, this ideological position was itself something of a complex mixture with individual inflections on various themes. In acknowledging evident European superiority in the sphere of instrumental action and natural sciences that were based on it, these writers occasionally fell into the trap of Orientalism itself, accepting a stereotype unfavourable to themselves and trying unsuccessfully to make it work against its inner logic. Chatterjee (1986) has argued this position forcefully.

Intellectuals fashioned two different, yet complementary, arguments against the idea that colonial rule constituted a conferment of modern civilization. Authors such as Bankimchandra Chatterjee, sensitive to the smallest inflection in cultural processes, began to point towards an irremediable limitation of colonialism's modernizing impact.

What was going on in India was not just a slower, less complete process of modernization. Modernity consisted of two processes or trajectories, the first one proper to the metropolitan societies, and another appropriate for the colonies. There was an undeniable likeness between the two, but it was the resemblance between an original and its travesty.[16] It was the Indian intellectual's relative unfamiliarity with the details of European history which alone allowed social change under colonial rule to be passed off as a re-enactment of the Enlightenment and the bourgeois transformation of Europe's social life. Familiarity with European history made the travesty of the likeness apparent.

Cultural critiques of this type were supplemented, in subsequent decades, by indigenous applications of political economy to an understanding of colonialism. Political economy, learnt from British education, was again turned into a trenchant critique of colonial economic exploitation.[17] Radical political economy showed a second type of internal limitation to the re-enactment thesis. Although it fell short of a fully worked out theory of imperialism, it showed how the faults of the colonial economic process were systemic, persistently long term,

---

[16] The great text of this critique is Bankimchandra's satirical work *Kamalakanta* and *Lok Rahasya*. Unfortunately, in most discussions the focus is exclusively on his novel *Anandamath*.

[17] The classics of this tradition were Naoroji 1901 and Dutt 1960.

and therefore hardly reducible to the greed of individuals, the failure of administration, or the notorious venality of the lower orders of bureaucracy staffed primarily by native officials.

It was gradually recognized that a third kind of response was required, one of breaking away from the embarrassing dichotomy of the early years, of simple acceptance or rejection. Significantly, it was appreciated that the major question was not one involving the relation between British colonialism and India, but rather one of fashioning an adequate theoretical response to the historical phenomenon of modernity. Accordingly, the focus of historical reflection would shift from the British empire to the civilization of modernity as a whole. And this critique of modernity coincided with a self-understanding that became eventually nationalist in the full sense of the term.

Undermining the intellectual legitimacy of colonial power is certainly a necessary constituent of nationalism, but this cannot by itself constitute a mature nationalist ideology. Nationalist ideas are directed *against* a foreign occupying power, but in order to be fully nationalist they must also have a more positive directedness *towards* a conception of what the nation is. Would it not be strange to characterize 'nationalist' a form of consciousness which has yet to decide what it is to be its nation? The worship of a nation, its semi-religious ardour, cannot be produced by an entirely negative critique of imperialism's political economy.

The sentiments, emotions, symbolic political acts and, finally, the pressure of its popular movements must be directed politically at an object—the territory and its people—through various contingent and complex processes, ultimately constituted by their collective imagination as the nation. Nationalism is an intensely poetic and dramatic affair, and at the heart of its historical initiatives stand the acts of an entire people, or acts initiated on their behalf. All national movements eventually conceal the provisionality and contingency of the process by which this people is formed in historical imagination; historical research, however, shows precisely their contingency, provisionality, and teaches us to be anxious about their fragile and reversible destiny.

Bankimchandra's work reveals the hesitations, false starts, and misrecognitions of the self which accompanied this unaccustomed business of thinking into existence a new collective self. Although he undoubtedly contributes powerfully to the fashioning of the shape of the Indian nationalist consciousness, his work shows three different solutions to the same question: who are the *we* that intellectuals speak on behalf of, and, paramountly, who are this 'we' who should oppose colonial rule?

The first answer was that this collective self was the Bengali '*jati*' led by its natural leaders, the educated bhadralok; in another version, after he lost faith in this collaborationist class, this jati was to be led by exemplary leaders emerging from the masses. His second answer, which negates the Bengali identity and looks for something much larger and more powerful, tends towards the Hindu jati. A third solution is to speak of the 'bharatiya jati', a nation of Indians. What is interesting is the possibility of applying the title of jati to all of them, and this indicates not so much a linguistic ambiguity in the writing of someone exceptionally careful in his use of language, as a semantic openness relating to the ambiguity of historical possibility itself.

If the Bengali jati is an unlikely candidate for successful struggle against the might of British imperialism, the search for a viable nation has to look in other directions. Bengalis did not constitute the stuff of a good nation not because they were lacking in sentiments of solidarity, but because they could not provide a credible opposition to the power of the empire. The enormous extent of the British empire, its much-vaunted reach, military power, and technical excellence, required a political bloc that was larger, weightier, and equally massive to take on an equal struggle against its resources. Bengalis were inadequate for such a historical enterprise.

Slowly, Bankimchandra breaks up the boundaries of this Bengali 'we', seen either upside down or rightside up, and seeks another configuration of 'we' among others who share similar grievances, similar hopes and passions, but who are more likely subjects of defiance against the indignities heaped upon them by colonialism than the spoilt and enfeebled Bengali intelligentsia. Three peoples appeal to him from this angle: the Rajputs, the Sikhs, and the Marathas.

In Bankimchandra's novels, Bengalis are often effortlessly replaced by characters taken from these regions and placed in their histories; though occasionally this pretence breaks down, and despite their distinctly un-Bengali martial prowess these characters continue to behave culturally in disturbingly Bengali ways. A powerful Rajput king observes, with scrupulous regard, the rules of matrimonial negotiation of nineteenth-century Bengali bhadralok (Chatterjee 1964).

There is a problem in this gerrymandering of the boundaries of selfhood or collective identity. True, the Bengali is taught with amazing quickness to say 'we' and 'ours' about Rajputs, Marathas, and Sikhs, and to include them in his/her references to his/her collective self. And, in this period of the rise of high Bengali culture, they gratuitously assume that the communities so included in the Bengali sentimental embrace would reciprocate this emotion of mutuality. Who indeed would not feel honoured by this Bengali gesture of inclusion?

In some respects this inclusive movement remains ambiguous, indeterminate between two very different constructions. The common thread among these peoples is of course their record of successful defiance against unjust and predatory power, but what is problematic is the identity of this predatory enemy. If taken literally, all these people fought against Muslims, in some cases also against the power of British armies, and Bankimchandra's fiction, for reasons which are only partially stylistic, plays powerfully on the anti-Muslim phase of their history.

These episodes can also be taken symbolically, non-literally, in which case, of course, when he pointed his finger at the Muslim he may have actually meant the British. However, this indicates two other possible ways of conceiving the nation to which Bankimchandra and his audience could belong—the first would be a national identity of Hindus which would treat Muslims as invaders and prevent their assimilation in the nationalist movement. But finally, there was also the last and the most attractive construction of the nation as the motherland—territorial, bounteous, benign, not discriminating between her Hindu and Muslim sons, and technically, the hymn to this motherland, *Vande Mataram*, fails to work statistically unless Muslims are included among those who raise their swords in her defence.

Bankimchandra belonged to the pioneering generation of nationalism, which means that the decision they found so hard to take, which caused so much agonized reflection, becomes routine for people who follow them. The decision it took them such a long time to take—in favour of a territorial nation—became decisively entrenched in later nationalist thought. Subsequently, when histories of Indian nationalist thought were written, Bankimchandra's generation was seen, correctly in its own way, as the founding generation of this nationalist tradition, erasing from this narrative all the hesitation, tentativeness, and anxiety which surrounded that choice. History is after all the story of what happened, and not of possibilities which came close to happening but did not.

Bankimchandra, along with his generation, thus illustrates the necessity of the distinction I advocate, namely, that between a mere *anti-colonial* consciousness and a properly *nationalist* one. I am arguing that the second can appear only when a particular identity for the nation has been chosen and has been met, due to a host of circumstances, with general popular sanction. Thus it showed the strong connection that the making of history has with thinking about history.

The nation in this period is literally a construction, an 'imagined community' (Anderson 1983); and, in constituting this community through this founding imagination, history, in its popular form, as an irreducible mixture of facts and fantasy (*res factae* and *res fictae*), plays a crucial part. There appears to exist a necessary inversion in nationalist historical discourse: ordinary popular consciousness regards this search for history as a search for the past narrative of a community, already constituted, that has existed before and independently of this narrative and can, in principle, exist independently of this storytelling. In reality, however, stories are not such negligible things. It is by telling these stories, by this construction of the past that this community, in exactly this shape and form, comes into existence. It is partly this narrative consciousness that determines the being of a nation.

This storytelling about a collective self represents an important contribution to the making of a nationalist mentality, an act of imagining, of conceiving things narratively in a radically different way. In earlier phases of colonial history, the defiance of Tipu, of the Marathas, or the princes of the north had happened as different, distinct struggles of political principalities and their often selfish rulers against equally selfish British expansionism.

When such desperate struggles were actually under way, the Bengali babu was contentedly enjoying the comforts of colonial subalternity. The trickle-down from British expansion for his class was not inconsiderable. In the 1860s and 1870s his gradual alienation from the British creates a new imaginative order which does not lead to political protest, but in a way of seeing earlier struggles as a single unfolding process of defiance. He appropriates other struggles and gives them a new meaning by fitting them into a new configuration. Struggles of Mysore, Marathas, Sikhs, and the northern royalty, carried on severally and without mutual recognition, were united in history books and novels, and eventually in the more intangible and powerful popular imagination.

Gradually, these are turned into a single process called and recognized as Indian history rather than (regrettably) separately regional or dynastic chronicles. The common element is the common denominator of negative presence of the British in all these stories—the common cause of the ruin of Tipu in the south, the Mughals in the north, and above all the undeserved neglect of the meritorious bhadralok in the east. The deprivations and injustices which they suffered, viewed from close quarters, were quite significantly different. Yet the fact that these were all due to the British gave these grievances ·a tangible character of commonness and formed the narrative mould of a most powerful sentiment.

Discourse of Nationalism

The advent of the Congress represents the next stage in the evolution of nationalist discourse. Indeed, the origin of the Congress is itself brought about by the cultural changes which took place in the mid-colonial period. The assertion of regional vernacular cultures was accompanied by the deep divide in the earlier more homogeneous cultures in which both traditional elites and subalterns participated in different ways.

This change can be illustrated by referring to elementary social practices. Formerly, both the learned Brahmin and the illiterate peasant performed *puja*, though in admittedly different styles, but they were bound together by a bond of intelligibility. Such a bond would be conspicuously missed in the case of a modern atheistic babu and the illiterate peasant. While the earlier situation was unequal and the practices were mutually intelligible, the latter case is one of inequality without such intelligibility.

The creation of a new class of Western-educated intelligentsia, assisted by the bounty of the colonial dispensation, which enabled them to acquire substantial economic assets apart from cultural dominance, altered the terrain of political discourse in basic ways. Increasingly, the new elite deserts the indigenous subaltern classes, forswears any kinship with them, turning historically into leaders without a following. Their isolation forces them to assume an increasingly mendicant posture towards the colonial authorities in the hope that the injustices of colonial political economy would be rectified by the unassisted power of rational arguments. They shared their discursive common sense with the British rulers, and they wished accordingly to rectify colonial suffering by shaming the British into adopting appropriate policies of reform.

Popular rebellions against British rule, not surprisingly, assume more pronouncedly folk, popular character, deriving their active leadership either from traditional elites ruined by colonialism or from among themselves—with the obvious disadvantage that the relatively narrow frontiers of regional consciousness proved to be the natural frontiers of their rebellions. As they often did not understand the scale and intricacy of the colonial structure well enough, and failed to build large-enough coalitions, the administration put them down with relative ease.

Tilak already represented a change in this fatal bifurcation in anticolonial discontent and showed a distinct petty bourgeois admiration for popular protests. But, it was Gandhi and his peculiar discourse which achieved a recombination of these increasingly diverging trends of anti-colonial dissent. His manner of achieving this is significant for an understanding of the subsequent trajectory of independent India, and has to be analysed with care.

Gandhi solved this problem of a disrupted, divided political inheritance with unprecedented originality. The difference between high and low culture, as has already been pointed out, was no new thing in Indian history; but the new distinction was not between high and low in the same register; rather, it became two incommensurable registers resisting mutual translation. Ideas of political reasonableness were being cut up in two. Resistance, under these conditions, had little chance of attaining really threatening social depth or spatial spread. Elite dissatisfaction spread thinly across India, but had little popular support. Popular defiance, occasional and intense, was usually restricted to small regions. It was easy for the colonial order to ignore the first and suppress the second.

To put the argument schematically, Gandhi gradually forged a new configuration of nationalism which, because of its carefully crafted semiotic dualism, could be considered reasonable from both orbits of discourse. An analysis of Gandhi's trial would reveal how carefully he arranged this double intelligibility of his political acts. What he said and did against the colonial state, in the full publicity of its courts in 1922, made sense in two different ways, but each way of making sense would have made little sense to the other.

Gandhi's acts at this trial could be read off without mystification or residue by the two different discourses about the political world. Politics could be seen as something absolutely central to the constitution of society, and this arena conceived as a field of instrumental and strategic action. Alternatively, the state could be seen, extending a traditional Indian mode of thinking, as something grand, spectacular, but distant; a far-off cause of much suffering but normally unamenable to the initiatives of ordinary men and women. Great men and women could occasionally arise and right its wrongs for some time, and they deserved support because they took on this great cause on behalf of the wretched and the inarticulate of the earth.

Acts that Gandhi undertook could make sense in terms of both conceptions of politics. The modernist intelligentsia could see in them the work of a shrewd colonial lawyer who carefully chose the terrain, the occasion, and the exact legal point of his struggle against British colonial legality, who posed to that legal system problems especially difficult to solve.[18] He could do so precisely because he knew that system inside out, and, as the unfortunate judge found to his profound discomfiture, he offered for judgement a curious mixture of compliance and defiance.[19]

The element of defiance made it dangerous for the colonial state to let his behaviour go unpunished; the accompanying aspect of meekness, non-violence, and acquiescence in legal penalties made it risky to punish it too harshly. That might incense Indian subjects and fail to be intelligible to public opinion at home, under the scrutiny of which all acts of the colonial administration were brought. A reading of this

---

[18] Consider, in particular, his handling of the judge in his 1922 trial.

[19] Gandhi pleaded guilty, and indeed went on to claim that he had gone much further in treason than the prosecution had maintained in its official charge.

kind, evidently plausible, would fall within the circle of modernist discourse—with a typically instrumental rationalist conception of the state, which reckoned by means of ideas such as political objectives, rational calculation of means, interests of individuals and groups, strategy, tactics, advance, retreat, manoeuvre.

Gandhi's defiance and its constitutive gestures could also be read in a radically different way. To ordinary Indian peasants, accustomed to the age-old experience of the irresistibility of state injustice and the ineffectiveness of the rhetoric of resistance except as a miracle, he appeared in a miraculous, already mythical light. He appeared as a Mahatma or gratuitous redeemer of the world's suffering, who had no earthly personal reason to enter this contest, but who had the courage, precisely the mark of the saint, to take the sufferings of ordinary mankind upon himself, and to suffer the indignities of others. Moderns would view him in a frame of the linear temporality of an unknown but hopeful future; a future which would be newly fashioned, which would be better than the inglorious past, because history is demystified to them and is seen as the sum of the conscious and deliberate acts of human individuals.

Peasants would often think they knew better, and treated such modernist futures with cynicism. For them he came in the frame of a traditional, intolerably long cyclical temporality, of endless cycles of eternal injustice and occasional relief that was miraculous, after which life was likely to settle back into the familiar tedious pattern of iniquity and suppression. Gandhi was the typical doer of the miraculous act which was at the same time both new and ancient, which happened only rarely, but was known to have happened earlier too in the lives of similar yet different saints in times of similar yet different darkness.[20] Although it had happened earlier, each time it took place again it had the sparkle, the newness of a miraculous deliverance. Thus, Gandhi's politics could be seen transparently from either side, but each side saw a different thing.

Gandhi's politics was dualist in a further sense. He reached his two audiences through the use of two separate registers of communication and persuasion. Gandhi wrote a great deal, for the middle class's medium of politics was language in all its wordiness. A politician was

---

[20] For an excellent account of how the popular image of Gandhi was formed, see Amin 1984.

known only by his/her words—speeches, articles, books, interviews, promises, retractions, prevarications, ambiguity, arguments—the whole intellectualist conception of a world approached primarily through words. To the majority of their illiterate countrymen and countrywomen the world of words, especially the written word, represented something wholly different, a world of denial, of disenfranchisement and hiding.

Words, when written, appeared to the peasant—used to the mendacity of the usurer and *mahajan*, the connivance of the petty official, deviously silent—a taking away of language rather than a giving, more akin to a conspiracy than to a universal and popular consultation. Spoken language, when it was not legally arcane or intellectually pedantic, was better, for it restored through the medium of mass meetings and political conversation some of the universality of languages. Even spoken language failed to cross other, more fundamental, barriers—when these were constituted not by natural but by conceptual languages.

Gandhi, unlike other politicians, circumvented this difficulty with the aid of two instrumentalities. Gandhi himself as the individual politician resorted to the use of other elements in the complex and wide semiotic register available in rural India; this included the symbolism of a whole range of non-discursive and non-modern ways of making meaning—from prayers to silences to dress to food, which for all their non-wordiness represented ideas and persuaded people by techniques that had been deployed for their persuasion for centuries. This, of course, appeared strangely retrograde and perverse to modernists of all types, but the strident criticism made against these elements of Gandhi's politics missed the point that what was significant in them was not their content but the semiotic form.

Besides this personal solution, the national movement solved the problem of the two circles of common sense by a different technique of translation. The structure of the discourse of nationalism, in its mature phase, crucially depended on a diglossia. Élites which gained political influence in different regions came together and formed an all-India coalition on the basis of a bilingual pattern of communication, speaking and writing in their regional vernaculars and in English. Partly, this made for a minimal translation of ideas from one circle of discourse to another. It is a major part of my argument that this essential diglossia is being destroyed in current Indian culture and is being replaced by exacerbating clashes between unilingual and English-using elite and equally unilingual but much less quiescent speakers of regional languages.

Despite his political successes, Gandhi's cultural achievement was limited. He did not create a single common sense out of the two conceptual languages which emerged in Indian culture through colonialism. His own style was too personal, too idiosyncratic, to form a structural base for a new, truly common 'common sense' which could become a part of the foundation of an independent Indian state. He remained more a hinge between the two discourses rather than became the creator of a culture of mutual translation.

In the history of Indian nationalism, Gandhi occupies a strange and paradoxical place. It is a matter of some surprise how a trend politically so central can be culturally so insignificant: while the movement was contesting the power of the British, Gandhi remained its central figure; after Independence, in the serious business of constitution-framing, adherents of his ideas caused amused and embarrassed comment. To put it somewhat differently, Gandhi the political leader won the unstinted adherence of a large majority of the nationalist leadership, but his thought failed to gain a similar influence, let alone dominance.

From the mid-1930s, Congress nationalism came to be affected by a new emphasis on social radicalism. Its popular support was unevenly spread across the regions of Congress dominance, but its moral critique of the indifference of earlier nationalism to questions of poverty and social justice was successful in introducing a certain tone of concern. It is not easy to gauge the consequences of this radical intervention in nationalist ideology: while it obliged everyone to speak of poverty and backwardness in a caring tone, perhaps it also taught politicians to indulge in rhetoric not seriously meant.

Radical nationalism had several different, regionally influential forms; but radicals constituted a fractious and unstable group incapable of working out coalitions among themselves, and therefore unable to realize the full effect of their weight. They never came to wield the influence they could have exercised had they stayed together. Mutual recrimination and fractious squabbling reduced each segment to ignoble compromises with ideological adversaries.

Communists pulled along in isolation, and their utter friendlessness in the 'peoples' war' phase imposed some curious decisions on them, making them appear to those less internationally inclined as untrustworthy collaborators with the colonial power. Socialists, left isolated in their turn by their visceral disapproval of communists and by communist isolationism, eventually came to find ironic solidarity with chauvinistic groups. Nehru, himself a part of the left, remained always variously estranged from the two other streams, and consequently helplessly dependent on Gandhi, and consigned his frustrations to the pages of his autobiography.

If we consider socialist ideology from the point of view of the attitude towards modernity of these different groups, a large measure of unanimity emerges despite some differences. They turned the problem that modernity had posed to earlier nationalists by means of a simple device. Marxism sensitized them particularly to the historicity of theoretical and practical forms; radicals thus refused to consider European modernity as a homogeneous process. Compared to their early nationalist forbears, they understood its internal stratifications, contradictions, oppositions. The radical theory of history, upon which all of them drew, emerged from the underside of modernity, from the side of its disprivilege and denial, its internal other; and, as Leninist theory emphasized, there was a natural connection of perceptions of history and collective interest between the internal other of modernity and its external other, the metropolitan proletariat and colonial peoples.

Following this tradition, radical nationalism effected a restructuring of the earlier dispute between Westernism and indigenism. Radical nationalism was primarily modernist. It accepted the universality of rationalist social thought, the idea that any human being was a potential utterer of its truths. It decided to take this offer of universalism implicit in Western rationalism literally at its word, and argued forcefully for enfranchisement within human reason of the dispossessed both in capitalist societies and in colonial countries.

Colonial radicals saw in this the opportunity of creating a new theory of potential re-enactment of European modernity. Socialism, i.e. modernity purged of its capitalist form, was universalizable. This time, it was not to be a fraudulent re-enactment under the aegis of colonial powers; rather, colonialism had itself become an obstacle to the re-enactment process. Once colonial power was removed, this re-enactment of modernity would become feasible at last.

The political thinking of late nationalism showed a renewed vigour of theoretical imitativeness, Leftists declaring as their major undertaking not the invention of a social theory, but an 'application', in the strictly imitative sense of this term, of their preferred radical doctrine—Jayaprakash Narayan and the communists, a version of Marxism; and Nehru, after an initial adherence to that, veering as he came close to his tryst with prime ministerial destiny, towards a British Labour version of parliamentary social democracy. And since, by a combination of political necessity and pure fortuitousness, the large section of the elite following Nehru came to control the apparatus of government after freedom, this specific theory was translated into the historical agenda of reconstruction of the new Indian state.

Nationalism since Independence

The strand of nationalism associated with Nehru has come under heavy and unrelenting criticism, partly an understandable cross borne by any political ideology that has won power; others can always criticize it from their position of ineffectual innocence. It would be interesting to undertake an initial classification of these criticisms, because these stem from extremely diverse grounds. However, as a preliminary classification, we must also distinguish between the genuine articles of the pattern of thinking associated with Nehru and a fraudulent extension of it that sought patronage and privilege in its name during Indira Gandhi's days in undisputed power.

Nehru's design, unlike its fraudulent successor, consisted of a serious proposal for the construction of a European-style social democracy under economic conditions of extreme backwardness and political conditions prevailing in the aftermath of nationalist mobilization. Two of its central theses have received a great deal of critical attention, and need simply to be mentioned here.

1. With nearly all other views of development of its time, it shared an excessively economistic conception of the idea of development, reducing all other elements in it to the status of corollaries. Ironically, it appears in retrospect that the relative successes of its economic plans are in danger of being erased due to its negligence of cultural reproduction processes.

2. Another central weakness of this design, which it partly shared with Soviet models of growth, stemmed from its tendency to rely too heavily on the instrumentality of the state, and to suffocate non-state institutions of civil society by theoretically equating the principle of public good with the institutional form of state control.

It negligently disregarded the possibility that state institutions could be effectively 'privatized' in particularly hideous forms, and become vehicles of private and sectional interests of a malignantly pre-bourgeois nature. This was particularly likely in India, given the great richness and variety of its long tradition of political tyranny of all kinds. The privatization of the benefits of the state—an institution which was supposed to counteract the injustices of the market—generated its own, even less accountable iniquities, and, additionally, made criticism of it even more problematic because of the equation of its ravages with the operation of the principles of social justice. But I shall confine my remarks to some other features of the form of nationalist thinking which carried Nehru's imprimatur.

Whatever the weaknesses of the productive and distributive principles of the Nehru model, it was generally assumed that its cultural programme (or rather, its lack of one) was quite adequate for the historical tasks that the nation faced. This nationalism was given implicit acquiescence even by its leftist critics, as it was assumed that it provided a secular base for the Indian nation state. I think this can hardly be taken for granted, and shall offer some critical arguments.

It can be argued that there is a strong connection between an ideology and a way of creating a narrative of the historical record, as these are crucial elements in reducing the threatening chaos of the social world in which people live into the reassuring form of an order. In this again, one significant element is how its own history, its historical self-description, is fitted into the larger narrative of world history that it wishes to tell. As this history is essentially political in character, its attraction lies not in its constancy but in its ability to adapt its structure to the political requirements of changing circumstances.

This will become clear if we compare the different stories that the Congress had told about itself during three stages of its career. In the actual course of the nationalist movement, Congress often faced strong competition from contending forms of nationalism: e.g. terrorist nationalism, the communists, or even Subhas Chandra Bose's Forward Bloc. Contemporary historical accounts of the Congress movement reflected such political strains; and consequently, its historians did not see these trends as part of itself separated by a regrettable but temporary misunderstanding; on the contrary, they often attempted to condemn these trends as anti-national simply because their construction of what nationalism was tended to be different from the Congress's.[21]

After Independence, there was a discernible shift in this political narration. Earlier on, the line of division between the Congress and other trends of nationalist politics used to be drawn with great sharpness; official histories written immediately after freedom, in the warm afterglow of victory, tended to blur such divisions. In the massive history by Tara Chand (1961–72), for instance, a significant rewriting takes place: anti-Congress trends are not distanced with aversion and mistrust; rather the allegiance that they enjoyed among dissenting groups is sought to be assimilated into the ideology of a triumphant Congress: a kind of retrospective generosity is extended to them in their new portrayal, and the sharp differences and controversies that actually erupted between them are played down.

Nationalist discourse thus produced, through its varying channels—school textbooks, official propaganda, the media, the ceremonies of remembrance, the symbolic sequence of holidays—a really composite pantheon of national leaders, not in an attempt to restore to this phase of Indian history its actual baffling diversity, but to appropriate them into a predominantly Congress past. The story of the national movement as a whole is slowly assimilated into the history of the Congress.

This history of history-writing is a matter of some significance for Indian politics and its relation with culture. By the 1970s, with Indira Gandhi's use of a more radical nationalist posture, the political requirement of nationalist ideology altered substantially. It was now useful to claim the heritage of the entire national movement as a pre-history of the Congress as refashioned by Indira Gandhi's distinctive new slogans.

---

[21] A clear example of such conflict can be found in the common treatment of the Communist decision to support the British war effort in 1942, against the nationalist call to quit India.

Accordingly, there was renewed revision of the history of the nationalist movement. The definition of nationalism was narrowed down to fit a strictly 'Nehruvian' vision of what Indian nationalism was, with a strong emphasis on secularism, socialism, the extension of principles of liberal equality towards social democracy.[22] There is no doubt, of course, that if it were open to choose our past, this is what we would like to choose; this is the sort of nationalism that many of us would have preferred.

Analytically, it is of signal importance that the nationalism of our preference is not confused with the nationalism that really existed, which was certainly less secular, less inclined towards social justice, and was often unenthusiastic about the observance of basic democratic practices. However, this was not a conflation that accidentally erupted in academic history at a particular point; rather, its picture of the past chimed in perfectly with the temporary cadence of Congress ideology under Indira Gandhi.

It differentiated itself from other trends in nationalism in today's India and served several ideological purposes.

1. It portrayed itself as the sole heir of the heritage of the national movement.
2. It condemned other trends as either communal or conservative and, therefore, by definition anti-national.

---

[22] I suspect that the canonical Nehruism of the 1970s was significantly different from Nehru's own ideological stance on several points: (i) Nehru, in his later writing, was far less enthusiastic about Marxist theory, and took great pains to stress that what he called socialism should never be confused with any version of Soviet communism; (ii) Nehru was far more scrupulous about the observance of democratic norms, despite admittedly glaring lapses. It is doubtful if he would have seen bourgeois democratic norms as obstacles to imminent social change, and rejoiced in their demolition during the Emergency. The 'Nehruvians' belatedly recognized the value of democratic norms when the Emergency caught up with them. But, despite their retrospective repentance, it should not be forgotten that this group provided the ideological justification for Indira Gandhi's destruction of constitutional controls over executive authority, probably in the expectation that they would be the secondary or tertiary beneficiaries of this concentration of power. Their motive for a self-serving invocation of Nehru's name is of course transparent; but to credit that with the badge of 'Nehruism' is to be unfair to Nehru.

3. By claiming that Indian nationalism had fought for the realization of the principles that Indira Gandhi (as it turned out, inconstantly) espoused, it sought to prevent its political opponents appealing to that fund of regard that an ordinary Indian had for this common nationalist historical legacy.

It can be argued that the original narrative of history, though less simplistic and less self-interested, contained massive misrepresentations of India's cultural history. Acceptance of the paradigmatic European models of nation-formation revealed how crucial the cultural unification process was for a nation. Given this model (if, in other words, this was regarded not as one type of nation-formation but its only possible, and therefore universal, form), it would appear embarrassing to admit that India was not a nation that was already formed culturally and merely waiting to be emancipated from British rule. It was still more embarrassing to acknowledge that, in strange and ironic ways, British rule created the preconditions for this nationalism by imposing systems of common suffering and common living under the colonial order.

It was politically more uplifting for the nationalist leadership to assert that this nation of India was formed by a cultural process which went back into immemorial antiquity. Nationalist ideology thus projected an exaggerated argument about India's 'composite culture', which was in the nature of a hopeful abstraction rather than a belief supported by a detailed and serious enquiry into India's cultural past. This encouraged a massive pretence on the part of the national movement and later by the national state that the question of cultural construction of the nation was left behind in the past, rather than lying still in the future. It made Indians believe that the imagining of the nation was an accomplished and irreversible fact; it did not have to be constantly presented and justified. Anyone who did not take the Indian nation for granted must be in clandestine collusion with forces opposed to India's national freedom. By encouraging this cultural default, the narrative of Indian nationalism (spawned by adherents of Nehru's vision) is partly to blame for the politico-cultural crisis that India's state order is facing today.

I would like to make a brief remark about social theory here. Colonialism and nationalism, each in its own way, placed the agenda of modernity firmly at the centre of Indian politics. Nationalism, as Gellner points out in his incisive if somewhat one-sided study, has an inextricable connection with the enterprise of modernity in the history of the West. Although its relation with modernity is more complex in the case of colonial societies, in the case of Indian nationalism this relation with aspiration towards modernity is clearly evident.[23] Nehru's nationalism viewed colonialism as the main obstacle to India's path towards a Westernized scientific modernity; therefore, in a paradox, removal of European power was the precondition for successful emulation of European history.

This strand of nationalism prided itself on its theoretical self-awareness, the central characteristic of its theory being the celebration of modernity. Yet, on reflection, there was an immense difference between the way emergent modernity appeared to the most intelligent and perspicacious observers in Europe in the nineteenth century,[24] and the way it appeared to its distant worshippers after the lapse of a century.

All major social theory in Europe emerged out of a cognitive struggle with a sense of bewilderment in the face of modern history: Marx's theory of capitalism, de Tocqueville's of democracy, and Weber's of secularism. Modernity, to those who lived through its first phase, seemed the most difficult word to understand and bring under social control. To the Asian modernists, modernity seemed attractive precisely because it posed no Hegelian riddle, it held no Rousseauesque terrors, nor did it require the massive Marxist intellectual enterprise of knowing history. Modernity was simplicity itself, a simple conflict between superstition and knowledge, error and science, in which, moreover, a benign history had arranged victory for science and truth in advance.

Koselleck (1985) has argued that modernity changed the human conception of the future in a new structure of temporal consciousness. Formerly, the future held no fears entirely different from the sufferings of the present, because, it was believed, as Machiavelli put it, 'men will

---

[23] It would be absurd to deny that substantial parts of the Indian national movement looked at the proposals of modernity with deep mistrust and moral repugnance. However, the general ideological tenor of the movement and certainly the ideology of the nation-state was decidedly modernist. For an interesting classification of trends of nationalist thought, see Parekh 1989: 11–70.

[24] Some of the major theorists of this modernity—de Tocqueville, Marx, and Weber—showed a deeply critical and mistrustful attitude to the concept.

live and die in order for ever to remain the same' (1970: 142).[25] Modernity destroyed this assurance of continuity and faced human beings for the first time with a future of a radical newness which deeply troubled conservatives and delighted revolutionaries.

As Arendt's (1970) work showed, the concept of revolution in its new linear sense was deeply connected with this novel concept of the future, coming to stand, in a strange etymological reversal, for exactly the opposite of what it literally denoted (Arendt 1970: especially 42ff.). History did not foreshadow the return of inevitable old patterns with minor variations, but the creation by human endeavour of unprecedented conditions—of states of political freedom, justice, and public happiness never conceived of before. It was not missed by some who observed the rise of this new politics of modernity that this new future contained equal dangers—unprecedented terrors for which there were no precedents of either preparation or prevention.

This new conception of the future altered the nature of historical knowledge, or its judicious use. History in the old sense became redundant at one stroke, lines of events would not be the same, the future could not be understood by studying the past. A new kind of knowledge of history had to take its place: it was a knowledge of processes, not learning about events. Rational social theory was to take over the function of explanation from earlier historical scholarship. Most of these theorists believed that it was possible, despite unprecedented complexity, to live in history with a form of prospective rationality. Social theory was supposed to provide this indispensable implement of living rationally under conditions of modernity. But, it could do so only by giving up the myth of re-enactments: the future was uncertain but still not unmasterable. People must not expect the past to be replayed in the future.

Modernity places the Indian in a similar historical position; yet the modernists' reading of his/her historical placement is radically different. While the actual problem with modernity is its ever-recurring unprecedentedness—that is, other peoples' modernity cannot entirely show the picture of our future—the modernist believes that its main attraction lies in the fact that it, in a manner of speaking, lets us into history's secret; through the European past, we know the script in

---

[25] *Discourses of Livy* (Discourse II, 'Concerning the Religion of the Romans').

advance. With the fading of this optimism, a new series of questions arises insistently: the specific ways in which capitalist production emerges in these societies, the peculiar twists of their democratic process. Is modernity ineluctable? Is it divisible? Can its inexorable logic be bent to the demands of rational, critical, equitable control?

These questions themselves pose the problem of the nature and configuration of historical knowledge in interesting ways. Historical knowledge in this context is always a knowledge of processes, not learning about the sequence of incidents but of the logic of structures. This would not mean looking at incidents in European history as precedents, and waiting like M.N. Roy for the arrival of our French or Russian revolution or Renaissance. This does not mean, on the other hand, giving up reading Europe's history, as chauvinist indigenism would advocate. For there is no other place to analyse the processes of modernity except in the historical annals of the West, and processes happen through events. Only in this way can we finally break out of the strange sentimentality of the relationship with Europe's history that lay at the heart of our nationalist discourse. Like de Tocqueville's description of American history, what we face today is unprecedented, but not unmasterable. Like him, in India, we also live in an age in which the past has ceased to throw light on the future. And we too face a new kind of undetermined time.

References

Amin, S. 1984. Gandhi as Mahatma. Gorakhpur District, Eastern U.P., 1921–1922. In R. Guha, ed., *Subaltern Studies III (vide infra)*, pp. 1–61.

Anderson, B. 1983. *Imagined Communities. Reflections on the Origin and Spread of Nationalism.* London: Verso.

Arendt, H. 1970. *On Revolution.* Harmondsworth. Penguin.

Barrier, N.G. Ed. 1981. *Census in British India. New Perspectives.* New Delhi: Manohar.

Bose, A. 1989. *India's Social Crisis.* Delhi: Oxford University Press.

Chand, Tara. 1961–72. *A History of the Freedom Movement in India*, 4 vols. New Delhi. Publications Division, Government of India.

Chandra, B., M. Mukherjee, A. Mukherjee, S. Mahajan, and K.N. Panikkar. 1988. *India's Struggle for Independence. 1857–1947.* Delhi: Viking.

Chatterjee, Bankimchandra. 1964. *Rajsinha* (in Bengali). In *Bankim Rachanavali, Volume I Samagra Upanyas* Calcutta. Sahitya Samsad.

———. 1965. *Bankim Rachanavali* (in Bengali) *Volume I*. Calcutta. Sahitya Samsad.
Chatterjee, P. 1986. *Nationalist Thought and the Colonial World. A Derivative Discourse* Delhi: Oxford University Press.
Cohn, B.S. 1987. The Census, Social Structure and Objectification in South Asia. In idem, *An Anthropologist Among the Historians and Other Essays*. Delhi: Oxford University Press, pp. 224–54.
de Tocqueville, A. 1974. *Democracy in America, Volume II*. Fourth Book, Chapter VIII. New York: Schocken.
Deuskar, S.G. 1970 (first published 1904). *Desher Katha* (in Bengali): Calcutta: Sahityalok.
Dilthey, W. 1974. *Selected Writings*. Cambridge: Cambridge University Press.
Dutt, R.C. 1960 (first published 1901–3). *The Economic History of India*. 2 vols. Delhi: Publications Division.
Dutt, R.P. 1970 (first published 1940). *India Today*. Calcutta: Manisha.
Foucault, M. 1972. *The Archaeology of Knowledge*. London: Tavistock.
Fox, R.G. Ed. 1977. *Realm and Region in Traditional India*. New Delhi: Vikas.
Gellner, E. 1983. *Nations and Nationalism*. Oxford: Blackwell.
Guha, R. Ed. 1982–9. *Subaltern Studies: Writings on South Asian History and Society. Volumes I–VI*. Delhi: Oxford University Press.
Joshi, V.C. Ed. 1975. *Rammohun Ray and the Process of Modernisation in India*. New Delhi: Vikas.
Kaviraj, S. 1990. Writing, Speaking, Being: Language and Historical Formation of Identities in South Asia. In D. Rothermund and D. Hellman-Rajanayagam, eds (*vide infra*).
Koselleck, R. 1985. *Futures Past*. Cambridge, Mass.: Massachusetts Institute of Technology Press.
Machiavelli, N. 1970. *Discourses*. Ed. B. Crick; trans. L.J. Walker. Harmondsworth. Penguin.
Mohanty, N. 1982. *Oriya Nationalism: Quest for a United Orissa 1866–1956*. New Delhi: Manohar.
Naoroji, D. 1901. *Poverty and Un-British Rule in India*. London: Swann Sonnenschein.
Parekh, B. 1989. *Colonialism, Tradition and Reform*. New Delhi: Sage.
Rothermund, D. and D. Hellman-Rajanayagam. Eds. 1990. Papers of Session on Asia at the German Historical Congress Bochum, 1990. Mimeo.
Roy, M.N. 1971. *India in Transition*. Bombay: Nachiketa.
Sarkar, S. 1975. Ram Mohun Roy and the Break with the Past. In V.C. Joshi. Ed. 1975 (*vide supra*), pp. 46–68.

Sathyamurthy, T.V. 1989. Terms of Political Discourse in India. Position Paper for the Conference on 'Terms of Political Discourse in India', Mysore. 30 June/2 July.

Sen, A. 1975. The Bengal Economy and Ram Mohun Roy. In V.C. Joshi. Ed. 1975 *(vide supra)*, pp. 103–35.

Volosinov, V.N. 1986. *Marxism and the Philosophy of Language.* Cambridge, Massachusetts: Harvard University Press.

Weiner, M. and Varshney, A. Ed. 1989. *The Indian Paradox. Essays in Indian Politics.* New Delhi: Sage.

4

Writing, Speaking, Being: Language and the Historical Formation of Identities in India

All civilizations have language but societies do not put this universal implement to the same use. Historically, language can hardly be treated as a homogeneous entity. It can be divided in many ways—into its various strata, its distinct elements, the differing types of competences which are gathered up into the general notion of a language. The social functions accredited to different strata of language in Indian civilization (though the situation in South India is different in some important respects) appear to be interestingly different from the European case; in this essay I shall try to analyse how language contributes to the formation, and rupturing, of social identities, and I do this by focusing primarily on the Bengali speech community.[1] This does not imply any claim to the exemplary or precedental quality of this particular case. Though the story of the relation between language and politics is bound to be different in the different language zones of South Asia's exceedingly diverse culture, these might reveal some similarity of processes, though not an identity of the exact line of events. In the last part of the essay, however, I shall speak more generally about the linguistic processes at work in the Indian nation state.

Language not only unites people, it also as effectively divides them. Another way of putting this would be to say that language is, socially, not merely a means of communication but also of deliberate

---

First published in *Nationalstaat und Sprachkonflikte in Süd- und Südostasien*, ed. Dagmar Hellmann-Rajanayagam and Dietmar Rothermund (Stuttgart: Steiner, 1992), pp. 25–68.

[1] A standard history of the Bengali language and its literature is Sen 1965.

incommunication. It causes not only feelings of identity but also of enmity: often the most indestructible barriers among people are 'walls of words'. By this I do not mean merely that the process of formation of one linguistic identity generates a sharper sense of differentiation from others: for instance, the more the people of a particular region become 'Bengalis', the more their sense of separateness from surrounding languages like Oriya or Hindi. This is evidently true; but this is not the only sense in which language creates incommunication. Language divides 'internally' as well, and not to pay attention to this process often distorts historical accounts about linguistic identities.

People 'having' the same language do not have it in the same way. Socially, linguistic competence confers on people capacities, and their absence correspondingly takes them away. Being Bengali is an identity coming out of a person's having the Bengali language; but clearly, all Bengalis do not have this language in the same way or to the same extent. Thus, they enjoy the political 'rights' of Bengaliness to a patently unequal degree: for some rights stemming from Bengaliness must be indivisible, but others are unequal and stratified. The *bhadralok* of Calcutta speak the Bengali standard language, one which has resemblances on one side with the 'high' language in which Tagore wrote his poetry, but also, on the other side of the cultural spectrum, with the language spoken in the bazaar by the fisherman, the maid in the babu household, or by criminals on the margins of urban Calcutta. And these are not rightly separated orbits sufficient in themselves but a complex of words pulled in different directions by the internal logic of each social practice. The historical existence of the Bengali language is a complex fact in which all these sublanguages (or linguistic subpractices) must find adequate and properly judged representation. Language as it is socially used thus has to be broken down into various subparts—high and low language, literary and common language, the *guru* (high, of greater merit) and the *chalita* (conversational) language (a special distinction of twentieth-century Bengali), the literates' and the illiterates' language. Such differences are not merely aural or cultural, but also political. Being able to use a language in certain ways enables a person to do certain things socially; others who do not possess such linguistic competence simply cannot perform them. Often, these people are reduced to varying states of dependence on those who are more skilled, and their access to the whole of the social universe is mediated by this latter group who can consequently control this tenuous access.[2]

The use of writing by moneylenders, the scourge of the indebted peasantry, is one example. And the peasants cannot be blamed if they consider writing not as a means of enlightenment but of oppressive mystification. Peasant revolts, historians have argued, show a particular intensity of anger against written records because they relate to the linguistic practice of writing differently. The complexity of the story of language and identities cannot be tackled without a sufficiently complex conception of the gradations of competence in language and its political effect. I shall call this the 'internal economy' of language.

The Structure of the Internal Economy of Language

The manner in which this internal economy was structured in traditional India seems to have been peculiar, and interestingly different from the European case. Jacques Derrida's work has emphasized the primacy in European culture of the grammatological, of the written over the spoken part of language.[3] This is asserted strongly, although in many European cultures the term for language comes from the Latin *lingua* or tongue, which might lead one to infer the primacy of the spoken inscribed in the etymology or language about language itself. But there appears to exist a more fundamental difference. The idea of *logos* in the Greek philosophical tradition clearly draws attention to language as a means of reasoning, of ratiocinative activity, giving this exceptional significance over other things that can be done by means of language. This is related, though this is not the place to try to show the connection in detail, to Gadamer's argument about the deep-seated privileging of the epistemological in Western cultural tradition.[4]

---

[2] Bernard Cohn has done pioneering work on these questions: see especially chapters 6 and 10 of Cohn 1987. An excellent discussion of language and political identity can be found in Dasgupta 1970.

[3] Derrida 1974: Chapters 1 and 2, argues this against earlier linguistic theories.

[4] Gadamer 1975.

The first difference is that in the classical Indian tradition though a great deal of attention is given to *nada*[5]—the originary form of sound, and therefore, the source of both language and music—and though it is occasionally equated with God himself, it seems to lack a clear equivalent to the typically European concept of the *logos*—speech, writing, reasoning, episteme, science. By contrast, the Indian philosophic and aesthetic curiosity appears directed towards *vak*—the irruption of the utterance which universalizes language rather than writing. Writing—inscribing something on a receiving medium—is as much to create meaning as to stain virgin space. The Indian tradition's way of treating writing is, in interesting ways, ambiguous. Writing is fixing, giving an idea a kind of material immortality, something that can be done only to the rarest, at least to the most significant, of thoughts, ideas of extraordinary importance in some sense, an exalted fate that common speech does not deserve. It is however possible to argue just the reverse of this case: material things are destructible, to consign ideas to material existence is thus to subject them to the law of decay and destruction. Towards writing the Indian tradition shows a strangely complex combination of reverence and mistrust.

There is a second analytical difficulty. The way Indian culture structures the internal practices of language cannot be adequately captured by a standard distinction between oral and literate cultures. Indian culture arranges the institutional transaction between literate-oral in very complex ways; here the distinction between literate and oral is not homologous to the one between educated and illiterate. Even the educated have their own traditions and institutions of oral performance. It is not that this culture does not know writing; rather, in spite of knowing writing from a very early stage of its history it clearly uses writing quite sparingly. This peculiar configuration of knowing the gift of writing, yet abjuring its use in social transactions, seems to indicate that in traditional Indian culture linguistic practice is governed by a 'theory' of distribution of functions between speaking and writing.

---

[5] There are references often in traditional Indian thinking to *nadabrahma*. *Nada* is the originary meaningful sound which is given great ceremonial significance in two of its cultural forms, the intelligent power of words and the sound of music, its aesthetic often begins with general considerations of this kind.

Some features of this functional distribution must be noticed before we come to a discussion of more modern history. First, the intimate connection so common in European culture between institutions, i.e. the extension in the scale of social practices in time and space, and consigning things to the fixity of writing, does not seem to obtain here.[6] Enormous and essential structures of social exchange and communication are entrusted to oral continuity rather than written codification. Although writing and speaking can both create continuity, their manner of doing so are different. In Indian society, except for the vast numbers of the directly productive classes of people, the upper strata depended on literacy and related means of social control. The upper strata required use of literacy for different functional requirements specific to the social practices they engaged in. Trading practices on any large scale required literacy and commercial records which could not be handled without literacy and numeracy among commercial groups. Wielders of political power depended on some amount of minimal administrative documentation: occasionally, there was evidence of impressive elaborate accounting of revenue resources of their realms.[7] Brahmins provided some of these services. But they were notoriously selfish repositories of the society's skills of literacy and learning of its practical applications, and they performed two types of essential functions. They lent their knowledge of literacy and its more specialized uses to the Kshatriyas or those who controlled political authority. A two-way traffic results from this caste monopoly of skills and cultural assets. Administrative ordering, deft use of the technical apparatus of legal principles, financial accounting, and bookkeeping require the use of these relatively rare and jealously monopolized attainments. Those who had formal political power depended on the Brahmins for these essential functional necessities as much as for more general moral legitimation. Caste barriers also constituted effective

---

[6] Some internal diversities in the tradition must be noticed. In the Buddhist tradition there was greater reliance on writing in order to fix the meaning of something especially valuable. The preachings of the Buddha are written down by disciples; but the Hindu tradition by contrast seems to be interested in inscribing significant ideas on the more quizzical tablet of memory.

[7] Both the *Arthashastra* and the *Ain-i-Akbari*, central texts for two different periods, point to habitual and widespread use of administrative records.

prevention against possible diffusion of these scarce resources and their increased availability to other groups in society. Secondly, Brahmins also performed the exceedingly important activity of rituals which ensured the imaginary continuance of the social order by keeping it supplied with its essential symbolic collective representations, and vital concepts for the construction of the collective self.

To be able to perform these materially and symbolically essential functions the Brahmins had to ensure that the relevant skills were reproduced in undiminished quality within their own caste. Relatively little of this function of institution-maintenance was given over to writing or writing-based forms of training. Although Brahmins had to be literate, a surprisingly large part of this training came to be not ratiocinative and written but passive and mnemonic.[8] Memory is never an unfailing implement for perfect or reliable reproduction. Dependence on oral continuity gave to these practices a peculiar character which may be read wrongly by social scientists. They confer on these continuing institutions the solidity and relative immobility common to similar institutions in written cultures. Here, because the internal mechanism was oral, and because there were rarely standardized written institutional histories, institutional continuity could be compatible with great flexibility. The eternal religion (*sanatana dharma*) can therefore keep changing constantly. Though this may not have ensured continuity the way writing would have done, it did have a compensating advantage. Reliance on memory fulfilled the historical need for flexibility within a formally rigid structure in a subtle and partly covert fashion. In reasoning activities no mnemonic reproduction could be perfect, a reproduction without variation, without slippages caused by simple incompetence, inadvertence, interpretation, or deliberate intent. Indeed, quite often the key to understanding the unchanging structures is the astonishing amount of unannounced change which these sanction. Rigid formal rules of social conduct were meant to ensure a remarkable degree of conformist continuity. Since these rules were uncodified and worked through an oral tradition, they afforded those who directed society considerable space for informal amendments.

---

[8] The difference is between the ability to think through a problem and the ability to reproduce from memory standard recipes. Even current Indian educational practice shows over-reliance on memory-oriented skills.

Sometimes a reputation for rigidity accomplished things in subtle ways which an actual immobility would not have done.[9] No wonder the record of Indian history is marked by a paradox—a rhetoric of immutability (as for instance in *sanatana dharma*, an eternal religious order invented in the nineteenth century) cut through by historical evidence of silent and surreptitious change. A good example is provided by the fascinatingly mobile history of the supposedly immutable order of castes.[10]

Traditional Indian society thus had a highly literate culture, but inside it literacy was guarded with great jealousy through institutional arrangements which strictly prevented its extension, so that it was always a strong sellers' market in literacy. Ordinary unlettered people carried on their daily existence through spoken vernacular dialects. In the nature of things, these vernaculars varied a great deal, and in most cases did not have standardized written scripts of their own before the tenth century. Above these productive and oral classes presided a bilingual elite which commanded the use of an esoteric language which could not be mastered by others due to caste prohibitions. The elite could carry on their own internal discourse (which could be either theological or political) in a language which had the strange quality of a partial publicity, with the dual quality of being public and secret at the same time.[11] It was public to insiders, but closed, esoteric, secret to outsiders who did not have the requisite skills. This had significant political results; because it made the scale of possible collective action

---

[9] The difference between the two forms of the caste system—of *varna* and *jati*—might have something to do with this.

[10] The sociological controversy about caste is instructive in this respect. Without denying Dumont's general claim that what is essential to caste is the ideological *form* of hierarchy, one can still admit the evidence of historical change through the process known after Srinivas as Sanskritization.

[11] Considerations of such things get unnecessarily embroiled in controversies about nationalist pride, accusations of orientalism, and such other judgemental disputes. Few social scientists in India have, for instance, pursued the question of the exact relation between what is indubitably common and what is conceptually public. Existence of commonness does not mean that this will be conceptualized as public space or public interest or public institutions. The work of Satish Saberwal raises this question (though not in this language): cf. Saberwal 1989.

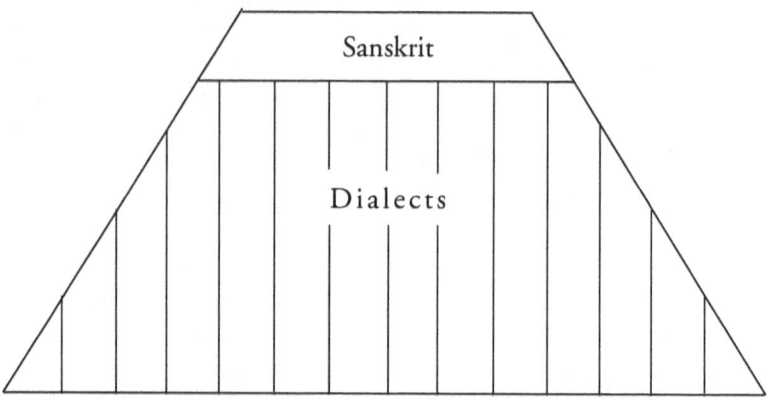

Fig. 1. Alterations in linguistic structures during medieval times

or consultation asymmetric between the elites and the subaltern social groups. While elite discourse could range across the entire subcontinent, the discourse of subordinate groups necessarily remained trapped in the close boundaries of their vernacular dialects. Thus, while conservatism and reaction could be subcontinental in spread, dissent was condemned to be mostly local. Only those reform initiatives were likely to succeed which used the implements of the elite discourse itself against its ideological structures.

Social and political changes in medieval times brought some alterations in the structure of language and literacy, but these were not so fundamental as to introduce changes in the linguistic economy. Two types of change occur. Due to the political power of Muslim rulers—a reality brahminical Hindu society could not ignore—Arabic and Persian came to slowly occupy a part of the exalted position of the earlier esoteric language—Sanskrit. But it was more a situation of power than of authority. As Muslim power became entrenched in North India, especially those social groups and specialized castes which traditionally used literacy in the administrative service of the government, now extended their skills to the new language of power.[12] It must be

---

[12] This linguistic configuration continued undisturbed down to the time of Ram Mohan Ray who was proficient in both Sanskrit and Arabic-Persian, besides his native Bengali and colonial English. It is remarkable how quickly

recognized, however, that this does not seem to have threatened the privilege of Sanskrit. Hindu society responded to the reality of Muslim rule partly through an attempt to marginalize the power of the state and eject it out of the circle of Hindu social practices, a move which succeeded in part due to the pragmatism of the rulers themselves. Although this could not wholly succeed, it did result in a sharper hiatus between the political power of the state, and social dominance inside these communities.[13] Power and prestige inside these communities remained intimately related to real or supposed competence in Sanskrit; officiating Brahmins may have had a tenuous grip on the intricacies of Sanskrit grammar, but this hardly mattered since the effectiveness of these practices was symbolic, not grammatical. Indeed, the stable political power of Muslim rulers and the process of conversion to Islam of those who used this to escape the repressive rigidity of the caste system set in motion two contrary responses in Hindu society. On one side this gave rise to a more frantic traditionalism, but on the other also to types of exchange with Islamic culture. A tendency towards utilitarian secular exchanges was discernible in the practices of castes like the Kayasthas who were given to government employment traditionally, or the trading groups who tended to treat all men equally as long as this served the objective of commercial expansion. But there were also the more intellectually grounded proposals for religious exchanges advocated by bhakti doctrines—at the same time more ambitious and vulnerable.

Religious developments have an intimate relation to our story of languages. Throughout this period there occurred a slow development of vernacular languages through the gradual separation of their emerging literatures from the high Sanskrit tradition. Comparatively little research has been done on this process; but the lines of development and their basic interconnections are clear. And it is instructive to dwell on this process because the radicalism of the reform religions displays

---

this heteroglossia is destroyed by the cultural processes of colonialism. By the time of Bankimchandra and Tagore, proficiency in Arabic-Persian and familiarity with Islamic culture are not required as marks of a cultured Bengali. The Bengali bhadralok elite had decided to give themselves a resolutely Hindu past.

[13] I have suggested elsewhere that the precolonial state was marked by the twin features of being spectacular and marginal: Kaviraj 1991c.

some peculiar features. The emergence of a vernacular literature does not indicate an immediate change in the narrative or imaginative content of literary culture, or a sharp, dramatic, conscious rupture with the classical tradition, however striking the disjunction may appear in retrospect. They arise haltingly, always making reverential genuflections in the direction of the high tradition and its texts, which they were eventually to undermine. These are not seen or begun as revolts against the logic of exclusion of the common people from aesthetic and religious seriousness built into the classical Hindu tradition. Rather, their first and most impressive texts are attempts to stretch the riches of this high culture towards the lower, culturally deprived orders. Their implicit justification would have been that, if religiosity and aesthetics were significant and valuable for all human beings, those without the use of Sanskrit should not be deprived of these values. As a consequence, these literatures assume a consciously subaltern relation between themselves and the high classical texts. The narratives around which these literatures grew were in most part old esteemed narratives from the classical tradition—the *Ramayana*, the *Mahabharata*, or similarly modelled stories of what in Bengal were called the *mangalkavyas*, which, though exalting unknown and upstart deities, do it in a style and form too easily recognizable as derived.[14]

One of the great texts on this translation of religiosity into a popular register was the *Ramcharitmanas* of Tulsidas.[15] Many of the complex and ambivalent properties of this new vernacular literature could be found in this, its acknowledged masterpiece. In neighbouring Bengali regions, too, similar texts were composed: the *Ramayana* by Krttivas and the *Mahabharata* of Kashiramdas were written out of similar cultural impulses, though in artistic quality they do not compare with Tulsidas's text. But Tulsidas himself, like a number of other lesser poets, was no mean composer of Sanskrit lyrics, and vernacular writers often had to legitimate their claim to serious attention by writing in the more exalted language.[16]

---

[14] *Mangalkavyas* were composed in honour of nonclassical Hindu deities like Manasa, the snake goddess, *Chandi*, and one of the best-known texts in this tradition is Mukundaram Chakrabarti's *Chandimangal*.

[15] Several English translations of the *Ramcharitmanas* are available: for instance, Prasad 1989 and Douglas and Hill 1971.

[16] A good example from Bengal, though in a later period, is Bharatchandra,

Despite this, vernacular literature's poetic traditions began an undeclared revolution. Within the formal terms of continuity with classical traditions in terms of narratives, forms, and texts, these 'translations' in the vernaculars were hardly passive cultural creations; and they gradually produced an alternative literature which told the same stories with subtle alternative emphases to alternative audiences. It founded a cultural strand that Namwar Singh has elegantly called a *dusri parampara*, a second tradition.[17] It has been pointed out quite often that the *Ramcharitmanas* was in several respects a deeply innovative text. Its ambition of taking the classical narrative to a common audience forced some alterations in the narrative and characterological structures. The humaneness of the idol is reinterpreted from a serenity that befits the almighty to an intimacy of a more accessible kind. As the epic is rewritten into the bhakti register, this gives a softness and sentimentality to the characterization which was lacking in the classical original. Modern interpreters of these texts sometimes make an anachronistic mistake by conceiving them in a style common to modern heterodoxies. Modern rebellions announce themselves even before they are wholly successful: revolutions in traditional cultures tended to hide the fact of their being revolts. They pretend to respect a continuity which they do not in fact practise. By declarations of continuity, however, they circumvent the censorship; precisely by their submission, they create a space for themselves in which the narrative axis, patterns of denouement, and delineation of characters all undergo a subtle transformation. Krishna, the incomparable warrior of the high tradition, becomes Krishna the incomparable lover. Ideas about union with god and his availability to his devotee go through the most radical change.[18] All the while this is accompanied by formal declarations of continuity, apparently testified to indubitably by the sameness of the narratives, the figures, the tropes, and the symbols. Yet, at the same time, in a slow, undeniable open process these religions and

---

who wrote some wonderfully innovative metric poetry apart from his larger works, *Annadamangal* and *Vidyasundarkavya*; but he, too, established his claim to poetic recognition by insignificant versification in Sanskrit.

[17] Namwar Singh 1975, in which the author's argument partly follows the critical work of Hazari Prasad Dwivedi, specially his reading of Kabir.

[18] I have discussed this with reference to Krishna and Radha in Kaviraj 1995.

their observance become public spectacles of a kind of defiance and heterodoxy.

These new texts could do this because they were practising an activity which was tolerated by the Hindu canonical tradition. The ascription of texts to mythical all-seeing sages was clearly a sanctioned device of collective writing, of having open-ended texts which went through constant proposals of embellishment and extension. This must happen of course in oral retelling of stories: but it does happen in written cultures like India in peculiar ways. Nameless poets tried to smuggle their favourite works into great texts to savour the ironical taste of an unnamed immortality.[19] Oral incantation made this possible to an even greater extent, creating something like a latent market of interpolations of which only those favoured by a wide public eventually made it into the text itself. Accumulations of this kind sometimes changed the narrative structure, *rasa* structure, flavour, or even the meaning of the work. Hinduism had a tradition of such *kumbhilakas*, of this strange form of plagiarism in reverse, of people claiming not someone else's work as their own, but their own as someone else's. Bhakti literature in its celebrated translations used this general sanction of free retelling to interpret a new religion into existence.

Gods and goddesses of the classical tradition retain their audience at the cost of this alteration of their character. The stateliness of the central divine characters is replaced by their accessibility and humaneness.[20] This principle of accessibility extends to the formal poetics of the compositions. The verses are composed in a simple and dignified language, in the most accessible of metres—in Bengali the *payar* for instance, the language and rhymes most suited for oral incantation by common people. Literary creations of the Vaishnava cult around Chaitanya displayed similar attributes and converted the figure of Krishna into a figure of love. Krishna's physical form, the idol itself, is transformed: the warrior form with four arms displaying the *shankha*, *chakra*, and *gada* somewhat softened by the residual *padma*, is replaced by the anthropomorphic symbol of the child, Gopal, or the

---

[19] The Sanskrit word for such writers is *kumbhilaka*.

[20] Though both in the Valmiki *Ramayana* and in the *Uttararamacharita* of Bhavabhuti, Rama is seen moved to tears, a demeanour not considered incompatible with his status as a hero or an *avatara* of Narayana.

adolescent Krishna of pleasurable and excusable transgressions. The predominant *rasa* is changed from *aishwarya* to the one of *vatsalya* or *shringara*—both in their different ways vehicles of nearness and indistinction. The language considered adequate for this religiosity is the vernacular. Like Buddhism much earlier, the bhakti movements favoured the lower language; but since these were touched by religiosity, this gave these tongues a new dignity. It will be historically misleading, however, to exaggerate this point; the extrication from Sanskrit remains incomplete in several significant ways. The Bengali Vaishnava *padavali* literature shows this ambivalence with remarkable clarity. Its poetic compositions hover between the clear folkishness of the language of Chandidas or Jnanadas on one side, and the comparatively sanskritized Bengali used by Govindadas. Both are equally indispensable parts of a single literary trend. Most interestingly, this linguistic tension is also reflected in the ways in which Chaitanya's life story is told by his biographers. Vrindavandas's *Chaitanyabhagavat* chronicles it in anthropomorphic terms, the extraordinariness of his acts marked by his miraculous humaneness. By contrast, Krishnadas Kaviraj's *Chaitanyacharitamrita* emphasizes the divinity of this existence, and sees in every act a metaphor of the order of the universe. It is hardly accidental that Vrindavandas writes in a limpid Bengali, while Krishnadas's work is only formally written in Bengali: in its more sombre moments it reminds us that we are in the presence of God himself by lapsing into appropriately complex Sanskrit, heightened by the erudite compositions in the more complex metre, *mandakranta*. Although Chaitanya is an avatar of Krishna he is saved from the heaviness of the classical type by the infusion into his image of Radha (because he is, according to Vaishnava theology, *radhabhava krishnaswarupa*). The figure of the feminine in the Indian tradition is often the symbol of the approachable, the popular, the proximate, the unthreatening and accessible. Because Chaitanya combines in himself the features of Krishna with the lovability of the feminine, he is an androgynous god, the deity of a popular religion which can capture the imagination of relatively subaltern peasant elements in the Hindu society of eastern India.

This indicates a further interesting fact about how people thought of themselves, and conferred self-descriptions on their relevant community. It is not only that the disengagement from Sanskrit is yet incomplete, and the continued popularity of the work of Jayadeva demonstrates its unassailed position as the norm for Vaishnava poetic compositions. More importantly for my central hypothesis, the poetry of Vidyapati from neighbouring Mithila is considered an inalienable part of the Vaishnava heritage. Given the later linguistic identity of this region as Bengali, both Jayadeva and Vidyapati would have raised problems of subsumption, as the first was an inhabitant of Orissa and the second of Mithila. If anything, this shows that despite the unmistakable beginnings of a distinctive vernacular literature, peoples' identity must have been primarily determined by their belonging to a religious sect rather than to a common speech group.

This suggests the following hypothesis. Between the two great layers of language, the upper layer of Sanskrit, and the lower layer of dialects in medieval times, a slow process of differentiation had begun. But the vernaculars were still held together in linguistic intelligibility within a linguistic structure marked by the commonness of Sanskrit at the high end and the easy neighbourly intelligibility of the dialects below.

Gramsci said a language contains a certain conception of the world. To put it another way, there is usually a strong historical connection between a natural and a conceptual language. Seen this way, the origin of vernacular languages appears to be intimately linked to an internal conceptual rebellion within classical brahminical Hinduism. Along with the emergence of a new conception of religiosity, based on a more intimate relation between man and his deity, this movement required a new type of language. To fulfil its functions, it had to be a language of transparency and nearness rather than of inaccessibility and distance. If the purpose of the act of worship was to underline the inequality between God and man, His infinitude against the vulnerable finiteness of all human capacities, the inaccessible sonority of Sanskrit achieved that perfectly. Bhakti Hinduism, like strands of European Protestantism, sought to destroy the brokerage of the Brahmins between the devotee and his god. The philosophical argument behind this was, as is well known, that the act of worship, the most significant act of attunement of man to God's universe, must be transparent and meaningful, and against the earlier semiotics of forbidding distanciation bhakti religion brought in a whole new semiotic of nearness and informality. All this could be accomplished only in a language which, although still distanced by the question of literacy, was closer to actual common speech in two senses. It was, first, a literature in the vernacular. Secondly, it was a vernacular written, though with an ineffable elegance, like the common spoken word. The idea was, in its ideal, utopian, perfect phases, like a pedagogy of the oppressed: poetry spoke a language of the people, expecting that over the long term popular language of worship and sensibility would be exalted by this poetry.

Later, when vernacular literatures were fully formed in colonial times, some of them, like Bengali, would often seek to confer upon themselves a history with a suitably impressive antiquity. In constructing these images of their pasts, they constantly gerrymander historical frontiers. Histories of Bengali literature, a required segment of the formation of 'cultured' Bengalis, standardly claim Vidyapati (from Mithila) and Jayadeva (from Orissa) as parts of their own history. Unlike what Gellner says about the histories nations construct of themselves, there is nothing really fraudulent about this;[21] for these were truly part of the genetic process of the formation of these cultures. But this also shows something equally and vitally true: that there was no Bengal in the modern sense. There was already perhaps an identity of the language, but no linguistic identity. Linguistic identity is not formed by the simple objective fact of some people having a common language; it lies in a more deliberate choice to see this fact as the essential criterion of their identity. The primary reason for this mild paradox—why the language existed without a linguistic identity of its people, I shall suggest—was due to the fact that it was a different kind of social world altogether. My argument is not that this social world 'lacked' some of the features that the modern world has; but that it was a world of a different kind, which we must try to understand by historical inference.

Language in a Fuzzy World

Elsewhere I have tried to approach this problem through a distinction between a fuzzy and an enumerated (in the sense of being counted) social world.[22] Traditional society is made up of a structure of groups which are, in some crucial cases though not in all, fuzzily conceived,[23]

---

[21] Gellner 1983.
[22] Kaviraj 1991b.
[23] Social groups have fuzzy ends or edges in a world in which differences are organized as spectrums rather than divided by boundaries. Arguments of this

of fuzzily conceived space,[24] and fuzzily sensed and imaged time.[25] It is impossible to develop a full argument here about the diverse ways in which the social world, social space, and social time are fuzzy conceptions, and further how these conceptions are interlocked. Indian society, as anthropologists have argued, is of course segmented. But these segments of the lived world do not seem to have frontiers as in any organization of modern social space. Villages do of course begin and end, and therefore have their boundaries, though here, too, in the most immediate form of lived space, there is a certain 'approximateness' and 'indeterminability'. Boundaries of villages, it has been pointed out for many regions of the precolonial world, were not drawn the way states would be represented in maps. It is important to stress that this traditional world is a world without maps, and is therefore devoid of a spatial mentality, inextricable from modernity, which thinks in terms of mapped spaces, and its corollary, measured distances. Inhabitants of the traditional world may thus be said to have a conception of farness rather than of calibrated distance.[26] Beyond the village, the boundedness of regions, subregions, languages, kingdoms is undetermined or indeterminable with modern precision. 'Boundaries' do exist, things, spaces, groups, do begin and end. But they tend to shade off, merge, graduate. It is a different way of organizing difference from the modern one with which we are familiar.

Language illustrates this principle of organization of difference very clearly. In the area lying between, say, Benaras and Puri, a traditional observer would have heard dialects slowly and imperceptibly changing, such that, with historical clairvoyance these could be ascribed to what would eventually become three distinct vernaculars—Hindi, Bengali,

---

kind, though conceptualized differently, are found in Fox 1977, especially the papers by Burton Stein, Bernard Cohn, and Ainslie T. Embree.

[24] Spatial perception could be similarly rendered into a traditional idea of farness against the modern sense of distance.

[25] Anthropological work provides sufficient evidence about a sense of time that is linear in relatively short spans, but whose edges become vague before and after a few generations.

[26] What I mean is that they may think of place X as 'far' Y as 'farther'. They would not have the means, much of the time, to say that X is 500 miles, and Y is 5000.

and Oriya. But it would be impossible, within that world, to determine where Bengali ended and Oriya began; in any case, the change would be decisively different from the standard modern organization of linguistic difference as this is fixed on to maps. Differences would shade off the way distinctly different colours are arranged in a spectrum. It is a world, to put it dramatically, of transitions rather than of boundaries.

Some other ontological features of this social world are of serious consequence for any understanding of politics. First, not merely are the boundaries hazy or spectrum-like, people and objects inhabiting this world are radically uncounted. It is also an unenumerated world. In this world, again, Hindus and Muslims would have perceived their difference (though I doubt they would do it in the modern way); Bengalis and Oriyas do so as well, just as do Shaivas and Vaishnavas. But they do not live in a world in which knowledge of how many Hindus or Muslims or Vaishnavas or Bengalis there are is a part of the commonsensical social knowledge determining patterns of social action. This has a crucial political corollary. Self-identifications are in some senses fuzzy and uncounted: thus, Vaishnavas do not know how many of them are there in the world, and they are crucially incapable of considering what they can do to force the structure of their social world to their collective benefit, if all who are like themselves act together.[27] Distinct languages can thus exist in this society without uniting or dividing people in the manner in which we familiarly see these processes in modern contexts.

Colonialism and the Growth of Linguistic Identity

British colonialism introduced decisive and irreversible changes in the structure of traditional society in this respect. The establishment of colonial power created a different structure of culture by a combination of deliberate policy and unintended consequences. Colonialism had to force social behaviour into recognizable institutional forms, which could be done only by introducing a new type of discourse. Colonialism did not allow to subject Indians any option in this matter; they were

[27] Kaviraj 1991b.

obliged, differentially according to their social status, to respond to its demands, identifications, and actions. Colonial laws and rules restructured Indian society in fundamental ways. Behind these laws there was a more fundamental conception of what laws were, how they related to the facts of the social world, a primarily bourgeois-rationalist discourse of legality. To understand and practically respond to the colonial-legal it was imperative for all Indians to understand this discourse; but it follows that the need was more intense according to their intimacy and involvement with colonial power. Sub-Brahmin groups seeking quick upward mobility through the pathways opened by colonial administration, newly-endowed landlords under the Permanent Settlement, and those armed with a university degree who could get professional placements in the new society had more to do with this system, and therefore showed understandable eagerness to enter schools, pass public examinations, read European history, and get a grip on these conceptual assumptions upon which the colonial institutional system was founded. For understandable reasons, they themselves, and to a lesser extent their colonial patrons, acclaimed this as their acquisition of the difficult, yet potentially universal, principles of rationalism. By contrast, other groups which, by choice or circumstances, had less to do with colonial institutions acquired less of this conceptual language, and eventually came to be derided by the babus for their lack of rational inclinations. Interestingly, it is not only the poorer and culturally deprived social groups which fell into this ignominy, but also those who, on account of cultural pride or other such non-maximizing grounds, remained within the institutions and practices of traditional culture. However, in general, colonialism imposed on society a radically new, unfamiliar discourse, a conceptual grid, an alphabet, without which these institutions were uninhabitable, unworkable, and unintelligible. Institutions are after all the external superstructure of practices, and by altering the logic of institutional functioning colonial rule also forcibly altered the structure of traditional practices and the social understandings that went with them.

Though early colonial administrations by and large followed a policy of non-interference in cultural affairs, there were strict limits to this tolerance. Colonial administrations could hardly dispense with one essential prerequisite of effective rule: intelligibility of this world to the rulers themselves. As a result of the unanswerable power that attached to the moves of the colonial administration in its days of dominance, even though sometimes these moves were misidentifications, they had real consequences. Gradually, colonialism introduced into this social world entirely unfamiliar processes and institutions drawn from the enormous cognitive apparatus that rationalism had by this time created in the West, by which alone the colonizers could make this world cognitively and practically tractable. Surely, colonialism was an enterprise of introducing modernity only in truncated forms.[28] However, one particular aspect of modernity the colonial state did introduce with effectiveness—the modern imperative of setting up social connections on an unprecedented scale. The extension of scale of social action brought in, as sociological research has amply shown, pressures towards standardization in varying forms.[29] European missionaries of the Srirampur (Serampore) College sought to fashion printed alphabets for Bengali, and by 1800 religious tracts meant to popularize Christianity were being printed at their press. These foreign pioneers of printing chose from among various styles of calligraphy, keeping in mind technical constraints, but once this contingent choice was made it came to have decisive standardizing effects on even Bengali writing. Ironically, the way generations of modern Bengalis would read and write their own tongue was fatefully decided by choices made by a peculiarly skilled Englishman.

The most significant standardization, however, occurred in the areas of spoken and literary language; and this begins the mysterious process by which a high literature which they would never be able to read nonetheless confers an identity on the illiterate. Calcutta, an unknown village before the advent of the British, came to acquire as the colonial capital unprecedented economic, administrative, and commercial eminence. The prime beneficiaries of the colonial social transformation either came from the society in Calcutta or journeyed there to remain close to the source of all colonial beneficence. The social elite resident in that city thus came to enjoy an eminence unknown in earlier times, and indeed, one which was structurally impossible. In a matter of less than a hundred years the Calcutta babu

---

[28] The economic aspect of this argument—that colonialism did not introduce a capitalist economy of the Western type, but a peculiarly distorted form—is too well known to require special mention.

[29] Cohn 1987. See the essay entitled 'Census, Social Structure and Objectification in South Asia'.

came to acquire an unequalled capacity to do social and cultural norm-setting, growing out of his opulence, and to screen demands made on the colonial administration. Slowly, the language of the Calcutta bhadralok, with occasional skilful mixtures from areas which had a reputation for particularly mellifluous accents, came to be regarded as the norm language for bhadralok Bengalis in all regions of this linguistic area. Of course, this norm-setting process could not have been completed without the print media. One of the reasons for lack of standardization in earlier language was the lack of scale-extension of any particular speech form. The arrival of printing altered this fact by exerting two types of pressures on its users. First, language had to be standardized not only at the material level of letters to be used in print; but also, this standard Bengali could then be dedicated to modern uses as the vehicle of high literature, of science, of serious intellectual instruction. Secondly, once this standard or norm language became established, elites or aspirants to elite status from other, more outlying, regions began to emulate its accents and written idioms. The gentry of Medinipur, presumably content in earlier times with speaking a dialect which kept them in close touch with their local lower-order brethren, and more significantly, in intelligible proximity with Oriyas, now began to read and speak like journals written in the norm language of Calcutta. Any claim to linguistic distinction in the traditional language-economy rested on the command of esoteric languages. Dialect Bengali would be spoken the same way by all social groups. Now the marks of distinction had to be entered into the vernacular itself. Traditionally, though the two languages, Sanskrit and Bengali, may have been placed in a relation of hierarchy, each language was internally more equal. Two changes now occurred in this structure. English quickly displaced Sanskrit from the status of esoteric language: Sanskrit was relegated to the position of an archaic tongue. More significantly, the internal economy of the Bengali language itself became distinctly more hierarchical. As an aspiring high language, Bengali, in its increasingly sophisticated form, came to have interestingly complex relations with Sanskrit and English, the two languages from whose tyranny it was supposed to emancipate its cultivated speakers. The resources of the colloquial language of the street—its early literary masters like Vidyasagar and Bankimchandra felt—were too meagre and insubstantial to carry the burden of such tasks. The more Bengali would replace Sanskrit as a high language, therefore, the more it would 'become' like Sanskrit in a sense, both in the direct sense of borrowing from its vocabulary, and being less accessible. Indeed, the new 'high' Bengali took on board a whole range of attributes from both Sanskrit and English, the two languages with which it existed in a relation of cultural contestation. Further, its internal economy would open up greater possibilities of hierarchy through the infinite refinement of 'literary' writing styles, and of 'cultured' pronunciation, an unfailing marker of increasing social differentiation.[30]

Sometimes this emergence of a standard Bengali and a culture of transaction of high functions in it rather than in Sanskrit or English is treated absentmindedly as a democratization of the linguistic field, a judgement to be taken with some caution. Within its incontestably democratic trends were lodged sharper inequalities of a new kind. The peasantry, the Hashim Sheikhs and Rama Kaivartas of Bankim's famous essay, stood no chance of comprehending the argument in which they figured, and which was made on their behalf—for no other reason but that they could hardly understand its Sanskritic grace.[31] Ironically, a speech community certainly grew up in nineteenth-century Bengal, as Bankim's *Vande Mataram* illustrated, with seven crores of Bengalis, a vast majority of them illiterate, prepared to worship their linguistic motherland, extending to her a form of reverence earlier reserved only for scriptural deities. Yet, though this produced a sense of political community around language or speech, it was anything but a community of the same speech.

This historical sketch, though obviously crude and minimal, helps us put to rest some prejudices that social science analyses of identity formation have uncritically picked up from later nationalist discourse. Both in mature nationalism and in social science, it is customary to seek systemic differences between traditional and modern identities. A vulgar Weberianism which almost always subtly informs nationalist

---

[30] Subsequently, Bengali showed an interesting line of development on this count. Through the radio and the great popularity of the Bengali film, the 'cultured' way of speaking Bengali has become since the 1960s very widespread. While this may have extended the 'civilizing' process in a certain sense, the diction and accent have become distinctly less significant social markers.

[31] Chattopadhyay 1964: 288.

thinking on this question often makes it out as if linguistic identities are primordial, while the national identity of India is modern.[32] This view is false, it appears, on two different counts. (i) The identities of region and nation are both products of the same historical-cultural processes which produced a mapped world out of the earlier fuzzy one. Political identities based on language are therefore equally modern though the languages on which they are based have a distinct historical existence from much earlier times. (ii) This historical imperative—i.e. both these are modern and historically intertwined, making it difficult to play one against the other—makes for a peculiar configuration of a two-layered identity for individuals and groups. A regional identity is subsumed in a larger national one—a fundamental historic fact that, later, more anxious and simple-minded forms of nationalist ideology have often sought to deny.[33]

Within Bengali fiction, Bankimchandra's work is fascinating, I have argued elsewhere, because he shows quite precisely how this consciousness is formed; how some crucial cultural choices are made, how within the newly formed intense consciousness of being Bengali critical weaknesses are perceived.[34] The sufferings of political humiliation and rightlessness are felt not to be a peculiar problem of the Bengalis, but common to all those who lived under British rule. Besides, if a credible political coalition was to be built up, which could effectively menace British power, a regional identity of Bengalis alone was unlikely to impress them. Authors like Bankim displayed what I have

---

[32] Nationalism in India has had a particularly strong connection with modernist developmentalism. As it develops, nationalist discourse decisively sides with modernity, and sees everything modern with approval and things 'traditional' with suspicion if not with straightforward hostility. Additionally, it often tends to consign all premodern forms to primordiality (in the derogatory sense of an aboriginal primitiveness). But it is useful to distinguish between two distinctions widely used in the literature. Primordial/modern is in one sense a chronological historical distinction. In a related but quite distinct sense, this may also mean a taking/making of identities: primordial identities are those people have to take, modern ones are those they make on their own, or so they would like to believe.

[33] This is a point that has been made consistently by radical left parties against the grain of mainstream nationalism.

[34] Kaviraj 1995: ch. 4.

termed an anticolonial consciousness before they chose their nation.[35] After considerable hesitation, and a few false starts, Bengali creative writing, by the middle of the nineteenth century, accomplishes a substantial gerrymandering of the boundaries of its imagined community. Initially, it appears that the 'we' who should oppose the British are to be Bengalis; but after considering proposals about making Hindus their nation, they eventually choose to be Indians. Reflecting this process graphically, Bankim breaks the boundaries of his initially restricted Bengali regional identity and begins to represent Rajputs, Sikhs, and Marathas in their saying of 'we', in their collective self-description. As parallel processes go on in other parts of the country, this contributes, by the beginning of the twentieth century, to the making of the familiar contours of Indian nationalism. Still, under this nationalistic configuration of self-consciousness, other identities of language, occasionally linguistically perceived ones of religion or subregional cultures, are always present in an indistinct and politically inactive state.[36] Much of current Indian politics revolves around how nationalism decides to deal with them—to attack and destroy them as competing attractions or to give them a place within its own internal architecture. Precedents of European nationalism, through which Indian nationalists initially sought to understand and think through their own world, presented an immediate problem. Successful European nations created, in most cases, culturally homogeneous states based crucially on the unity of one language. Indian national identity seemed to 'lack' one of the main prerequisites of a modern nation, a feature which helped them to weather periods of political adversity.[37] Indian nationalism and its

[35] What I mean is that their decision to oppose British colonialism comes chronologically before they decide who this 'we' was—Bengalis, Hindus, Indians?

[36] The connection of Urdu with Islam, and of Punjabi more recently with Sikhism. Yet, it is interesting to note, with Khubchandani, that Urdu, especially Hindustani, is the language of a culture rather than of a religion. Similarly, those who equate Punjabi too closely with the Sikh religion forget that there is a Punjabi-speaking people in Pakistan, and there is a Punjabi 'diaspora'. Khubchandani 1991.

[37] Curiously, any historical or social feature that Indian society has that is different from standard forms in European history is seen as a feature it does not have; its presence is seen as a lack and theorized consistently in this fashion.

state inherited from its inception a 'language problem': i.e. the problematicity of its cultural formation in the absence of a single unifying language. Two ways appeared to be open to it and the state it aspired to establish after Independence was achieved. One arguable, but unlikely, road was to pursue a single-minded strategy of cultural homogenization based on the primacy (others would call it domination) of a 'majority' language. This would have implied trying to solve the cultural problem by a Soviet model: the only drawback was that the conditions for its practical realization did not exist. Hindi did not have a statistical absolute majority in India, nor was its political supremacy firmly established by the cultural processes of nationalist politics. It was therefore the second solution which was taken up by the national movement—a strategy of accepting the legitimacy of linguistic self-identifications of people in their regions, giving it a place in a second order identity of Indian nationalism and using a critically significant political diglossia.

The Nationalist Diglossia

The nationalist movement used two cultural devices to solve this difficulty of according legitimacy to regional identities but still requiring a second order self-identification of people as Indians. In its mature stages, it generated a plausible and powerfully articulated narrative of India's immemorial past, a logic of cultural unification lodged in the essentials or the depths of Indian history, into which, through the creation of a 'composite culture', Muslims were integrated in medieval times. Nehru's *Discovery of India* was of course the classic of this narrative construction which saw the imagining of India as having been accomplished in the past.[38] As part of an anti-imperialist ideology, it had an understandably powerful appeal, though in my judgement the exclusive reliance on this narrative for solving all problems after Independence has had a deleterious effect on political thinking. This logic of creating unity within plural strands, the ecumenical tolerance which gradually absorbed others into an extended notion of the self, was felt to have created this imagination and its practical institutions already in the past; British colonialism disturbed its continuity only temporarily. This implied that once the national state was achieved, this buried cultural imagination of India would again come into its own. This became

[38] For a critical discussion of this narrative structure, see Kaviraj 1991a.

a deeply held and widespread belief that undergirded much nationalist practice of mobilization and state-building. Nehru's text, written at the moment of its imminent triumph, was a systematic and passionate statement of this narrative of culture; and I think Nehru's curious inattentiveness to cultural construction cannot be explained without understanding how seriously his generation believed in the story they had told themselves. As I said earlier, as an empowering narrative for the nationalist movement this picture of India's past was immensely powerful. For rational reconstruction of the state, in the less romantic period after freedom, this narrative was more a hindrance to realistic policy than a help. It put the process of the cultural construction of the nation in the past, rather than in the future; it saw that as an accomplished task rather than as a requirement to be fulfilled if India was to stay together as a nation state. It encouraged forgetfulness and negligence about the cultural reproduction process in all its forms—in everyday life, social practices, and education, its most significant institutional form.[39]

But this narrative structure was supported by a deeper cultural arrangement that was more directly linguistic, which determined and mediated crucial political relations, and decided who could, literally, speak to whom. To rejoin my earlier argument, the mixed elite drawn from the educated, bilingual intelligentsia of different regions found themselves within a triangle of cultural or discursive exchange—exchanges with the lower orders of their regional people, with peoples of other regions through their leaders who were culturally and politically similarly placed, and exchange with the British, apart from the more general and exalted need to receive information about scientific developments in the Western world. The most effective and economical means of dealing with this set of discursive demands was a diglossia or cultural bilingualism.[40] Through political experimentation, the national movement came to settle on this device of political culture quite

---

[39] Though there is no space for outlining this here, my argument requires as a complement a critical discussion about educational structures, practices, and policies.

[40] Any observant student of Indian culture would notice the common prevalence of diglossia and heteroglossia. After the coming of colonialism, the typical structure of Indian bilingualism is English-vernacular rather than vernacular 1 and vernacular 2.

fundamentally. Common training in English education, with a common syllabus, common cultural preferences and tastes, and common biases provided the preconditions for this situation, but it was cemented by the evident functionality of this arrangement for the growth of an Indian political movement.

Some consequences of this invisible cultural fact deserve some mention. It ensured in an oblique and unobtrusive way a kind of elite domination of the higher levels of nationalist mobilization, even though subaltern dissent against colonialism was more extreme and visceral and middle-class defiance more careful and circumspect. The linguistic economy partly guaranteed that despite this, it was only the middle-class elements who would provide the all-India leadership. Vernacular speakers could storm into the leadership of linguistically homogeneous areas, but there their political stars stopped climbing. Compulsions of this kind, working not through the explicit and usually resented logic of social class or status, but the subliminal agencies of language and communication, introduced an elitist counterweight into the inherent populism of the nationalist movement.

This diglossia was also politically rational in a narrower sense. Indian culture, it is often remarked, is characterized by an easy heteroglossia. After the entry of English education on a large scale, the situation stabilized into a fairly common structure of diglossia among the educated. A pure Indian bilingualism (i.e. using two Indian languages equally fluently for serious intellectual activity) was not very common among the elite: bilingualism rather meant the ability to use a vernacular and English. This meant that a bilingual person was not thickly aware of cultural or political development in only two areas; under this arrangement, he was of course thickly aware of his own vernacular-based regional culture, but also thinly of all others. The success of nationalism was made possible by political conceptual co-ordination between the various vernacular regions. However, often this bilingualism was internally uneven; those who could use these languages were unequally fluent in them. This yields a structure similar to the flower-shaped arrangement suggested by the Dutch sociologist of language Abram de Swann, with the inconvenience of having widely irregular-sized petals.[41] The petal representing Hindi would account for about

[41] The floral model is used in de Swann 1988: ch. 3, and used in a discussion on India in idem 1990.

40 per cent of India's population next to those of comparatively small languages like Kashmiri or Manipuri. The recent admission of the political significance of some languages which cannot he ascribed specific regional or spatial location, like Nepali or Sindhi, would make the structure of actual linguistic exchanges still more complex. Additionally, such bilingualism is bound to be in individual cases asymmetric: a speaker would not have equal competence in both, and since competence confers and abridges rights and capacities, each would thus support the cause of the language he is more proficient in. For individuals, thus, we should write not only that person X has E+V, but also indicate a certain slope or precedence: E/V or V/E, because these would, in political action, make a material difference.

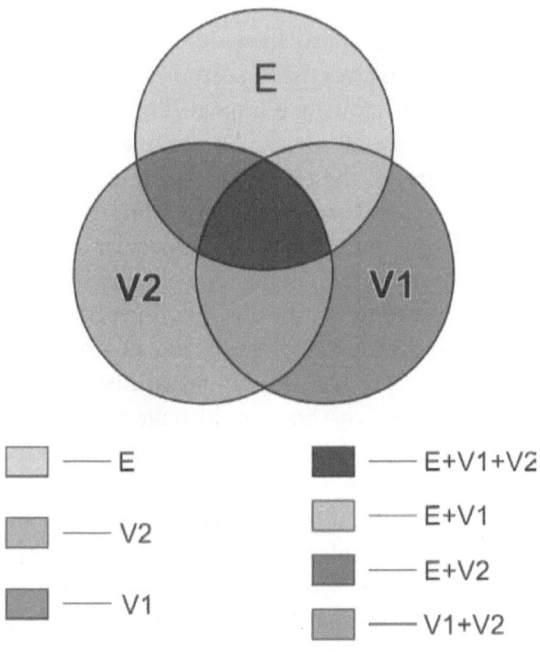

Fig. 2

Language thus acted as a necessary process of filtration, or 'gatekeeping'; it would filter out inconvenient, extreme, radical, intransigent demands from subaltern social groups from reaching higher bodies. This was no small factor in enabling the higher decision-making

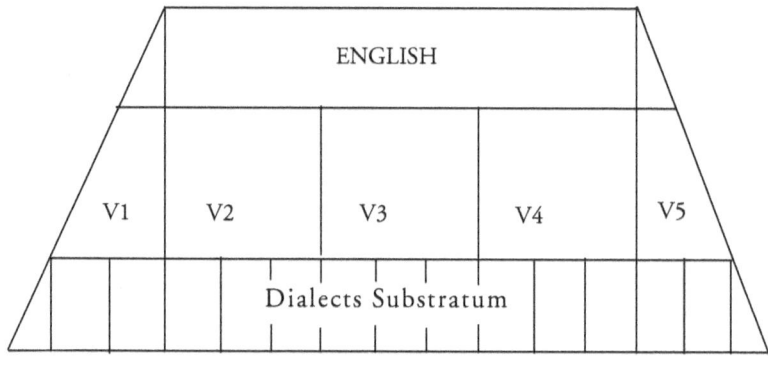

Fig. 3

bodies to maintain their immaculate middle-class ambience of restraint, and polite gentility. This gives rise to a certain paradox of participation. Certainly, the English-knowing bilingual elite represented the largest number of people from all vernacular regions; but this implied an inverse relation between the extent or width of representation and its intensity or intimacy. Conversely, seen from the point of view of ordinary people living in the dialect or vernacular spaces of the pyramid of speech, the further their demands were carried into the political world by their representatives, the less the control they could exercise over them.[42] The Indian people became, like democratic people elsewhere, the generalized reason, the universal justification for things done in their name which they would have found largely incomprehensible. The greatest example of this paradox was the constitution. It was apparently part of their tryst with destiny to give themselves the longest, the best, and the most intricate constitution in the world: there is a minor irony considering the fact that over 70 per cent of the country was illiterate and had no clear idea of what they had been given. Making a constitution of this kind was a strange but historically inevitable mixture of giving people unprecedented rights and also keeping them securely out of their reach.

[42] In democratic theory a distinction is commonly made between delegation and representation. Something like this also exists in the Indian national movement, though this is seen as two pragmatic forms rather than two theoretical positions engaged in explicit debate.

Language and Politics after Independence

What is remarkable in this story of language and the conferment of identity is a paradox that emerges in a comparison between pre-Independence years and the time after Independence. Abstractly, it appears that the cultural problems of nationalism can be handled better when the ideological force of nationalism is assisted by the material power of the modern state. Yet, on an historical view, it seems that the Indian national movement, when it had to contend with the enmity and obstructiveness of the colonial state, tackled some cultural processes better than the nation-state. In certain ways, the guiding logic of the complex network of culture, language, identities, and discourses seems gradually to slip out of the grasp of the state, leading to a further paradox. The state is becoming increasingly powerful in technical and material terms and at the same time abjectly ineffective in regulating, let alone solving, cultural conflict.

The Nehruvian elite, which inherited effective control after Independence, faced a complex initial situation. Indeed, the issue of an official or 'national' language occasioned some of the most acrimonious debates in the Constituent Assembly. Its proceedings also showed another ironic fact: how deep the influence of European precedents was on the minds of the Indian intelligentsia. On the language issue, the assembly saw a division between moderates and Hindi extremists centred on three major issues: (i) whether India should have a national language, and if it did whether it would be the broad ecumenical form of Hindustani, or a Sanskritized Hindi, (ii) what would be the status of English, how quickly this mark of foreign subjugation was to be phased out and replaced by the national language; and (iii) the largely symbolic problem about the system of numerals to be adopted. A nation, it was argued by those who favoured Hindi, must have a national language; and this could only be an Indian language. Of the various Indian languages, since there was, 'unfortunately', no clear majority language, this place should go to Hindustani or Hindi as the language spoken by the largest plurality. Strong and insistent demands were also made in the Constituent Assembly for having a Hindi version of the constitution adopted as the original in place of the English one. Interestingly, even moderates on the language issue conceded the idea of having a single language being a precondition of firm, unassailable nationalism. Eventually, however, the Assembly adopted a more complex, if less decisive, line in favour of what was known as the Munshi-Ayyangar formula, which pragmatically reflected the structure of discursive exchange which underlay the national mobilization.[43]

The influence of European examples was so deep that it determined the manner in which the constitution-makers framed their question. A single language, one of the prime features of European nationalism, was missing in the Indian case: the nation-state lacked a common language. Pragmatically, with their comparative knowledge and historical sense, however, the Nehruvian leadership realized that the cultural form of Indian nationalism must be different from the European norm. Nehru's government pursued a policy of gentle exhortation on the significance of Hindi as an official language for the union government and communication between states. The actual use of languages in government, however, diverged substantially from its declared policy. The introduction of large-scale economic planning, and the related emphasis on science, technology, and the processing of standardized information naturally increased the subtle forms of power exercised by the high bureaucracy simply on account of their inabilities and preferences. They could converse more easily in English and carry on these intricate activities more conveniently without the acute problems bound to be raised by translations many times over between the vernaculars. English became more entrenched in the bureaucratic and private managerial echelons after Independence because the earlier political compulsion of using vernaculars to underline self-respect had less relevance. To those outside the charmed circle of English education, this gave grounds for the complaint that India was reconquered for English after Independence.[44] The language of India's nation-building was, unfortunately, English.

The first wave of regional disturbances that the new state faced was not of its own making: it may have contributed to their occurrence

---

[43] For an excellent account of the debates on the language issue in the Constituent Assembly, see Austin 1966: ch. 12.

[44] One of the telling examples of this was the alteration in the structure of school education. A strong emphasis on symmetrical bilingual education in the period from the 1930s to the 1960s produced a fairly distinctive school system

only by forgetting the promises the Congress had made. Congress acknowledged during the freedom movement that administrative boundaries instituted by British rule were arbitrary, and had to be reordered after Independence. After 1920 the Congress organization decided to work on the basis of linguistic provinces rather than of administrative boundaries, implicitly reinforcing the commitment. Events at the time of Partition and the experience of constitution-framing may have made the ruling group more cautious in this regard. However, the original organization of states was, by the mid-1950s, facing serious disaffection in some parts of India. The structure of this disaffection is interesting. Initially, regional discontent did not arise in all parts of the country simultaneously, but only in those parts in which some communities had, under the colonial dispensation, enjoyed subcolonial advantage over others. Early opportunities of colonial employment had imparted a peculiar class structure to Bengali society, since Bengalis had supplied the entire demand for middle-class bilingual professionals not only for the Bengali-speaking areas but for the entire northern and eastern parts of the empire. In the Madras Presidency Tamil enjoyed largely similar superiority for similar reasons. Linguistic groups who were disadvantaged by this naturally hoped that with the end of colonialism such privileges would also disappear. Strong regionalist sentiments arose over Congress tardiness and hesitation. Although this caused temporary embarrassment to Nehru's government, some peculiarities in the situation made the eventual transition to linguistic states remarkably easy and smooth. The actual grievance was against the regionally superordinate cultures rather than the central government. The moral strength of the case of these regions was matched by the weakness of their adversaries. Besides, constitutional rights, unlike material resources, were not scarce or restricted things, and thus the achievements of the rights of one group, instead of threatening, furthered the claims of others.

---

in the areas that had enjoyed the differential advantages of colonial education. This was gradually replaced by a flourishing privileged private sector of English-medium schools and an underprivileged state sector of vernacular schools. Because of the strong correlation between the acquisition of English language and chances of good middle class employment, there has been a constant demand for rapid expansion of these 'public schools'.

Interestingly, although the Nehru government conceded these demands, and gave it a generalized form by instituting the states reorganization commission, Nehru himself expressed some forebodings. First, he thought living in mixed, multilingual administrative units would provide education in common living and reduce linguistic chauvinism.[45] Secondly, he anticipated difficulties in administratively applying the principle: areas like the north-east have in fact proved chronically difficult to settle linguistically.[46] Yet Nehru agreed to linguistic reorganization because of the undeniable force of the argument of democracy—that use of the vernacular in administration would bring government closer to the people, because that was the language they were illiterate in. In the case of the demand for a Punjabi *suba*, he persistently refused to grant it because he thought this was merely a communal divide under a thin subterfuge of language.

The reorganization of states on the basis of language still left major difficulties. In some areas, like Assam, linguistic groups were too mixed to allow for their clear administrative disentanglement without making the units too small. Even such reordering has not, much afterwards, solved the question of enclaves within majority languages. Hindi remained anomalously placed inside the constitutional structure, since it was stretched from Bihar to some parts of Punjab. This might have encouraged some kind of interest coalition among its speakers, and since their resources taken together would have been quite substantial, this may have renewed the conflicts of the Constituent Assembly once more. A potentially difficult situation was avoided precisely due to the internal divisiveness of the Hindi language area. Hindi was historically less standardized than other vernaculars,[47] and several of its subregional forms could claim to be much more than mere

[45] Occasionally, such ideas went to an unpractical extreme—as in the case of the intensely unpopular suggestion for the merger of Bengal and Bihar. For Nehru's thinking on linguistic states, see Gopal 1979: ch. 12.

[46] Professional linguists sometimes argue that the idea that there should be sharply defined territorial boundaries not only for nation states but also for linguistic units inside them was unsuited to the Indian situation and bound to cause problems. Cf. Khubchandani 1991.

[47] For a discussion of the issues involved in the Hindi-Urdu-Hindustani debate, Khubchandani 1991, and an earlier account in Dasgupta 1970, chs 2 and 6.

dialects of some general norm language,⁴⁸ though *khadi boli* from early on made known its pretensions to that status.⁴⁹ Apart from the problem of the standard, Hindi was riven by the acrimonious dispute between a Sanskritized Hindi and a Persianized Urdu tearing apart the spontaneous historical form of Hindustani, the language in which most people actually spoke in North India. This was also the form more easily intelligible to neighbouring vernacular speakers, and in which much of the high literature was written. Internal dissensions within Hindi led to a circumstance which turned ironically to be beneficial to the new state. The potential mobilization for Hindi as a 'national' language which would compulsorily replace English, and make India look more like a unilingual European nation-state, failed to gather momentum because it was hard to decide which kind of Hindi would enjoy these privileges of universal aggrandisement. After 1956 the union government has faced infrequent difficulty from this direction, except for some areas like the north-east, where linguistic determination of state boundaries has remained intellectually unconvincing and politically contested.

One of the major features of Nehru's development policy that has escaped serious critical attention was its economism: a superstitious belief in the powers of economic growth to dispel all evils like rays of light in the enveloping darkness of traditionalism. Thus, although individual members of that early governmental elite had impressively high cultural attainments, their dedicated economism made them deeply negligent about processes of culture. While economic processes were minutely analysed, alternative policies assessed and debated, they did not see cultural processes or institutions as serious objects of either historical reflection or deliberate policy, except in terms of budgetary allocations. Unattended cultural reproduction processes, left to the violence and malignancy of both a vicious market and unprincipled state manipulation, have now produced something like a massive counter-revolution of culture. In the rest of this essay I shall

---

⁴⁸ Maithili has caused endless debates on this count—whether it was a dialect of Hindi or a separate but closely related language.

⁴⁹ Even this has to be qualified, because during the early development of modern Hindi literature eminent figures like Bharatendu Harishchandra had suggested *khadi boli* as the form of prose and *brajabhasha* as the form for poetry.

try to present a bare outline of this process and its relation to the crisis of the state.

If states, to be durable, have to depend on something like a common consciousness, the Indian national state faced an obvious difficulty, not so much because of the multiplicity of its languages as due to the fact that there were two rather different types of 'common sense' about the world that were lodged in the English and the vernacular segments of its culture. True, serious transactions had begun between these two orbits of common sense in the nineteenth century and during the freedom movement. But such exchanges remained unfinished and irregular. As India did not have a natural coincidence of a common culture and a common language, the quotidian self-recognition of its citizens depended crucially on an argumentative and ratiocinative process which could be fashioned by education and deliberate cultural policies. Such a self-recognition of Indianness is primarily a conceptual construction and is to be produced and maintained by means of cultural arguments quite different from the easy recognition of a collective self given in the mere utterance of a natural language. It has to be an indirect, second-order process, quite distinct from the process of linguistic self-recognition, of creation and stabilization of a political common sense. Identity in India must have more than one layer. From this point of view, Nehru's government and its successors have consistently misconstrued the historical function of education. Due to their deeply economistic reasoning, they considered education an input in the creation of skills necessary for a modern economy, and entirely missed its more fundamental common-sense-forming role. These roles are performed by different levels of the educational structure. Technological education was given nearly exclusive priority, including science education as its base, and naturally also higher education. This led to a state of affairs in which, while a large number of middle-class graduates were trained to be engineers, medical practitioners, or planners, the large majority were not trained in being Indians. Such training, sorely missed in recent years, has been left to the canned patriotism provided abundantly and free of charge with the television news.

The later evolution of Indian politics has shown such superstitious belief in the enlightening powers of economic processes to be fallacious. Economically upwardly mobile farmers have not become more kindly towards other rural classes—their traditional neighbours in the daily life of the countryside.[50] Professional middle classes have not shown increased comprehension of others' justified demands on the resources of the state.[51] Under the primitive capitalist conditions that exist in India, greater economic prosperity does not seem to increase a group's understanding of the overall requirements of distributive justice: rather an insensitivity to distributive questions may produce the drive for strong commercial enterprise. In general, economic growth simply failed to radiate the kind of illumination and understanding expected of it by the development model.

Cultural defaults of the nation-state, begun in the absentmindedness of Nehru's government, were intensified by successor regimes. While all governments paid ceremonial attention to high culture and art, made larger budgetary allocations to higher education, they considered their responsibility completed by such exertions and showed little interest in organizing social reflection on the relation between democracy, poverty, and culture. These delicate processes were thus left to an increasingly chaotic and iniquitous market of cultural skills and goods whose spontaneous trends were 'corrected' by an increasingly arbitrary state which specialized in correcting injustices by other injustices rather than the unaccustomed intellectual practice of following a judicious policy over a long term.[52] Indian cultural life saw the emergence of a progressive intelligentsia whose only vocation in life, after pursuing individual self-interest, was to lead the Indian people, especially the indigent, to liberation—but it had forgotten to pick up their language. Those who spoke those languages often had political horizons too narrow to consider national interests, and were mired by pulls of regional or subregional selfishness. The contradiction between the two

---

[50] The demands of rich farmers show this insensitivity quite dramatically.

[51] The middle class's hostility to any suggestion of redistributive moves was reflected in its violent reaction to the declaration that the recommendations of the Mandal Commission would be partially implemented.

[52] This is reflected in the irrationalities of the schools system. Public schools, run on lines of merciless private enterprise, treat these institutions as business propositions with high fees, impossible entry criteria, and a quality of training which is hardly commensurate with the expenses or the advertisement. Government schools, starved of basic resources and plagued by bureaucratic controls are not allowed to stabilize into any reasonable pattern by the appallingly arbitrary way in which changes are made in their educational schemes.

common senses, lodged largely in English and the vernaculars, has now assumed close-to-crisis intensity, bringing the conceptual basis of the Indian state to great strain. The process of the imagining of India has fallen a victim to quietly effective processes of bifurcation and heterogeneity. The neglect of education—leaving it to the market—meant a chasm between high and low culture; incompatible with the logic of democratic politics, this has persisted. Entrant elites at the state levels of the Indian federation, drawn from farmer groups, perceived this system, with some justification, as one of cultural or linguistic untouchability, an English-based caste system. On the other hand the urban elite, systematically withdrawing from the diglossia into exclusive use of a coarsening functional English, reacted negatively, often showing their paradoxical belief that only those who could not speak in any Indian language could be safely called Indian nationalists; others were assigned derogatory ethnicities like Punjabi, Bengali, Bihari, Tamil, etc. The unplanned and unorganized spread of vernacular education, which is often distinctly inferior in quality, accentuated this process. The diglossia that had formed the cultural basis of the national movement has tended to fall apart. Educational differentiation has led to a situation in which a monolingual English-using elite is faced by an equally monolingual vernacular aspirant group contesting its power with increasing urgency. Both languages suffer coarsening in this friction, though it is the slow slide of English into functional inelegance which is most observable.[53] Thus the discursive structure of nationalism is being broken down in two ways. First, the English-using managerial elites at the top of the pyramid are getting distanced from the vernacular-using lower slices, failing to perform the task of creating and disseminating a nationalist common sense which must not be an ossified collection of ideas from past nationalist leaders, but an active configuration of ideas which all negotiate. Secondly, since in

---

[53] I would argue against some enthusiastic linguists that while the Indian way of using English must be legitimately different, the question of linguistic elegance should not be confused with this. Elegance or distinction is achieved when language rises above mere functionality, and can express complexity and subtlety of ideas. From this angle one can find a clearly perceptible coarsening of the linguistic culture. And it is not the inadequately bilingual speakers who are responsible but the parasitic, culturally sterile, and imitative elites whose only language is this vulgarized, subliterary English.

our model the major part of the exchanges between the vernacular segments did not occur laterally, but through the bilingual top, these vernacular sections are coming into increasing friction.[54]

By and large, till recently, the Indian state has faced relatively infrequent difficulty from linguistic separatism. Common peoples' quotidian linguistic identities seem to lie quiescent in a pleasant, inoffensive, taken-for-granted kind of way, until they become vehicles for other types of grievance through a malignant elective affinity.[55] Though both the Assam and the Punjab problems show pronounced linguistic aspects, in these disturbances the linguistic demand exists in interestingly complex relation with others.

One can also glimpse the emergence of a different sort of problem in Indian politics which might revive the question of Hindi chauvinism in a new form. Since Indira Gandhi's victory in the general elections of 1971, directly populist rhetoric had been rather faint in Indian political discussion. Populism has in recent times seen a great revival, forcing democratic issues on the political agenda of the nation, mixed in a distinctly Tocquevillesque fashion, with dangerous disregard for norms of institutional circumspection. Mrs Gandhi spoke in the name of the great majority of the poor; others now speak in the names of the equally great majorities of the 'backward castes', of the neglected Hindus, or the insulted, disprivileged speakers of Hindi, the language of the majority of Indians. We saw earlier how the question of what to do with Hindi was alleviated by the other one of what was Hindi. Since Independence, the situation has changed in several ways. The first is the noticeable retreat of Urdu into the cultivated middle-class parlour, under the assault of a state-patronized and Sanskritized Hindi. Because of the evident disruption of the nationalist diglossia it has become possible now to claim that the division of the rich and the poor, of the

---

[54] It must be seen, however, that this model is meant to be an ideal-typical construction. Exchanges took place bilaterally between regional cultures: e.g. Bengali literature (especially the novels of Bankimchandra Chattopadhyay, Rabindranath Tagore, and Saratchandra Chatterjee) were widely translated in other languages. My point is that the primary political exchange happened systematically through bilingualism of the elite.

[55] Khubchandani 1991 makes this point about Punjab. Despite the creation of a Bengali-speaking Bangladesh, there was no noticeable urge on either side for a sentimental merger.

urban exploiters and the rural sufferers, the upper castes and lower, are all translatable into the symbolic divide between English, the language of the undeservingly privileged, and Hindi, the speech of unmerited suffering. A significant recent development has been the declaration of four chief ministers of northern states that Hindi should displace English in official administrative functions. They explicitly demanded that it should be used in inter-state communication, and as the exclusive language for entrance examination of various types of government and semi-government bureaucracy. Its major supporting argument is that insistence on English artificially and unjustly wrongfoots speakers of Indian languages—an entirely understandable idea up to this point. Yet their demand is not that linguistic iniquity should be ended, but that it should be turned in favour of native Hindi speakers. They should enjoy the privilege that belonged to English users because they constitute the ironic majority of 40 per cent of the Indian population. Clearly, this would not be perceived as equitous by those who do not speak Hindi, only a proposal to disadvantage others. English, they would claim, is more equitous because it places all Indians in a position of equal disadvantage.

Undoubtedly, in the past forty years India has seen a process of uneven but also unprecedented enfranchisement of the common people. Language rights constitute a vital part of this process—the right to protest becomes attenuated if it is not a right to protest in one's own language. Through the processes of democracy, identities have undergone rapid reconfiguration, and political groups are naturally trying to split and recoalesce identities in ways preferable to themselves. Communal elements have put forward the considerable appeal of a Hindu majoritarianism. In response, the Janata Dal advanced a consolidation, also majoritarian, of backward castes, splitting the potential Hindu coalition on caste lines. The proposals for Hindi majoritarianism, though statistically on somewhat weaker grounds, bear interesting connections with Hindu communal sentiment. Historically, the trend most dangerous for the survival of Indian democratic government will be a process of mutual attraction, a fatal elective affinity, between various forms of majoritarianism, a coalition struck between differently grounded majoritarian demands. Indeed, as some people have argued at different points in recent history, the majority demand of a Hindu state, instead of the present one based on 'Western' secularism and the majority demand for a Hindi-dominant state, can coalesce because the two groups of beneficiaries of such privilege would overlap to a large degree. 'Being Indian' has involved a multi-layered identity in which the upper and more general identification subsumes, but does not nullify, the less general and particular ones. The new majoritarian trends threaten this historical form and the specific equilibrium that the nation-state has tried to give it. In a major irony of history, although most of these forces and their political leaders see themselves as being uncompromisingly anti-English and anti-Western, they wish, despite their strident indigenous rhetoric, to replay a European paradigm of nationalism in which being Indian must find confirmation in speaking Indian and writing Indian. If such a convex majoritarianism gradually takes shape, convex because this puts the majoritarianism of religion on top of that of language, compensating the statistical inadequacy of Hindi by the overwhelming dominance of the Hindus, this can really fatally threaten the cultural presuppositions of the Indian nation-state. That would illustrate the disruption of a democratic state by the unqualified and uncomprehending application of an equation between democracy and majority rule. For democracy cannot exist without the rule of the majority; but equally, it cannot exist as only majority rule, unmodified by other subtler, juster, latent, equitable principles which make it not only the most acceptable, but also the most delicate and perishable among forms of modern governance.

References

Austin, Granville. 1966. *The Indian Constitution: Cornerstone of a Nation*. Oxford: Clarendon Press.
Chattopadhyay, Bankimchandra. 1964 (rpnt.). *Bangadesher Krishak*. In *Bankim Rachanavali*, vol. ii. Calcutta: Sahitya Samsad.
Cohn, Bernard S. 1987. *An Anthropologist among the Historians and Other Essays*. Delhi: Oxford University Press.
Dasgupta, Jyotirindra. 1970. *Language Conflict and National Development*. Berkeley: University of California Press.
de Swann, Abram. 1988. *In Care of the State*. Cambridge: Polity Press.
―――. 1990. Political and Linguistic Integration in India: Monopolistic Mediation versus Language Integration. Draft paper presented at seminar on Changing Relations between State and Society in India and Trends Towards Emerging European States. New Delhi: 5-9 March.

Derrida, Jacques. 1974. *Of Grammatology* (translated by Gayatri Chakravorty Spivak). Baltimore: John Hopkins University Press.

Douglas, W. and P. Hill. Trans. 1971. *The Holy Lake of the Acts of Rama.* Bombay. Oxford University Press.

Fox, Richard G. Ed. 1977. *Realm and Region in Traditional India.* Delhi: Vikas.

Gadamer, Hans Georg. 1975. *Truth and Method.* London: Sheed and Ward.

Gellner, Ernst. 1983. *Nations and Nationalism.* Oxford: Blackwell.

Gopal, S. 1979. *Jawaharlal Nehru*, vol. 2. Delhi: Oxford University Press.

Kaviraj, S. 1991a. The Imaginary Institution of India. In Partha Chatterjee and Gyanendra Pandey, eds, *Subaltern Studies VII.* New Delhi: Oxford University Press.

———. 1991b. On the Construction of Colonial Power. In Shula Marks and Dagmar Engels, eds, *Foundations of Imperial Hegemony.* Oxford: Oxford University Press.

———. 1991c. State, Society and Discourse in India. In James Manor, ed., *Rethinking Third World Politics.* London: Longman.

———. 1995. *The Unhappy Consciousness: Bankimchandra Chattopadhyay and the Formation of Nationalist Discourse in India.* Delhi: Oxford University Press.

Khubchandani, Lachman M. 1991. *Language, Culture and Nation-building.* Shimla: Indian Institute of Advanced Study and Manohar Publishers.

Prasad, R.C. 1989. Ed. and trans. *Ramacharitamanas.* Delhi: Motilal Banarsidass.

Saberwal, Satish. 1989. *India: The Roots of Crisis.* Delhi: Oxford University Press.

Sen, Sukumar. 1965. *Banglar Sahitya Itihas* (in Bengali). New Delhi: Sahitya Akademi.

Singh, Namwar. 1975. *Dusri Parampara ki Khoj* (in Hindi). Delhi: Rajkamal Prakashan.

5

The Imaginary Institution
of India

India, the objective reality of today's history, whose objectivity is tangible enough for people to try to preserve, to destroy, to uphold, to construct, and dismember, the reality taken for granted in all attempts in favour and against, is not an object of discovery but of invention. It was historically instituted by the nationalist imagination of the nineteenth century. The exact form this reality took was one among many historical possibilities in that situation, though the fact that only this line of possibility came to be realized is so overwhelming that it is now difficult even to conceive of some of the others. To say this is merely to assert that it is a historical object, and it is essential to speak about the contingency of its origins against the enormous and weighty mythology that has accumulated on its name.

To understand nationalism as a historical reality it is essential to step outside the history that nationalism gives to itself. Undoubtedly, this historical description is not entirely homogeneous, and its axis shifts according to the political demands and exigencies of different periods. Still, there is a clearly identifiable narrative which, despite all its internal variations, can be called the nationalist history of nationalism. This essay does not deal with the complex history of this narrative structure, but only with a brief, comparatively early, stage. This is a stage in which some decisions were taken that turned out to be crucial for the

First published in *Subaltern Studies VII*, ed. Partha Chatterjee and Gyanendra Pandey (Delhi: Oxford University Press 1992), pp. 1–39. I have benefited from comments made on an earlier draft by David Arnold, Partha Chatterjee, and, particularly, Gyanendra Pandey.

later development of Indian nationalism. Its analysis might reveal some interesting features in the formation of nationalist discourse and its strategies of self-presentation.

History writing about Indian nationalism meant, for a long time, compiling in increasing detail accounts of those political events which constituted this complex fact.[1] Ideas did of course figure in that account, often in large and dominant ways.[2] But they related to these events in a direct, almost linear, fashion; and in order to relate in such unproblematic ways these had to be large, general, abstract ideas which were amenable to such causal/quasi-causal attribution.

To tell the story of nationalism, they were narratively committed to a telling of a particular kind: an account which separated out of the great chaos of varying ideological events a single thread, and showed nationalism arising and moving to its destiny.

By its nature, this conception of nationalism had to be homogenizing: what I mean by this inelegant term is that although these scholars were often conscious that people opposed the British with ideas that were differently inflected, grounded, expressed, coloured, stylized, motivated, the major purpose of the concept of nationalism was to point to their level of historical similarity. This does not necessarily deny the presence of other strata in these ideas or other possible and appropriate descriptions. But, clearly, what got emphasized (and not unwittingly, because this point was written into the historiographical programme) were the points of similarity, the sense in which all these Indians were doing the same thing with these ideas.

In recent years historical thinking has tended to turn in some measure away from large, holistic, totalized histories of nationalism. The shift is expressed in several ways, and at the risk of excessive simplification we could say that historical attention has tended to turn from political history to cultural history, from events to discourses, and even inside the history of ideas from the content of nationalistic thought to a more sensitive understanding of its forms. But discourse is a

---

[1] It is essential to make a distinction between single and complex historical facts, because of the different ways in which causal explanatory statements can be made about them: see Hempel 1974.

[2] Evidently the movement is identified in terms of the collectively held ideas of its members and supporters.

much used and often ambiguous term, not because it does not indicate anything clear and specific but because it is indeterminately situated between several possible and justifiable meanings. Discourse is a general name for a number of possible types of functions or operations with words. Any study of discourse must not be blinded by the simple dichotomy between event and discourse, but be sensitive to the stratified, internally complex and ambiguous formation of discourse itself. This essay focuses on one particular element, or figuration, of discourse—the narrative.

This figuration, though previously neglected, seems to me of some importance. It is generally conceded that the idea of nationalism stitches together, in ways that are not seriously and minutely analysed, social groups, or communities of people. Formerly, these groups and individuals would not have considered themselves as one single people, having a single political identity.[3] After the emergence of nationalism, they somehow do. It is necessary to investigate this 'somehow', to probe into the various discursive formations within nationalism. This is not to question its consequence, but to enquire into its structure/formation. Indian culture is particularly rich in narrative traditions; and narratives traditionally performed the political function of producing and maintaining cohesion. Religious denominations and sects would maintain their distinctness and internal cohesion by the adroit use of storytelling. Hinduism implicitly recognizes the political character of these stories. To keep a sect outside the pale and make contacts with it taboo, it is narratively shown that their deities side in the interminable battles between the gods and demons with the *asura* camp. For purposes of diplomatic truce all that is required is the interpolation of an amorous episode between a formerly demonic figure and a nubile goddess from the Hindu pantheon. The *mangalakavyas* of Bengal are gigantic operations of such manipulation of boundaries. It is hardly surprising that in this society, humming with political narratives, the nationalist movement would be quick to see the considerable political possibilities of narrative persuasion.

---

[3] I do not wish to enter the controversy about whether there was a pre-existing *cultural* identity. I take it that there was. But even those who advocate this view would not deny that this was not political, which is enough for my argument.

Self-description of Nationalism

Ideologies seem to have a close connection with the narrative function; and this in turn relates to historiography. Indian nationalism is not merely an object of historical enquiry, but a political object—a movement, a force, a party, an establishment, a cultural interest,[4] an ideology and, finally, a state. And it is the nature of all political ideologies to try to coerce enquiry about itself into an agenda constructed by it.[5]

Historically it is not surprising that this movement had to create a sanctioned, official history of itself. This consists of half-truths favourable to the contingent political configuration within the movement; this history is an intensely political process. But it is important to break down the abstraction of the national movement itself, and of a large formation like the Congress, in order to see the politics that are constantly at play inside historical accounts. Even within a seemingly homogeneous history, it is often essential to ask whose history this is, in the sense of history *for* whom rather than history *of* whom, because there are changes in the telling. Within seemingly homogeneous history there are conflicts between tendencies, the axis and the periphery, the mainstream and the embarrassing fringe, the self and the other. From being the inheritor of one stream, albeit the major one, such a history takes a small, subtle, perhaps historically inevitable step towards claiming to be the inheritor of all.[6]

Clearly, an operation of this kind requires an axis of some sort, a central trend round which the complex and diverse material is organized. Such displacements go on continuously; and there are appropriations within appropriations. In the rewriting (though it must be

---

[4] This can be derived from the common Marxist concept of ideology, though there are not many detailed arguments on this point or this part of the ideological process of creating and reinforcing similitudes.

[5] I take the point Marx makes in the *German Ideology* about the French Revolution to be true of all successful ideological movements.

[6] It is possible to argue that some movements gain a real universality, e.g. the bourgeois political formations in the French Revolution. In cases like the Indian national movement, bourgeois trends fail to achieve such discursive or political hegemony. However, they still aspire to it and try to create it retrospectively by slowly occupying the history of the nationalist movement as a whole.

seen that any writing is rewriting) of the history of nationalism, this axis has been first the Congress, and more recently, inside the Congress, its Nehruvian stream. By the latter stage, all earlier figures are essentially measured according to their fit with a Nehruvian model of being nationalist. Admitting that those whose mental world was often communal could also be nationalists—indeed sometimes the more hysterical ones—disturbs the harmony of this official universe. This construction underestimates the alarming extent to which the power of Indian nationalism emerged from, or was a merely politically redescribed or redirected form, of the power of violated religious sentiments.

It was not merely that the great and complex canvas of Indian nationalism was reduced to a meagre symmetry; even within the works on single individuals scholars were barred, by their ideological self-censorship, from discovering interesting asymmetries. It was not customary to consider any relationship of obliqueness between a political figure and his historical work. It was improper to make any suggestion that nationalists may have written one thing and done something else, failed in their courage, wisdom, or rationality, or any of the many different ways in which human beings are known to fail.

The Question of Anachronism and Periodization

In recent historical work we find some questioning of this homogenizing history. Against the earlier history of homogeneity, we are now being offered a history of difference. A first level on which this new research has tried to restore a sense of complexity in history is by restoring the difference of epochs or periods of the anti-colonial struggle against the strong teleology of official narrations. Therefore, some remarks about an anachronistic history and its typical moves would be in order.

At first approximation it might seem that nothing is simpler than capturing the content, context, and texture of thought or mentality of a historical moment.[7] In fact, however, its achievement is not unproblematic. For the moment is already appropriated in a double sense by the

---

[7] One of the most persistent and insightful enquiries into such questions is Gadamer 1975.

flow of history itself—an ontological appropriation by its consequences; by the foregrounding of other events and imposing a sense of self-evident correctness to the Whiggism of the later point of view; and an epistemological appropriation which is built into the basic structure of what could be called the 'natural' historical consciousness. Thus, it is not the simple empirical presence of the historical moment that is naturally available but its Whiggish view which exalts in any past epoch the function of producing the present over the function of being what it was. In other words, this Whiggism is not just an object of cognitive reproof of the type that is appropriately reserved for errors.[8] The flow of time, the ontological structure of historical existence, encourages such Whiggishness. It must in the act of being rejected be given its due respect.

Anachronism uses the presumption that earlier periods and cultures were structured like our own in their institutions, practices, discourses, meanings, and significations of concepts, etc. Thus the whole universe of significations and causalities of the modern period (however the 'modern period' is identified) are thrown backwards on them. Historians tend sometimes to forget that there is a requirement of minimal distanciation before objects of the past can begin to be properly described. Quite often the worst appropriation occurs not in the process of evaluative judgement but in the apparently innocent act of describing.

The conceit of the present, the precarious ontological privilege that it enjoys over other times, is expressed often in another, subtler, and more fundamental fault of historical vision. This is the temptation to believe that the only function of the past, its only conceivable justification, was to produce the present. According to this procedure, only those aspects of the past are given great descriptive salience which seem to have some causal affiliation with events and structures of the present time.

All nationalist discourse after the coming of Gandhi tries to answer the implicit question: how can Indians best defeat and remove British rule? Arguments about home rule, dominion status, complete independence, for example, are all different answers to the same historical question. They fall, to use Gadamer's metaphor, within the same

[8] Ibid.: 258–74.

horizon of political history,[9] a concept that usefully but undogmatically distinguishes between the possible and the impossible. On closer inspection it appears that, in earlier horizons of anti-colonial discourse, this question is entirely absent. If we turn to the historical horizon inhabited by Bankimchandra or Bhudev Mukhopadhyay, this question, at least in this form, does not lie within the orbit of possibility of their thinking.[10] *Paradhinata*—subjection to alien rule—is both too fresh and too overwhelming to permit such unfeasible thoughts. Alien rule is a kind of *a priori* of their thinking, a deeply hated limit which they, for all their hatred of it, are not able to transcend. All possible thought operations are consequently carried out taking that condition for granted. These authors remain within these limits not because they like British rule. In some ways their rejection of a colonizing Western rationalist civilization often goes deeper and is more fundamental than that of later nationalists; but they simply do not see the end of colonial subjection as a historically feasible project. For them the epochal historical question, around which all social reflection revolved, was: how did a civilization with such varied resources become subject to colonialism? But this was a question very different from the one of how such subjection could be politically ended. It is important to remember, methodologically, that they are not answering that second and later question in the negative; the question does not get asked within their discourse.

Anachronism distorts our historical judgement by making it appear that the question around which their thinking was structured was also the self-evident one of later, maturer, nationalist thought. What, on this view, can be a more central, a more natural theme of nationalist discourse than the end of imperial subjection? Besides, how can we call a discourse 'nationalist' until it has the courage to pronounce that elemental defiance? Those who argue on these lines make, in my view, an initially correct point, but fail to draw the correct conclusion. They assume that the thinking, or more diffusely the *mentalite*, of these generations was nationalist, but of a weak, hesitant, compromising kind. But this is unconvincing. Indeed, their discourse is not really

---

[9] Ibid.: 269.

[10] A very detailed and textually scrupulous account of what the horizon looked like can be found in Raychaudhuri 1988.

nationalist in the narrow sense if the internal conceptual condition for use of the adjective is the presence of the idea of a determinate nation with clear boundaries, unambiguous principles of inclusion, established by a clear act of choice. Later we shall see that there are substantive reasons as well for withholding this common description.

But the argument of homogenizing nationalism is so plausible and forceful that it is difficult to remain unaffected by its seduction. Ironically, historians who strenuously avoid the company of ordinary nationalism for ideological reasons do on occasion fall into its methodological trap. Once we admit the plausibility of the homogenizing view we agree to the fundamental mistranslation of the two questions as strict equivalents; then, it is impossible to keep away from standard anachronistic answers and judgements. If the later question resounds everywhere in the history of colonial societies, it would seem that writers of an earlier period were answering it in the negative. In cruder versions of such history writing the thought of a writer who considered freedom politically impossible but found colonialism so hateful that he could not stop dreaming about it would be firmly shown to be a collaborator of British rule. This must happen if history is inattentive towards the way in which time and experiential horizons slowly shift and construct a paradigm-like internality of questions, answers, procedures, presuppositions, defiance, and conformity. In that case historical horizon is not a metaphor, but a real rigorous historical concept. Otherwise, we slide very often into the notorious difficulties of reading silences.

There is a second form in which the infelicity of anachronism recurs in the analysis of Indian nationalism. An anachronistic view would imply that when we are looking for the history, i.e. the origins, the earlier stages of Indian nationalism, we must encounter it in some suitably smaller, paler, or otherwise immature form, a smaller-scale version of the later fully-blown nationalism. In early periods we would thus expect to meet a paler version of patriotism, not the burning enthusiasm for one's country that is felt apparently by later Congressmen or their intellectual representatives. This view finds it much more difficult to acknowledge a patriotism for something else as an ancestor for Indian nationalism because today those two patriotisms would be politically opposed. Surprisingly, it appears that there is no such necessary connection between being patriotic and being Indian. Indeed, historically speaking, this configuration of consciousness becomes nationalist before it becomes Indian. Happily, Indianness is not entirely an afterthought; but it is certainly a later occurrence. Had it been only an afterthought, this Indianness would have been a mere insubstantial pretence and a large historical movement and a constitutional democratic state after Independence could not be hung on that wispy thread. Because it was an historically available identity, though of later origin, it could perform such historical tasks. Anachronism, by pretending that it was an identity existing from immemorial times, encourages unjustified optimism; an appreciation of its more recent and comparatively precarious historical career would imply the chastening idea that this people have not been used to being Indian for very long, and political policies must take into account its recentness.

The state of Indian history and historical consciousness in this regard appears to be closely parallel to what Gramsci said about a similar phase of the invention of Italian nationalism, within which there was a similar conflict between two strands. One, the more romantic and surely the more narratively effective, was the strand of immemorialism, drawing shaky and doubtful lines of continuity from Italy's Roman past to its present misery. A second strand acknowledged the modernity and constructedness of Italian identity. Due to disruptions in Italian history, similar in some ways to colonialism, 'the past does not live in the present',[11] Gramsci says regretfully. 'It is not an essential part of the present; in the history of our national culture there is no continuity or unity. The affirmation of continuity or unity is only rhetorical or amounts to mere evocative propaganda. *It is a practical act which aims to create artificially that which does not exist.*'[12] Unfortunately, Gramsci too occasionally falls into the false objectivism of believing that such a consciousness is mere imagination, failing to note, against the grain of his own thought, that such imaginings—encrusted, crystallized, entertained for a long-enough time—would produce 'objectively' or naturally existing consciousness.

What Gramsci says about the fragmentation of history is true of India as well. It is true that each century has its own literature, but it

---

[11] I take this to mean that some of the features of Italian life were not the products of its own indigenous historical evolution.

[12] Gramsci 1985: 253. My emphasis.

is not true that those literatures are produced by the same 'common' people. Any attempt at a generalization of a 'past principle' is therefore impossible, and would at the same time both unite and tragically divide the people; precisely because what is invoked is a new people. They are Indians, neither the continuation of the earlier Hindus, nor of the Muslims; nor is it true, as is sometimes said by well-meaning histories, that there were no frictions or distances between these communities. For even if their earlier relations were peaceable, the social principles on which such peaceableness was based would be archaic and practically unhelpful in modern times. Every move to appeal to an older large identity—Hindu or Muslim—was bound to create unities which were far more difficult to unite into further integrative forms.

Because of this fragmentation of earlier history,

> a unilinear national hagiography is impossible: any attempt of this sort appears immediately sectarian, false, utopian, anti-national, because one is forced to cut out or undervalue unforgettable pages of national history... There is nothing of the sort [a national history] in Italy where one must search the past by torchlight to discover national feeling, and move with the aid of distinctions, interpretations and discreet silences... The preconception that Italy has always been a nation complicates its entire history and requires anti-historical intellectual acrobatics... History was political propaganda, it aimed to create national unity—that is, the nation—from the outside and against tradition, by basing itself on literature. It was a wish, not a move based on already existing conditions.[13]

The Discovery of a National Community

The intractable modernity of the new identity of a nation, especially a nation mobilized to act for itself, constantly troubles the thinking of early nationalists. They have not yet named a community which would take the responsibility of opposition to colonialism. Curiously, far from there being a united India, an immanent nation which is repressed, the processes of consciousness themselves show to what extent nationalism is a historical product of colonialism, how, in spite of their fundamental difference, colonialism was a historical precondition for

[13] Ibid.: 256–7.

any modern nationalist consciousness. Thus the responsibility, the role, the character of nationalism emerges earlier in history than the community which will perform this responsibility; the responsibility is born before its agent. And contrary to what is said in the common hagiography of the Indian nation, what this community will be is a matter of some confusion and occasionally of dispute. It is possible for early writers to speculate about a Hindu or a Muslim community filling this role, as much as a territorial identity of a radically new order.

Since these writers have still not chosen their nation, it is more appropriate to call the political consciousness of this phase by some other term, for instance *anti-colonialism*. But it is an error to think that until nationalism in the latterday sense arrives, there is no political consciousness. To equate the political and the nationalist is once more a powerful instrument of nationalist ideological accounts. It disallows any opposition to colonialism other than itself, any dissent organized on other lines the title to oppositional glory. Yet any involvement with the structure of colonial power—the whole range of political things in the colonial world from its political economy to its world of significations to its politics of language, the battle between the high language of colonialists and the vernacular—must be seen as political. No doubt the language of politics often tends to be subtle and symbolic. Politics often becomes a contest over the use of language, a matter of defiance of linguistic and symbolic norms. Indeed the whole world of colonialism seemed perfectly suited to a theatre of a typically Austinian defiance.

Due to the overwhelming nature of colonial control, intellectuals of that early generation had to know extremely well how to do things with words: indeed, words were the terrain on which most politics was done. Despite their symbolic and subliminal character, the political nature of such linguistic performances should not be ignored. Politics in colonial society is a world of performatives. Of course, these are not performatives in the strong sense in which Austin writes about them, where there is a constitutive relation between the word and the act, i.e. to utter the word is to enact the act which goes in that name.[14] But, it seems, in the world of politics there is a context-related way of doing

---

[14] The kind Austin called 'constatives' in his detailed typology. See Austin 1975: 3.

things with words. The more things are proscribed and excluded, and deprivations attached to acts, the more, it appears, uttering a word can become a performance of defiance. It is in this sense that such utterances are political, although no overt, external political acts follow immediately from them. And that it is idle to expect matching acts to issue forth from the words is signalled by the style, manner, and quality of enunciation of the words themselves. Paradoxically, this is expressed both in the surreptitiousness with which they are uttered, in the frequent play of humour, and also a certain daring in eventually deciding in favour of the utterance, not the ultimate subterfuge of silence.

In this early phase, then, we find a form of consciousness/discourse which is genetically related to mature nationalism, but is distinctly different from it. If it was fashionable to take structuralism so seriously now, one could have said this is a difference between genetic and structural relations between two discourses. It also shows the proleptic temptations in thinking about such contiguous and genetically connected periods.[15]

Though not nationalist in a strict sense, this consciousness is anti-colonial because there is hardly any doubt about its dark and anguished opposition to colonial domination, and the destiny it had imposed on Indian society. In fact, their opposition to colonialism is cast in the same pessimistic mould as Rousseau's rejection of civilization,[16] one reason perhaps why so many of this generation found Rousseau more to their liking than rationalist enlightenment thinkers.[17] Colonialism is so pervasive and ineluctable an experience for them— they are so convinced of its being evil and so convinced that it could not possibly be defeated, that for those who remained unreconciled to its positive value it wrapped their whole world in a shadow of melancholy. Still, this is not, strictly speaking, nationalism. The rejection it represents is more intuitive and visceral, a feeling of historical pessimism

---

[15] For a detailed account of such proleptic temptations, see Skinner 1988.

[16] On the view that Rousseau rejected a bourgeois civilization, although he saw its historical ascendancy as inevitable.

[17] Bankimchandra Chattopadhyay, for example, shows great admiration for Rousseau, calling him the third great *samyavatara*, an incarnation standing equal with the Buddha and Christ.

and anguish without any clear ideas about recourse, let alone programme. It feels almost blindly, believes, and hopes colonialism would have to be opposed; but it is hardly clear about how and by whom, following what strategic conception.

Anti-colonialism, in the sense in which I am using the term *faute des mieux*, is very different from the usual one in which Marxists commonly use it. This structure of thought is a merely oppositional attitude towards colonialism, and if we gather up all its historical characteristics it is more a cultural critique, a resentment against ignominy rather than a political-economic rejection of its civilizing pretensions. Its melancholy does not begin to turn into optimism before it changes into nationalism proper. From being a negative reaction to colonial power, it turns positively into a consciousness of a new identity. It must be seen, however, that this something which it supports is not present to it in an objective form. It has got to be constructed, imagined into existence. And the pessimism of anti-colonial consciousness arises partly because of its failure to find easily an adequate social base for its dissatisfaction and its critique. Hostility against colonialism, which is all-conquering, is felt from the ground of older, limited, fragmented identities—of regions, Hindus, Muslims, Bengalis, or rather babus—none of whom in their thinking about history seemed to have much of a chance of success against the colonial machine. For that historical optimism to emerge, they had to find a new identity; although this identity is produced by gerrymandering earlier ones, someone like Bankim could say cleverly that this identity, this new 'we', has never been defeated, because it has never opposed colonialism historically.

In this phase of anti-colonialism, or whatever more elegant name is given to this structure of consciousness, the writers are expressing a primarily negative idea. There is, however, an interesting side to it which we must explore. Even palaeolithic nationalism requires some collective subject; the ignominy of colonialism must be seen as a suffering that is collective, of a collective subject which is larger than, and which envelops, the author. For this is a thought-form which is by definition collective, its syllables can be uttered only by a collective subject or on its behalf, to use the Foucaultian trope of *enonciation*.[18]

---

[18] See Foucault 1972: ch. 4.

But the remarkable thing is that the collective subject is not related to developed nationalism by a relation of standard ontogeny. It is not a smaller, weaker, thinner, earlier form of the same subject that will be called the nation. The nation, in India as much as in Italy, is a thing without a past. It is radically modern. It can only look for subterfuges of antiquity. It fears to face and admit its own terrible modernity, because to admit modernity is to make itself vulnerable. As a proposal for modern living, on a scale quite unprecedented (both in terms of sheer spread and the sheer power of good and evil it can do to itself by establishing a modern state), in a society still knowing only one legitimizing criterion—tradition—it must seek to find past disguises for these wholly modern proposals.[19]

Narratives are always related, explicitly or otherwise, to some sense of self. Narratives can never be rational in at least one sense of this universally admired but elusive criterion. A rational view is, to use Thomas Nagel's elegant phrase, 'the view from nowhere'.[20] A rational case is one that is made on nobody's special behalf. Narratives are always told from someone's point of view, to take control of the frightening diversity and formlessness of the world; they literally produce a world in which the self finds a home. Or, it would perhaps describe the process better if we say that around a particular home they try to paint a picture of some kind of an ordered, intelligible, humane, and habitable world. Since here we are talking about collective narratives, this anchor is in the identification of a *collective* self.

Anti-colonialism is originally pronounced by traditional collective selves, communities which were given in terms of earlier, more segmented, social definitions. At this stage, the community which performs this *enonciation,* or hopefully will in the near future, remains curiously indeterminate. It is a rather unclear 'we' which is invited to do this. Indeed, it seems that late-nineteenth-century writers were curiously uninterested in spelling it out, in turning their attention towards an analysis of the strengths and weaknesses of this group, and suggesting a political theory for forming it into an ideal strength adequate to its enormous task. The intellectual process is not directed towards a self-enumeration of the collective subject, still left hazy,

[19] Gramsci 1985: 235.
[20] Nagel 1985.

immediate, primordial. Arguments are typically concerned with undermining the ideological claims of the colonial administration and its collaborators, that strident claim which particularly irritates Indians that the British were civilizing a savage people. These are concerned with the acceptability of the modernity—truncated, opportunistically edited, and abbreviated—offered historically through colonialism. Often it discusses the comparative principles of organization of the two social orders.[21]

Later, this 'we' becomes coterminous with Indians; but the process through which this happens is instructive. Indianness, along with other attributes and entities of the social world, is also a historical construct. Actually, this India was new, but it required the delusion of an eternal existence. And interestingly, it was European writers writing on India as part of a counter-Enlightenment movement who constructed this India and presented it to Indians looking for an identity.

This is no small irony; and it indicates a web of intellectual complexity which has to be unravelled with sensitivity to discrete individual trends. The 'picture' of India or 'the Orient' that emerged in the seventeenth and eighteenth centuries, and which came to fatefully affect Indian social discourse and the self-images lying at their base, was not a simple image produced by a single, unproblematically homogeneous movement.[22] Besides, although the general outline of this picture was repugnantly orientalist, much of the actual detail was produced by a tendency which, though perhaps romantic, was not 'orientalist' from that point of view, but rather sought to create a picture of the Orient which would provide a foil to the West, point out its inadequacies, or in some cases a standing rejection of the monopolistic claims advanced by dominant forms of rationalism.

Whatever its source in Western scholarship or Indian publicistic material, this pretence of Indian antiquity was entirely necessary and

---

[21] To do this was fairly common though systematic comparisons were rare. In Bengal two eminent examples of such comparative sociology are the works of Bankim and Bhudev Mukhopadhyaya. Bhudev is more concise and systematic; cf. Raychaudhuri 1988.

[22] Said (1978) tends at times to produce such an impression. My criticism is not that such impression is entirely false; but that it is correct in specified and limited logical circumstances.

at the same time largely false. Accordingly, it is impossible to assume innocently the mythology of nationalism that this India was suppressed (i.e. it must exist in order to be suppressed), and gradually won the strength, the cohesion, a god-gifted political organization and leadership, to rise to consciousness and freedom. In fact, this historical process was a less linear and far more tentative affair.

If Indians thought as Bengalis did earlier in all respects, there would have been no Indian nationalism. The 'we' of the Bengali intellectual, even when exhorted to fight against British injustice, was initially a very limited and rather parochial thing. Intellectuals specialize in sensing injustice and discrimination and are regarded by rulers as quite generally an ungrateful tribe. They can become disaffected in strangely diverse ways, apart from having their applications for furtherance turned down, or melancholy residence for eighteen years at the same rung of the bureaucratic ladder—the principal reason Anil Seal identified for the great novelist Bankimchandra Chattopadhyay turning to writing.[23]

Disaffected intellectuals initially complained only about specific and concrete cases of injustice, and thought that those who would appreciate their sense of ignominy were people like themselves—educated, middle class, comfortable beneficiaries of the colonial order. Politically, the prospects for such an organization, made of affronted Bengali babus, as some of them realized, could not be very bright. A trade union of disgruntled civil servants could hardly take on the British empire. Generally, babus, though conscious of the political ignominy of subjection, considered its material benefits adequate compensation for such abstract injury. Consequently, they bent their energies first towards self-promotion, and what was left of them towards social reform. To become practical at all, the programme of opposition required a sense of injustice that was abstract and general, which could be shared by a larger group whose social joys and sorrows were differently produced from those of the Calcutta babus.

In Bengal, the first step towards this was taken when colonialism was seen as the cross to be borne by not just the babus trained at Presidency College, but by that abstract, as yet entirely unselfconscious, collectivity called the Bengali community as a whole—*bangali jati*. In the earlier stage it was assumed that the more numerous and hazier part

[23] Seal 1968: 118.

of this 'nation', its non-babu segment, must march in mute obedience under the generalship of the garrulous urban commanders. But in Bankim's later works we can already detect a suggestion of unease, and anticipations of a romantic reversal of this relationship—of an elite following a people in movement, a people whom they must follow, as Disraeli said, because they are their leaders.

As a nation, however, the Bengalis turn out to be a great disappointment. The historical and contemporary resources of the Bengalis appear woefully inadequate for a task as daunting as taking on the British empire. If the past was any indication of what the future would be, their history did not promise much martial defiance. Driven by such considerations, anti-colonial intellectuals do something historically fateful: they break down the boundaries of their 'natural' 'we', and begin to extend their 'we-ness' in different directions in a desperate experiment in coalition-making. Many of them, including Bankim, thought seriously of deploying the 'we' of the Hindus with different degrees of perplexity, guilt, and defensiveness. That appeared as an immemorially old 'we', already available for use, though a politically unified Hinduism looked suspiciously artificial. Later, this 'we' came to be coterminous with what is generally known as India, though traces of earlier unreconstructed identities still clung to this new one. The Rajputs, the Marathas, the Sikhs gradually came to secure a place in this process of widening the collective self. And this extraordinary inclusion is achieved by opening out the narrative contract—Bengalis entering into narrative contract with communities who had nothing really to do with them in the past, constantly gerrymandering the boundaries of their national collective self.

Interestingly, the British could write 'histories of India' much more unproblematically than their Indian imitators, for they wrote of an India that was externally defined, a territory contingently unified by political expansion. To define the boundaries of British India was a simple operation; this merely required looking at the latest map of British annexations. By contrast, the India that Nehru so painstakingly discovered was an India more difficult to define, for the nationalists he represented sought to demarcate its boundaries by a more elusive internal principle.

To give itself a history is the most fundamental act of self-identification of a community. The naming of the Indian nation, I wish to suggest, happens in part through a narrative contract. To write a history of India beginning with the civilization of the Indus valley is marked by an impropriety. An India internally defined, an India of a national community, simply did not exist before the nineteenth century; there is, therefore, an inevitable element of 'fraudulence', in Gellner's sense, in all such constructions. 'The history of India' is a massively self-evident thing to write about and this powerful transformation of something that is fundamentally insecure into something aggressively self-evident is precisely the mark of an ideological construct. It is ideological because there seems to be no other reasonable way of writing the history of these historical objects.

In this case, the fraudulent and the imaginary are merely re-descriptions of each other. If we leave it at Gellner's model, we leave our analysis of nationalism peculiarly incomplete. It is rather pointless to call it fraudulent if there is no hope of a proper, true, entirely objective history. Fraudulence presupposes the possibility of an in-principle undistorted account. Of course nationalist ideologies often effect major distortions of history, and surely such untruths have to be shown and rejected. But there seems to be involved in this process a different problem which, for want of a better term, we may, after Gadamer, call 'the principle of effective history'.[24]

The Construction of the Past as History

In treating history as the memory of a people, as a discourse in which a people retells to itself its own past, we seem at first to come up against the sort of impropriety that Gellner has criticized so forcefully. The lore of the Celts, to make the point with brutal simplicity, was nothing more than the Celts' lore, not the early history of the British people. For the United Kingdom is a much later construct; and there is something quite false in saying that object X's history can cover a period in which there was no object X. The only possible defence of such accounts could be that we treat them as histories of spaces rather than of peoples. But the histories that nationalists write are paradigmatically *peoples'* histories. By the same token, accounts of the exploits of the Satavahanas or the Tughluqs were the accounts of those dynasties, and on a doubtfully charitable view, of the people they ruled. Clearly, therefore, there is a logic of illegitimate appropriation in the standard

[24] Gadamer 1975: 267–74.

way of writing the history of India, starting with the civilization of the Indus Valley, which is seen with some justice by our neighbours as the early history of Pakistan. Of course, the Mohenjodaro story being the early history of Pakistan is no less absurd or plausible than some others being the early history of India. It is remarkable how evenhandedly the British could divide between querulous subjects of their empire things as intangible as antiquity. As we go on, however, the Gellner thesis runs into some difficulties.

The first oddity is that if Gellner's view is taken with complete seriousness, no history of India can be written before the nineteenth century even on the most optimistic view of the matter. Some would wonder if it can be legitimately written of the period before 1947. The trouble is that this way of thinking would make the writing of history entirely coincident with the existence of cultural self-images.

This dilemma has been present at the heart of nationalist social reflection: this is reflected in the difficulty nationalists have in choosing between two accounts of what happened in the national movement. One view is that it is in some sense a pre-existing immanent nation which rises to consciousness and eventual freedom; and the task after Independence is to defend a nation whose conceptual and emotional existence is in fact historically unproblematic. At the same time, nationalists cannot quite give up a second view, which implies that an indeterminately defined people came to acquire a state, and the nation is to be built afterwards by this state and those of its leaders whom we particularly admire.

It is true no doubt that by appropriating the history of the Satavahanas we are acting undemocratically, without consulting them as to whether they would have liked to be included in our history. Surely this is a discursive disenfranchisement of the Satavahanas from being Satavahanas, which they most unambiguously were; we turn them into ancient Indians, begging the question if something that was born in the nineteenth century could have a biography leading back a millennium. But there are two further difficulties. First, we can do little more than remain conscious of this retrospective structure of historical accounts, and take care that it does not lure us into subtle empirical falsification. It is unlikely that we can do more. For, secondly, if we take the Gellner view to its extreme point, it would issue in the rather inconvenient principle that only Satavahanas can write histories of Satavahanas with any undistorted historical view; and since no

Satavahanas are around now, given this theory of authenticity they must, in the interest of truth, be condemned to historical nullity.

Indeed, the history of the past would become impossible in a radical way. The condition of writing a 'correct', objective (as opposed to fraudulent) history would be that historical identities must not be transformed or gerrymandered. It has been shown with great persuasiveness that the historic destiny of events is to live through their effects, which confer on them an ironic ineradicability. It is impossible to disentangle the history of occurrences from the history of their effects; we therefore always live within 'effective history'. To use a more analytic style of reasoning employed by A.C. Danto,[25] the adding of every single significant line to earlier historical drama or narrative rearranges the structure of the narrative itself.

The birth of a male child to Motilal Nehru, barrister, successful lawyer in the Allahabad high court and a nationalist, has to be reconceptualized a hundred years later as the birth of the first prime minister of India. The event still 'happens' in 1889 but its conditions of significant description get irrevocably altered in 1947. If this is the given structure of 'historical being' and consequently the only adequate form of historical descriptions, there is hardly anything we can do to rescue the Satavahanas from the clutches of modern historians. The modern historian must know that they are, very narratively indeed, early Indians; the historian cannot maintain that this is more than narratively so, because then he would pretend that he does not recognize the conditions under which he is thinking.[26]

Such perplexities of narrative description about history were well known to Bankim's generation; for they were responsible for many of the narrative forms in which Indians today habitually mould their history. Bankim is an excellent example of how effectively and with what consistent opportunism this narrative principle can be invoked and forgotten. Some writers—Bankimchandra Chattopadhyay and Rabindranath Tagore foremost among them—are wholly clear about the double nature of the imagined community. It is not merely others

---

[25] See Danto 1983.
[26] Cf. Gadamer's critique of Diltheyan objectivism in Gadamer 1975: 192–214.

in the present, previously unrepresented in the ambit of a collective self, who are included now; this holds true of peoples of the past. Bankim uses this with a delighted deceitfulness in his arguments, denying that Bengalis were ever conquered, because there were no Bengalis at the time, i.e. the temporal boundary of what he considered to be his 'we' did not stretch back into that period of disgrace. This does not stop him from claiming undoubted descent from the more ancient Aryans who, on standard evidence of territory or race or culture, must stand in very doubtful kinship indeed to the modern Bengali. This is possible of course because we are dealing with imaginary history, not an academic one.[27]

Fuzzy and Enumerated Communities

Imagined communities can place their boundaries in time and space anywhere they like. It is not always reasonable to look for objective criteria for these things. Another way of saying this would be that the objectivity they often display is a historical form of objectivity. It is impossible to justify the objectivity of the entire narrative, but easy to see the difficult objectivity of its consequences. But there is another point to be made about imagined communities. Whether imaginary or real, this way of conceiving a community is a very modern and unprecedented theoretical device. Acquaintance with European history since the Renaissance surely helped intellectuals to use this idea and devise an appropriate form of this for themselves. To understand its implications let us first try to set out clearly what is involved in this claim. Imaginary or real, these arguments describe and conceive its community in ways

---

[27] This could raise interesting questions about the nature of time in these different types of accounts. History in the academic sense assumes what is sometimes called a linear, internally homogeneous, calibrated time. Given this temporal structure, distances cannot be reduced by any imaginative conceptual technique. The present time is equally calendrically distanced from past times. Its impersonal distances cannot be abbreviated or otherwise infringed by affection. The time of myths does not have this 'calibrated' quality. Present times can feel closer to *ramarajya* or whatever other stretch of the past appeals to the imagination. Remembering and forgetting imposes a very different sort of order on mythical and imaginary narratives; and its partisans would be able to provide a clear enough rationale for this order.

that are quite different from earlier, more genuinely communitarian, ways of conceiving one.[28]

Let us call the earlier conceptions of community *fuzzy*. As this is bound to be a contested idea, let me try to be clear about what exactly fuzzy means in this context. Any idea of community is based on an idea of identity, which is predicated in turn on some conception of difference. People who lived in pre-modern social forms had of course a strong sense of community, usually more intense than those of modern societies. They handled their daily experience of social complexity through some system of rules by which people could be classified as similar or different and dealt with accordingly. As contacts with people of other groups were relatively infrequent, it did not require an elaborately developed theory of otherness. Groups in which people lived had the quality of what sociologists like Tönnies would have called primary, i.e. groups to which one does not have to make an interest-actuated decision to belong. This undoubtedly reinforced the quality of self-evidence of the relations they were made up of. Crucially for my argument, these were communities (*gemeinschaften*) in Tönnies' sense. Living inside them fostered a feeling of intense solidarity and belongingness, but the most important principle of communityness is that the solidarity is not based upon a convergence of interest, which distinguishes *gesellschaften*.[29]

There is an interestingly paradoxical connection between the theories of *gemeinschaft*/*gesellschaft* and the processes of nation formation. The theory derived from Tönnies places great emphasis on an interconnected set of dichotomies: between modern and traditional social forms, solidarities based on interests and on community, the unlimited possibility of extension of *gesellschaft* associations and the 'naturally' limited contours of *gemeinschaften*, the contractual dissolubility of 'societies' and the indissoluble primordial nature of community belonging. This, in turn, can be shown to have some connection with Weber's distinction between the constant perfect—ability of rational actions, and the repetitiveness of traditional acts—for that is what keeps the boundaries of communities more or less constant.[30]

---

[28] Using these terms in the sense given to them in social theory by the work of Ferdinand Tönnies, cf. Tönnies 1971.

[29] Ibid.

[30] Weber, deriving it from Tönnies, provides a similar distinction in Weber

The Imaginary Institution of India

Despite the considerable resources of this distinction, there appears to exist a more complex dialectic between community and nationalist modernity which tends to be underplayed in the use of such a strongly dichotomous model. To understand this historical relation we have to produce a mix of the different and in some ways clashing insights that Gellner and Anderson's separate arguments provide. Modern nationalism commonly arises out of an aspiration to control the forces of modernity, and is therefore affiliated to the rise and growth of *gesellschaft* organizations. If modern nationalism is seen to be affiliated to these processes of transformation of social forms, this produces a paradox. Historically, these organizations tend to erode—either explicitly or by subtler, undeclared processes—the earlier types of smaller, tighter, closer organizational patterns. Yet, in a sense, nationalism tries to steal, to use Marx's phrase, the poetry of primordiality from them, to try to argue about and justify itself through a wholly illegitimate discourse of immemorial aspirations and indissoluble community. Nationalist movements usually try to show the nation, actually a product of a conjuncture of modernity, to be a community which was lost—to be regained. Quite often this regaining requires large-scale political sacrifices which ordinary people are unlikely to accept if they calculate their political actions in a purely rationalistic accounting of individual cost and benefit. The language of monadic individuals and their purely calculating contractual interests does not suit the rhetoric of passion—blood, sacrifice, remembrance—that nationalism as a movement requires.[31] So, although a modern phenomenon, nationalism must speak a 'traditional' language of communities.

Let us now turn to another question: the relation between the nation and those identities which historically precede it, and with which it must be partly at least in competition. In the argument influenced by the modern/traditional opposition, sometimes the relation is seen in excessively dichotomous terms. These arguments ascribe to

---

1947. He simply mentions nationalism as a solidarity relationship without discussing the embarrassment this can cause this theory: Weber 1947: 136–7.

[31] Literature, poetry, and especially patriotic songs are good examples of this. In Bengali, a particularly telling illustration is the poetry of D.L. Roy, and his poem of ultimate excess: *dhanadhanye puspe bhara amader ei basundhara/ tahar majhe ache des ek sakal deser seral se je swapna die tairi se des, smrti die ghera.*

pre-existing community identities a certain inexplicated 'pregivenness'. Communities (which, it must be seen, refer to a principle of organization, rather than one form of groups) are called primordial, and the way that term is used amounts to an effective denial of history.

Ostensibly, primordiality indicates an organization which is so resistant to change as not to be transformed across historical time. In fact, however, much that is declared primordial and historyless turns out to be historical on closer inspection.[32] Occasionally, these may actually be recent constructions which, like fake antiques, are bestowed an artificially produced look of decay. In pre-modern societies, antiquity is given such high value that constructed things might include in their principle of construction itself a mechanism that seems to erase their historical age. Recently founded dynasties are in particular need of showing their ancestry from the descendants of mythological heroes.

Sociological arguments about Indian nationalism often impose the dichotomous model rather mechanically, to affiliate nationalism with all forces that are modern and 'forward looking'. Often the place of communities in this general model is taken in the Indian case by the region defined around a distinct language, and the quality of being natural, pre-given, primordial, is conceptually conferred on it.[33] This way the dichotomy between the region and the nation doubles the paradigmatic oppositions between tradition and modernity, *gemeinschaft* and *gesellschaft*. Ironically, if we look at the evidence, it appears that the question—which is prior, the nation or the region?—turns out to be false, or at least not very helpful. Actually, the region, though culturally more homogeneous, is as much a historical construction as the nation. More startlingly, in some cases, the formation of a linguistic region is not of much greater antiquity than the coming of an anti-colonial consciousness, for the rise of a distinct regional language was related to some developments linked to colonialism. This is particularly clear in the case of the Bengali language.

---

[32] The power of this idea is illustrated by Marx's hypothesis about an Asiatic mode. Even Marx, whose thinking is so scrupulously historical, was willing to believe in unchanging village communities. Marxist historians have found this hypothesis unhelpful.

[33] The political implication of this is obvious: it can damn any mobilization around linguistic identities as primitivist, anti-modern, etc.

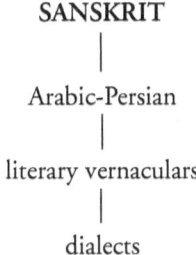

Even Bengal, a most culturally self-conscious region, has difficulties in fitting a model of a long pre-existing language and a sense of 'Indian' nationhood that is relatively recent. In defining regions, language is usually the most significant criterion. But this language—which confers on the region its unity and its name—is not a given.[34] Before the British came, the linguistic map of 'Bengal' would have been quite confused and unfamiliar. The use of language was stratified in several ways. For some purposes, traditionally, Sanskrit served as an inaccessible elite language; for others, Arabic and Persian. The inaccessibility of these languages to ordinary people was complemented on the other side by their universality among the elite. Thus the structure, in linguistic terms, would generally replicate the structure of agrarian societies that Gellner outlines in his *Nations and Nationalism*.[35]

Characteristically, an arrangement of this kind would offset the numerical advantage of the lower orders by their horizontal division, and conversely, compensate for the relative smallness in number of the privileged by their cultural homogeneity and political cohesiveness. Against the clear singleness of Sanskrit and Arabic-Persian, traditional vernaculars do not display a strong normative form. The core of the vocabulary consisting of Sanskrit, *apabhramsa*, and *desaja* words makes for a relatively easy way of speaking the vernacular. Below the layer of the esoteric languages, thus, there exists an implicit equality of dialects. As languages are not standardized, it is hardly possible to use these as standards by which to identify the regions that speak them. A large number of dialects existing in neighbourly difference covered a

---

[34] Elsewhere I have tried to critically analyse the standard narrative constructions of 'the history of Bengali literature', which seeks to confer this antiquity on the regional identity of Bengal: Kaviraj 1990.
[35] See Gellner 1983.

region. Drawing a linguistic map was a difficult if not an impossible affair, because the frontiers where one language ended and another began were bound to be hazy. The dialect spoken in north-western Bengal would be hardly different from neighbouring Maithili; in the south, the language of Medinipur was insignificantly different from that of Orissa.

Subsequently, the new literate elite created by Western education gradually drop the courtly Arabic/Persian or the priestly Sanskrit as languages of high culture; they try to create a high-culture Bengali via the structural, sometimes even syntactic, imitation of English. Gradually, through the historical selection of the privileged dialect of some area, this elite gives rise to a new norm language. The growth of printing, and the possibilities of standardization it contained, helped this norm language to be consciously adopted by the elites of the sub-regions; so much so that they become gradually ashamed to utter the dialect which would have been, in an earlier era, the cultural flag of their region. Once such a 'high' language develops, all dialects can now be differentiated from it as lower-order languages. Only now is it possible to draw a linguistic map of a region with some amount of clarity, since what happens in Bengal is repeated in the appropriate regions of Bihar and Orissa by similar norm-setting processes around a similarly constructed Hindi and Oriya language. In less than a hundred years an area which was covered by a mass of small dialects gets restructured linguistically into two or three regions using the highly self-conscious languages of their respective high cultures.

In fact, this constructedness comes out clearly in attempts at fashioning a long history which Bengali high culture of the modern time gives to itself.[36] It is only in the period after the eighteenth century that some identifiable historical ancestor of modern literary Bengali can be found. But this culture requires a high ancestry; and consequently, this highly confident literary culture gives itself an interestingly idiosyncratic and opportunistic genealogy. It is interesting to see it move in the tangled antiquities of a few contiguous and fluctuating regions to do its shopping for its historical past. For such purpose it happily appropriates Buddhist *dohas* from Nepal and the splendid poetry of

---

[36] There are innumerable examples, because this self-identification becomes a part of the school syllabi and is quickly universalized. A good example of this sort, though very different from the textbook variety, is Sen 1965.

Vidyapati as the undoubted ancestry of modern Bengali literature. We should not therefore be misled by the impressively ancient ancestry that regions and their languages press upon us. Often, the process by which the region comes into being is not much more ancient than the ones which make the Indian nation appear some years later, and sometimes the contributing processes are the same. Thus the dichotomy between a *new* nation and an *ancient* region, partly imposed on our thinking by the structure of reasoning of modernization sociology, should be seen more critically.

Let us return now to some aspects of what we had earlier called the fuzzy community. In several ways, the communities in which people saw themselves as living were fuzzy compared to the community of the nation that is now proposed. This does not imply that earlier individuals did not know how to handle social complexity in the form of the presence of others in their own life experience. They would meet other individuals routinely inside their villages, or sometimes in non-standard ways, as on pilgrimages. On all such occasions, they would have at their disposal fairly elaborate sets of rules for differentiation by which their responses to others would be determined. If the other person belonged to one level of his community—say, his endogenous caste group—he would know exactly what to do with him. However, such precision did not extend to other aspects of a person's identity or community: it was directed to only certain types of activities and practices.

Apparently, it might never occur to members of these communities to ask how many of them there were—of the same caste, of Vaisnavas, or Saivas—in the world. A different form of this fuzziness would be a relative lack of clarity of where one's community, or even one's region, ended and another began. On being asked to name his community (*samaj*),[37] such a person could take, depending on the context, the name of his village, neighbourhood, his caste, his religious denomination—but hardly ever his linguistic group, not to speak of a nation.

Thus, earlier communities tend to be fuzzy in two ways in which no nation can afford to be. First, they have fuzzy boundaries, because some collective identities are not territorially based. Religion, caste,

---

[37] It is interesting to note that originally the term *samaj* meant something indeterminate, like the common meaning of the English word 'community'. Bengali did not have a term to designate the abstract concept of a society; later the word *samaj* is given this meaning by convention.

and endogamous groups are all based on principles that are not primarily territorial. Indeed, there would be a sense that the 'region', the world that is near, is set within a world that is large, far away, vast and limitless, but both the nearness and the vastness would be fuzzy in the same sense. People would be hard put and indeed could not be bothered to tell where the near ended and the far began.

Secondly, part of this fuzziness of social mapping would arise because traditional communities, unlike modern ones, are not enumerated. The most significant implication of this is the following: they did not see historical processes as things which could be bent to their collective will if people acted concertedly on a large-enough scale. Since they did not ask how many of them there were in the world, they could not consider what they could wreak upon the world, for their collective benefit—through collective action. They were thus incapable of a type of large action, with great potential for doing harm as well as good, which is a feature of the modern condition. Living in an unmapped and unenumerated world may have allowed them to live ordinarily in non-aggressive proximity (though one should not underestimate the ability of older societies to do surprisingly large-scale collective harm). Their sense of community being multiple and layered and fuzzy, no single community could make demands of pre-emptive belonging as comprehensive as those made by the modern nation state.[38]

The boundaries of nation states cannot be fuzzy in the same way. Indeed, the territorial attachment of modern states is sometimes so intense as to be rationally incomprehensible, as evident from the cheerful intensity with which modern nations fight wars for control of uninhabitable land. Second, a parallel principle, the national community, must be enumerated; nations must know how numerous they are. It is not surprising that in the discourse of Indian nationalism the question of numbers figures so prominently.

If there is an argument which underlies earlier defiance of British rule in India, it is the simple and intuitive one that points to the alienness of the new rulers. It implies the impossibility of a good moral claim of an outsider to rule an alien people. It must be seen that the

---

[38] Indeed, one of the principal controversies in modern Indian politics has centred around a satisfactory arrangement of identities. Are other identities compatible with the identity of the nation?

The Imaginary Institution of India

colonial administration worked in ways which sought to create an ideological justification for itself, and sought to answer such objections. In this justification utilitarian social theory played an interestingly complex role.[39] Of course the use of utilitarianism can be explained in a simple historical manner. At the time British colonialism took root in India, and began to see itself as a political rather than a large trading enterprise, the discourse of social theory in England was dominated by the utilitarian debate. Although utilitarian theory had many critics, there is no doubt that it came to have a deep and gradually pervasive influence, a kind of subtle presence which spoke continuously if indirectly behind practical arguments and arrangements, the mark not of philosophical truth as much as of a sociological triumph. It is hardly surprising therefore that utilitarian theory would be found at work in the arguments of British administrators and ideologues.

It appears however that this was not the only reason for the presence of utilitarianism in the political disputations of the time. Some specific arguments of utilitarian theory made it particularly useful for justifying colonialism. Traditionalist theories of political rule, of the Burkean variety, obviously could not establish a good moral title for the colonial rulers of India. Rights-based theories of the early type would have been equally inadequate: it would have required impossible ingenuity to argue a case in favour of a natural right of the British to rule India. Utilitarian theory was remarkably free of such handicaps. Since the logical form of utilitarian arguments are consequentialist,[40] these could be put together to advance a convincing justification of colonialism, at least to the new elite formed by Western education. Alien rule could be questioned on moral grounds of a traditionalist type: those who rebelled against British rule in 1857 could be said to have been guided by a theory which could be given a Burkean form. The entry of utilitarianism in Indian political discourse rendered such arguments obsolete. British rule, it was now argued, conferred on its Indian subjects a whole range of new civilized means of life, starting from the railways and scientific education to the most crucial gift of all—a stable political order.

---

[39] Stokes 1964 is the most detailed account on the subject.
[40] For the consequentialist structure of utilitarian arguments and its theoretical consequences, see Smart and Williams 1973, and Williams 1985.

Large numbers of the babus converted by their education to rationalist thinking ornamented their collaboration with colonial power by aggressive utilitarian reasoning. Bankim himself asks occasionally about the distinctly ironical joys of being oppressed by an indigenous tyrant, and the defence, on grounds of independence, of a traditional order which involved so much degradation and suffering. The title to rule and the justification of power are not to be decided by prescriptive or traditional principles. These are primarily pragmatic matters. Simple tradition could not justify the existence of governments, and created no valid right to rule, certainly not the flimsy—and to some barbarous—idea that indigenous tyrants are preferable on patriotic grounds to foreign reformers. Thus this phase of high colonialism was justified by a structure of utilitarian arguments pointing to the modernizing consequences of British rule. It was not easy to move to a criticism or defiance of British rule unless the argument of the greatest good of the greatest number could be taken away from the colonial administration.

Utilitarians among the babus, justifying reformist collaboration with British rule, would have contended that support for traditional Indian society was backward looking and sentimental. Against this, a new argument advanced by intellectuals of Bankim's generation was that utilitarianism could be faulted on two historical points. First, the claim of the universal validity of the norms of life that enlightenment had set up could be denied. Second, utilitarianism shared with most strands of rationalist thinking on society an untenable belief in an almost total malleability/constructivism of society—going against sociological traditions associated with the names of Montesquieu or Henry Maine which pointed out that the logic of a social order limited very seriously the ability of legislations to construct social action into new forms. Increasingly, the more critical intellectuals of this generation moved towards a view of this kind.

Bankimchandra Chattopadhyay was original in adding a third insight to these. The superiority of the enlightenment ideal depended on the implied premise of re-enactment. Only on the premise that it was possible to re-enact the history of capitalist modernity in the colonies, and the further supposition that colonial reformists intended precisely that, could the babu rationalist argument be admitted to be serious. Bankim, through travesty in particular, contested these fundamental beliefs. The colonial administration, he argued, was not seeking to recreate an order modelled after European modernity; and in any case, structurally, colonialism allowed only travesties to be re-enacted.[41] Occasionally, he would also give a more radical twist to the greatest good idea, by asking literally, and subversively, what good this gift of modernity had brought to the greatest number, the peasantry.[42]

As a consequence of these ideas, there is a marked shift in political discourse about colonial rule; for the first time, this discourse qualifies in the narrower sense to be called *nationalism*. If colonial power cannot be justified by rationalist utilitarian arguments, the terrain of political discourse, and consequently of practice, must shift decisively. The central problem now is not why India became colonized, or even whether alien rule could at all be justified. It is already decisively concluded that alien rule cannot have rational justification and must be opposed. Now the concern shifts to whether it is possible to oppose it in practice, and what principles of organization would be most effective in doing so. Moreover, it now becomes essential to ask which collective subject, or on behalf of which collective 'we', the individual subject should begin to oppose British rule. Anti-colonialism becomes modern nationalism only when it is able to make this transition, moving from a discourse on the earlier question to the new one, and *when it has been able to identify a nation.*

By the end of the nineteenth century this identification is becoming possible in several ways; and accordingly the political discourse becomes distinctly less unhappy. When the question of the identification of the nation is asked, the move from a fuzzy to a clear, enumerated community becomes crucial. Enumeration becomes significant for two reasons: first, it is a source of great psychological strength to restate the tremendous numbers included in this 'we', reflected in the fourteen crore armed hands that Bankim makes Bengalis raise in defiance, though this involves the unorthodox procedure of equipping each of them with two swords.[43] But this is an evocative slip—its sole purpose is to create a sense of invincibility by this deft, if suspect, multiplication. Second, it is a matter of great political significance to

---

[41] See *Kamalakanta*.
[42] See *Bangadeser Krsak*.
[43] '*Dvisaptakotibhujaihdhrtakharakarabale*'.

know this collective subject. The appeals that might rouse it to action depend to a large extent on how its boundaries are drawn. This process must be accomplished, at least in principle, before we can talk about a nationalist consciousness in the narrow sense. It is deeply ironic to call those nationalists who have not yet chosen their nation. If they are nationalists, their mode of being so is distinctly different from that of a later age and should not be absent-mindedly assimilated into that.

Finally, there is another fundamental relation at work in this discourse: between nationalist thinking and the rationalist discourse of modernity. By introducing modernity in their intellectual world, doing much institutional change in its name and making modernity the last argument in its own justification, colonial education forced these people to take up considered stances about the whole project of enlightenment modernity. It is its partial acceptance of a modern theoretical view of the world, especially enlightenment's social epistemics, which demarcates this stage of nationalist thought from earlier less historically conscious patriotism against English 'invaders'. One reason why numbers are so important is because of the new view of the social world created by rationalism and urged upon them by colonial education and propaganda.

Obviously, Indians did not become patriotic for the first time in the nineteenth century, but they invented a new way of being patriotic, a new object to be patriotic for. Gellner is right in pointing out that nationalism arises with and within a larger movement and intellectual configuration of modernity in which one of the major regulative ideas is the possibility of pursuit by newcomer peoples of the life, liberty, and ironical happinesses of industrial modernism. Most theories see and abstractly recognize the typical configuration called modernity—industrial technology, capitalist production, a territorial sovereign state, a regime of rationalist cognition, and rational-technical epistemics about the social world—but actual sociological enquiry has given disproportionate attention to one prominent hypothesis about these interconnections. Both Marxist and anti-Marxist theory has put much greater effort into the proof or disproof of capitalism accompanying nationalist aspirations, to the exclusion of its other connections.

In Europe at least there was a clear connection between the nationalist doctrine's urgency of enumeration and the rationalist theoretical view, its attempt to live in a world that is wholly, unsurpassably, classified, enumerated—a world securely distributed into tables. Clearly, this is part of a programme of bringing the world under control by precise cognition, turning every little piece of information into social technology. Nationalism, once it came into its own, through its massive and obedient instrument of the national state, continues to press on with this relentless project of enumeration—the endless counting of its citizens, territories, resources, majorities, minorities, institutions, activities, import, export, incomes, projects, births, deaths, diseases. It counts, it appears, every conceivable quantifiable thing. No doubt this is helped in most cases by the bourgeois character of this nationalism—the easy, intuitive transfer of a language of *possession* from individuals to the more problematic individuality of the nation. But while it happens, it seems self-evidently true that nations possess territories and citizens in the same way as individuals possess their goods.

But this also shows us a paradox in the discourse that this configuration sets in motion. The nation-state is conceived often as part of a modern configuration, as an apparatus that the people need to bring the forces of modernity under control. The language of this kind of society is a deeply individualistic language which speaks of atomistic individuals who enter into relations with each other on the basis of a purely rational calculation of advantages. The most rational of such actors is of course the free rider. It is possible to work out an easy form of Olson's paradox of collective action to assert the impossibility of national movements.[44]

On the other hand the nation is also, invariably, conceived of as a community. This is the point of paradox. National groups, although they are *gesellschaften,* must at least in the romantic period of their rise against foreign control, present themselves to themselves (because usually they are their own primary audience) as a *gemeinschaft*. It is at one level a coalition of group interests which wishes to merge into an

---

[44] See Olson 1971: ch. 4. In his well-known argument, Olson shows that if the good for which a group is mounting a collective action is indivisible, it is rational strategy for each single individual not to work for the collective good. In this way they would avoid punishment or costs, while they cannot be, in the nature of the case, excluded from the benefits. Thus, individuals can reason that they will not actively work for independence, but since they cannot be excluded from independence when it comes, they would enjoy its benefits anyway.

overwhelming combination against the ruling power; but apparently it must pretend, because of the newness and unprecedentedness of this sort of collective action, that it is an immemorially ancient community. Actually, it must be a bond of secular interests, but in ideology it must be represented as a mystic unity of sentiments.

Is the nation, then, it will be objected, unreal; is it not something 'objective'? The view I put forward does not deny the objectivity of the nation, but displaces its meaning and asks for a softening of the concept of objectivity. Things that exist in history are often objective only in this way, and only to this extent: perhaps to grimly scientific minds an objectivity of a very vulnerable, unsatisfactory kind. Since a primary means of communities reproducing themselves is to tell stories about themselves, it is not surprising that narrative structures predominate in nationalist discourse. But there are limits beyond which a narrative way of thinking cannot extend.

Alasdair MacIntyre has shown how narratives can help in negotiation of the world's complexities and contribute to the existence of a whole, unfractured, communal existence.[45] It is only when a society has a general consensus about its objectives and the moral order of the universe that narratives can do this job. This, when seen in the perspective of nationalist history, yields an interesting point. Common opposition to colonial dominance often imparts to the 'community' of the national movement a genuine moral consensus of this kind.

It is remarkable, but hardly surprising, that the narratives of nationalism speak about some things in social destiny and not others. These narratives are explicit and detailed about freedom, sacrifice, glory, and such things, and usually very vague about the more concrete and contestable questions of distribution, equality, power, the actual unequal ordering of the past society or of the future one. Narratives here are above all practical things, interpretations of the world and its history which issue in a call to change it. Its pragmatic objectives are incompatible with such fractious stories of production and distribution. After the achievement of independence, these narratives have done their work; if pressed into the service of providing an order to the nation and its state, they begin to falter. Such productive and distributive arrangements can be justified or questioned by a new type of

---

[45] See MacIntyre 1981: ch. 15.

discourse—a discourse of social theory. The new period, to misuse Marx's phrase, 'cannot draw its poetry from the past'.

How important this storytelling form is, for political conviction, is shown by its persistence. Even in people in whom it is least expected, it tends to reappear. Among the political leaders of Indian nationalism one of the most clear-sighted and convinced about a theoretical orientation was Nehru. Indeed, in his *Autobiography* he laments that Indian nationalism lacks a theoretical view of politics.[46] Yet when Nehru writes he provides a complex design of three interconnected narratives—of the world, of the nation, and of the self. Thus the narrative form was impossible to get away from, not because of any intellectual lack in the writers but because collective existence as much as collective actions create their ideological support by great narratives.

On Narrative Contract

The telling of a story brings into immediate play some strong conventions invoking a narrative community. Ordinarily, these are coincident in terms of their frontiers with social communities of some form: societies, particular groups, sometimes movements aspiring to give themselves a more demarcated and stabler social form. To some extent all such communities, from the stable to the emergent, use narrative as a technique of staying together, redrawing their boundaries or reinforcing them. Participating in a movement quite clearly involves accepting something like contractual obligations, and, I suspect, some of this affiliation of individuals to movements counteracting a monadic individualism is accomplished by narrative contracts.

Narrative does not therefore aspire to be a universal form of discourse. It draws lines, it distributes people, unlike rational theoretical discourse which attempts to unite them in an abstract universe of ideal consensus. Narratives are not for all to hear, for all to participate in to an equal degree. It has a self in which it originates, a self which tells the story. But that self obviously is not soliloquizing or telling the story to itself. It implies an audience, a larger self towards which it is directed, and we can extend the idea to say that the transaction of a narrative creates a kind of narrative contract. For the recipient of narrative

[46] See Nehru 1936.

cannot be just anybody: it is only some people belonging to particular categories who are privileged by the narration. As P. Acharya has shown, Muslim children could not come easily under the narrative contracts held out by Abanindranath Tagore's wonderfully coloured folktales; there are very real frontiers of indifference and contempt which would keep them out. The nationalist storyteller confers the bounty of the story on the elect, those who are rendered eligible by the conventions of the story. Nationalism clearly uses the contractual character of the narrative to extend its ideological message. Across segments of society, across generations, across all political divides it creates a vast, constantly open, and constantly renewed political contract.

The Nationalist Critique of Modernity

Historically, the great enterprise called the enlightenment had met three historical frontiers, separated from each other in terms of space and time. It had an internal frontier on the underside of bourgeois society, between the elites and the productive classes within European capitalism. A second frontier lay between its victorious, conquering colonial power and the peoples it subjugated and reduced to political ineffectuality and cultural silence. A final frontier is reached today when that civilization itself feels exhausted and has produced an interesting and complex internal critique.

Capitalism, Marx said, was the first universal social form, at least the first form capable of a possible universality. It imposed, on most people with whom it came in touch, certain peculiar forms of suffering. These several sufferings at the various frontiers of capitalism gave rise to critiques in which those who suffered at its hands tried to make sense of their history. In a sense, each critique analysed and held up for criticism aspects of suffering related to capitalism which were opaque, unperceived, and unreported to the others. But as critiques they are potentially connectable; they, as it were, waited to meet each other. It is only now, in the writing of history, that such a meeting is possible. In this, the critique of an aggressive, uncritical, all-conquering rationalist colonialism by the early nationalists is a necessary part. And it is only when these critiques are stitched together that a true map of the unhappy consciousness of humanity, when capitalism reigned, can be put together.

At least three different types of theoretical problems emerge from a study of anti-colonial thought in the nineteenth century. Intellectual responses to colonial rationalism did of course vary widely across the great expanse of the world of European colonies. Every civilization, from tribal societies endowed with tight, highly economical sets of symbolic resources, to ancient cultures reduced to an unaccustomed subalternity, was forced to think of its present as history, and make some sense of what colonial rule did to its society. Bengali intellectuals of that early generation thought in ways specific to themselves and to the resources they had at their command. Similar moves must have been tried all over the world. Until an intellectual history of anti-colonialism is compiled, the history of colonialism will remain unfinished.

Not surprisingly, the history of this third critique is largely unwritten. This is partly due to an absence of the constitution of its object; this third discourse must be first constituted as a historical object before it can be seen to deserve a history. Of course the materials for this history are distributed over several discrete disciplines—the history of nationalism produced by historians, political thought systematized by political scientists, rituals, and folk customs reported by anthropologists, myths collected by ethnographers. To have the materials is not to have a history; this is because history is preceded by a theoretical question, it must philosophically constitute and defend the object which it will write the history of.[47]

Unless the people who are subjected to colonialism are seen to engage in such an enterprise which—despite evident internal differences between periods, between high and folk culture, between the great tradition and the small, between the anti-colonialists and the nationalists, between the radicals and the conservatives—is still seen as one, as a single, whole, historical enterprise, its history cannot be written.

The first general point that emerges is to recognize the seriousness of this enterprise, and to respect its authenticity. Serious historical reflection can exist in non-theoretical and non-historical works. What I wish to emphasize is the originality and distinctness of this intellectual enterprise; what was going on inside these intellectual performances was not just an attempt to counter or criticize Western theories of social organization by the use of concepts and argumentative structures

---

[47] This theoretical constitution of the object of historical enquiry is often done by other disciplines, or by the general intellectual culture.

taken from Western theoretical discourse. Its originality lay in the fact that this critique was attempted from outside this orbit or circle of discourse; this originality is essentially an acknowledgement of the distinctness of Indian discourse, the assertion of the abstract possibility of other universes of theoretical reflection.

In modern social theory the point is quite often made that different societies could be said to have different internal standards of rationality.[48] It is also fairly common to speculate about what indigenous traditions, silenced by European colonial power, might have said had they commanded resources of argumentation comparable to European social theory. Sometimes this is artificially arranged by making tribal witchcraft speak the language of modern analytic philosophy in a pretended dialogue with the ideas of modern science. Yet these discussions remain abstract and historically insubstantial; for these depict what discourses could have happened, not what was really said by real people in real historical situations. The discourse of Indian nationalism in its early stages shows that we do not always need such ahistorical constructs in seeking a view of an 'other'. In colonial times there existed not only colonized cultures which spoke limited hermetic languages and which had narrow and undifferentiated horizons of thinking; there were also other cultures, with considerable internal resources of historical self-reflection, which do not require such generosity of external construction of what they may have had to say about colonialism and the imposition of Western modernity. Colonial cultures like India carried on much real as opposed to hypothetical reflection about their history, comparative rationality, and the validity of the claims of a universal reason.

If this is so, why does mainstream social theory carry on as if these societies, after their moments of colonization, were entirely divested of discourse? As if, even when there were undeniable episodes of defiance, these were in some sense violently material, unprefaced, unaccompanied by any discursive negotiation of their world of subalternity?[49] Certainly,

---

[48] This is done most notably in the work of Peter Winch (1990).

[49] Historians have along with other mainstream social scientists, traditionally neglected discourse, in their immersion of the narratives of the economic and political events. Anthropologists were, by contrast, more attentive to these

in recent years this indifference in Western social theoretical discourse has been modified to some extent: relativists in anthropological theory and criticisms of orientalism, particularly Edward Said's influential work,[50] have made some amends for this absence, this erasure of one side from the intellectual history of the colonial world. But these critiques, it must be emphasized, are part of the discourse of Western social theory, attempting to restore some balance in its view of the world: they do not provide the necessary representation of the other discourse. These do not write the history of the discourse of the colonized, but point to its existence, and indicate the space where it must be entered in the historical record.

In historical fact, the Orient is never reduced to silence: indeed, it constantly gives vent to its resentment against colonialism through an enormous range of expressions from insults, dishonesty, graft, opportunism, gossip, to social reform, political programmes, mass mobilizations, movements, but also serious historical reflection. This is often done in languages, styles, and concepts which would be unrecognizable in terms of Western social theory, and are consequently treated as being equivalent to historical silence. Probably, this is not due only to difficulties of language, but to a theoretical difficulty as well. Discourses constitute planes or orbits in which ideas and arguments are made, heard, and contested. But the most significant thing is that there is no single unruptured plane on which all such circles of discourse coexist and can be heard by each other. More often, these are like circles which exist on different geometric planes. Arguments like the anthropologists' or Said's critique of Orientalism are oppositional ones within Western discourse; however much they abstractly advocate the cause of native rationality, they do not represent or read these discourses.

In writing the history of the discourses of the colonized we must guard against the mistake of misrecognition, translating its concepts into its nearest European equivalents, like romanticism, socialism, bourgeois theory, etc. It has proved persistently difficult in any case to

---

questions. Consequently, it is not surprising that new forms of history writing, for instance *Subaltern Studies*, but also some others, use a great number of the anthropologist's tools.

[50] See Said 1978.

use evaluative characterizations like 'conservative' and 'radical' when discussing these ideas. They are often articulating positions for which in a strict sense there are no names in Western social theory.

Conclusion

The foregoing argument has made a number of points about narrativization and history, using the two concepts each as a foothold for a critique of the other. I have used the term narrative itself in two different senses; but this need not create confusion because these are easily distinguishable. The first and more ordinary meaning of narrativizing or telling a story is to construct fictive entities or fictive connections. This is reflected in the sense of the term storytelling which indicates often that someone is making something up. Evidently, that kind of 'storytelling' cannot perform the functions expected of history as an academic discipline, whose justification is in being true in the strong sense. However, narrativizing has another meaning which indicates its colligatory function.[51] By colligatory I mean the essential act by which historical accounts join incidents (accounts of facts) or processes in a sequence: $a - b - c - d$, and so on; emphasis on the colligatory element in history would shift attention to the arrows between the facts, the relation between a and b, or the more indirect one between a and c.

Historical narratives claim to bring the material of history under control by two equally essential processes. Certainly, the primary process is to make sure that the accounts of the incidents themselves of a or b are true. But even entirely true accounts of incidents do not colligate themselves entirely on their own. Narratives claim further to bring history under control by separating not only the true from the false, but also the formless from the ordered. It says typically that b happened after a; but clearly b's following a is not a self-evident affair. It must be accompanied by an implicit classification of events into classes and then say b followed a in the relevant class of happenings. Even within that class there may be other events over which b is preferred for mention, for which again reasons must be advanced. Every event is ascertained within a story or something like a story sketch.

[51] The term 'colligatory' is taken from Walsh 1974.

While it is necessary to ask whether our knowledge of the first level entity is reliable or not, and this is a question of its being true or false, we should recognize that, at the second level, it has to be inflected into a criterion of adequacy. There are many ways of colligating facts, and the reason why one colligation cannot reduce others to falsity is that no colligating performance can be descriptively complete. Thus, apart from the factual, empirical content of history, there would always remain the colligatory one, about which one can speak a language of justifiability under *some* conditions, but not the finality implicit in a language of strong bivalence. It is not only the choice of *a* or *b* out of a whole lot of other candidates that is political. The space lying suggestively between *a* and *b* and *c*, teeming with objects not selected for mention, is also intensely political; and these empty spaces of unmentioned incidents is worrisomely like fiction. Thus those used to speaking the rather more extreme language of deconstruction could say that an element of exclusion is always implicit in the mentioning of historical facts. Every item of truth is surrounded by large spaces of 'absence of truth', events, processes, experiences, entities about which such truth is not uttered, in fact not even sought. The interstices of every narrative are filled with semblances rather than truth. Thus the telling of true stories in history would not rule out the telling of other stories different from the first which are also true.

This has some connection with the nature of the criticism offered here against nationalist history. Criticism is in a sense a relation of dependence, as the Indian philosophic term *uttarapaksa* indicates so graphically. Critical history is not interested in the destruction of nationalist historiography in its entirety. History is not an enterprise which can be begun from the beginning: it is 'always already' begun. It comes into the world which is already marked with errors, and it can erase the errors only after inheriting them.

It is unpractical to believe that the new kind of history will successfully throw out older history. The task of the historian is like the work of somebody who partially rebuilds a house (which is an excellent metaphor for history because people do live inside it). He does not put a system in on an empty space brick by brick. There is a structure which already exists, and it cannot be wholly dismantled because he needs to live inside it at least partially; his criticism is to attack it brick by brick, taking a brick away and putting another in its place. After some time, with a large number of bricks changed, this would constitute a structural change in what is called history. Even when the whole structure is replaced (is that possible?) there would still be a memory of the earlier structure precisely through its absence; with the proviso that this is the fate waiting for the new history as well. This is not surprising. It simply confirms the idea that the business of writing history is also a part of history.

References

Austin, J.L. 1975. *How to Do Things With Words.* Boston: Harvard University Press.
Danto, A.C. 1983. *Narration and Knowledge.* New York: Columbia University Press.
Foucault, Michel. 1972. *The Archaeology of Knowledge.* London: Tavistock.
Gadamer, Hans. 1975. *Truth and Method.* London: Sheed and Ward.
Gellner, Ernest. 1983. *Nations and Nationalism.* Oxford: Blackwell.
Gramsci, Antonio. 1985. *Selections from Cultural Writings.* London: Lawrence and Wishart.
Hempel, Carl G. 1974. Reasons and Covering Laws in Historical Explanations. In Patrick Gardiner, ed., *Philosophy of History.* London: Oxford University Press.
Kaviraj, Sudipta. 1990. Writing, Speaking, Being: Language and Historical Identity in South Asia. Keynote paper for the section on 'Identity in History: South and Southeast Asia', German Historical Congress, Bochum, 27–29 September 1990. (Forthcoming, South Asia Institute, University of Heidelberg.)
MacIntyre, Alasdair. 1981. *After Virtue.* London: Duckworth.
Nagel, Thomas. 1985. *The View from Nowhere.* New York: Basic Books.
Nehru, Jawaharlal. 1936. *An Autobiography.* New Delhi: Allied Publishers (rpnt. 1964).
Olson, Mancur. *The Logic of Collective Action.* Boston: Harvard University Press.
Raychaudhuri, Tapan. 1988. *Europe Reconsidered.* Delhi: Oxford University Press.
Said, Edward. 1978. *Orientalism.* London: Routledge and Kegan Paul.
Seal, Anil. 1968. *The Emergence of Indian Nationalism.* Cambridge: Cambridge University Press.
Sen, Sukumar. 1965. *Bangla Sahityer Itihas* (in Bengali). New Delhi: Sahitya Akademi.
Skinner, Quentin. 1988. Meaning and Understanding in the History of Ideas. In James Tully (ed.), *Meaning and Context.* Oxford: Polity Press.

Smart, J.J.C. and Bernard Williams. 1973. *Utilitarianism: For and Against*. Cambridge: Cambridge University Press.
Stokes, Eric. 1964. *The English Utilitarians and India*. Rpnt. Delhi: Oxford University Press.
Tönnies, Ferdinand. 1971. *On Sociology: Pure, Applied and Empirical*. Chicago: Chicago University Press.
Walsh, William. 1974. The Colligatory Concepts in History. In Patrick Gardiner, ed., *Philosophy of History*. London: Oxford University Press.
Weber, T. 1947. *Theory of Social and Economic Organisation*. New York: Free Press.
Williams, Bernard. 1985. *Ethics and the Limits of Philosophy*. Glasgow: Fontana.
Winch, Peter, 1990. *The Idea of a Social Science and its Relation with Philosophy*. London: Routledge.

6

A State of Contradictions: The Post-colonial State in India

No story of the European state can be complete if it does not take into account its effects outside Europe. Francois Guizot's classic history of the European state requires a supplement.[1] His magisterial account presents the picture of the state inside Europe's own history, but the story of the European state has an equally significant counterpart, a history that happens outside. Outside Europe the modern state succeeded in two senses—first as an instrument, and second as an idea. First, the organization of European societies produced by the modern state was an essential factor in Europe's ability to bring the rest of the world under its colonial control. Here the state functioned as an immense and unprecedented enhancement of European societies' capacity for collective action—in raising military resources, producing the economic resources which undergirded its military success, focusing on clearly defined strategies of control and conquest. In fact, when other peoples began to reflect on the reasons for this astonishing success, they often settled on this as its intangible but indispensable instrument. Premodern forms of political authority were utterly inadequate in dealing with the power of the modern European state. It could be restrained and eventually effectively opposed only through a movement that organized the power of entire populations against European colonial regimes.

The European state also succeeded a second time as an idea. Successful nationalist movements, after decolonization, enthusiastically

First published in *States and Citizens*, ed. Quentin Skinner and Bö Strath (Cambridge: Cambridge University Press, 2003).

[1] Guizot 1997.

accepted the idea of a modern society centred upon the state's sovereignty—a principle of social construction entirely different from traditional ones. Except for a few odd individuals like Gandhi and Tagore, nationalists did not object to the presence of the modern state, only to its being under European control. With Independence, they did not wish, except in a few cases like Gandhi, to 'abolish' the state, but to use it for their own purposes. After two hundred years of colonialism, the European state receded from India, but the idea of the state brought in by colonialism continued its triumphant career. Eventually, the gigantic transformations of third world societies after decolonization, for good or for ill, were driven through by this modern instrumentality of the state. In the absence of other forces—such as great revolutionary social classes like the bourgeoisie or the proletariat that played such an important role in European social transformations—it was the state which almost entirely arrogated to itself the power of proposing, directing, and effecting large-scale social change. There might be great debates about judging what the state has done; but there is no doubt that it has been the single most powerful collective agency in the recent history of these societies. That is why the state is central to the story of non-Western modernity, and Western colonialism is central to the story of the non-Western state.

This essay is not about the post-colonial state in general, only the historically specific form it assumed in India. It is thus necessary to spell out what can be generalized from the Indian case and what cannot. First, although India is a single country, its numerical significance is obvious: what happens to its people politically represents the collective experience of about a third of the non-Western world. Second, as there is little dispute today about the desirability of democracy, the Indian case is particularly important. It is one of the most successful cases of democracy outside Europe. But the 'success' of democracy is an ambiguous idea: it is possible to give it a minimal or an expansive interpretation. The narrow and minimalist reading is simply the continuance of a competitive electoral system of government: if this system continues uninterrupted over a long period of time, that draws applause as a success of democracy. But there can be an alternative, Tocquevillean reading of democracy's success—which is not just a continuation of a system of government, but the capacity of this government to produce long-term egalitarian effects. In India, democracy has been a remarkable success in both these senses. First, in a highly diverse society, divided by religion, caste, classes, languages, the democratic system has functioned without interruption or popular apathy for nearly six decades. Second, and more significantly, this institutional continuation of democracy has produced a fundamental social transformation which is in some respects startlingly different from the European social processes. Thirdly, if democratic institutions spread and achieve success in the non-European world, these will produce historical results depending on the forms of sociability available in each historical context. Such cases of possible democratic success are likely to follow trajectories closer to India's than to modern Europe's. To understand the prospects of democracy in the future, the story must include the Indian case alongside Western narratives of the nineteenth century.

This essay interprets 'post-colonial' as indicating not the trivial fact that this state emerged after the colonial regime departed, but in the stronger sense to mean that some of its characteristic features could not have arisen without the particular colonial history that went before. I also believe, unlike some other political scientists, that political change in modern India cannot be studied fruitfully except in a long-term historical perspective. To understand the unfolding story of politics and the state today, it is thus essential to start with the historical transformation of political power in the age of colonialism.

Modernity in India, and perhaps also in other European colonies, was largely a political affair. All commentators on European modernity point out the significant, if not originary, role that transformations of the production and economic processes played in the making of European modernity. I wish to suggest that in India, by contrast, the causal powers of economic change were far more limited. The type of capitalist development that eventually took place was determined to a large extent by political imperatives of state control. The colonial state created the conditions for early capitalist development, rather than the other way round. Modernity came to India by the political route, through the introduction of a new activity called 'politics'. Indeed, the activity was so new that in many vernaculars it is still colloquially referred to by the English-derived word 'politics', rather than by an orthogenetic term. This new activity assumed primarily three forms in successive stages of modern Indian history. Initially, it entered with the establishment of new institutions of colonial rule, eventually crystallizing into a colonial state/regime. Sociologically, 'politics' was an activity which involved British rulers and Indian elites who engaged in transactions of power with them. In the second phase, its scope was extended through the popular nationalist movement from the 1920s, when Indians from other social groups and classes took part in this as a large, encompassing, transformative activity. Although most Indians were affected by this form of politics, their participation and capacity to behave as actors depended on class and education. Nationalist politics, in spite of its wider appeal, remained more the politics of the wider educated elites, much less of the ordinary Indian peasantry. Curiously, even after Independence, this structure continued unchanged for about two decades. Since the 1970s, in another serious transformation, the business of 'politics' has become much more expansive, with lower-class politicians bringing the concerted pressures of their ordinary constituents into the life of the state.

What were the central processes in this transformation? Why has politics of a discursive, representative, democratic character succeeded in India? The basic argument of this essay is controversial, but fairly simple. There can be no doubt that in the last two hundred years Indian society has undergone a most fundamental transformation. The central point of this change, in my view, is the transformation of a society in which 'imperative co-ordination', to use Weber's inelegant but useful phrase, was achieved through a religious system based on caste, with comparatively little role being played by the state, to an order controlled by the state—its institutions, its laws, its resources, its functionaries, and its place in ordinary people's imagination. In premodern times, control over the state was relatively marginal to the narratives of significant social change. The most significant upheavals in traditional Indian history were not dynastic or regime changes, but the challenges to the religious organization of society through the reform movements of Buddhism and Jainism against ritualistic Brahminism in ancient India, or the rise of bhakti cults against Hindu orthodoxy in late-medieval times. By contrast, from the middle of the nineteenth century the state's role has been absolutely central in the passage of social change. The colonial state ended in 1947, but the new way of organizing social life through 'politics', making the society state-centred, has not merely continued but expanded its jurisdiction over all aspects of social life. The 'European' state thus still dominates modern Indian life in those two senses. The institutional apparatuses introduced into Indian society by British colonial power have not been dismantled, but massively extended. Secondly, the idea that to be modern is to live through the state, to organize society through this central institution of power, has had a great vindication—ironically through the demise of colonial power itself.

Following this main idea, I shall present my argument in three parts: the first will offer a brief outline of the arrangement of social power in traditional (pre-colonial) India; the second will describe the changes brought in by colonialism and Indians' transaction with its initiatives; and the final section will analyse what has happened to this state after Independence—by its becoming a 'nation-state', and the manner in which principles of democracy have been interpreted by social forces in India.

II

Colonial power came to an Indian society which already had a long-standing and intricate political organization. Much of northern and central India had been under an Islamic empire for nearly six centuries.[2] Yet the presence of Islam in India was special. In most other societies, a conquering Islamic power had converted the people and transformed indigenous social practices and religious doctrine. In India the irresistible military power of Islamic dynasties learnt to coexist with the immovable social structure of the Hindu caste system. Indian society thus had a dual structure of power, composed of a strange crossing of Hindu and Islamic principles, From very early times, 'Hindu' society (an anachronistic description for a collection of different sects united by a single sociological order) had an explicit and intricate arrangement of social power structured in a caste order.[3] Caste represents a peculiar structure of social power which tends to circumscribe the jurisdiction of political authority. Caste, as is generally known, has two forms—the

---

[2] See Bayly 1989. For a different argument, and based on a different regional perspective, see Dirks 1998.

[3] Al Biruni, the great Islamic scholar, despaired of discovering any doctrinal singleness in the Hindu sects, but decided, brilliantly, that the key to their unity lay in a sociological order of Brahminism. Al Biruni 1914.

formal, ritualistic structure of the four *varnas*, and the effective sociological structure of much more numerous *jatis*. Social anthropologists usually give less importance to the formal varna structure, but it is significant for one central reason. It shows that at the centre of the caste order is a scheme of an *asymmetric* hierarchy, which separates the goods that ordinary human beings seek and value in mundane life, and segregates groups according to these. The underyling theory behind the caste order implied that the primary values/goods of human life were ritual status/religious prestige, political power to rule over society, and the economic power to control wealth. The central logic of the varna version of the caste system was to separate the social groups which exercised monopolistic control over each of these human goods. The social order of castes ritually separated the fields of intellectual authority, political and military supremacy, and commercial wealth.

These arrangements meant that, by contrast with the aristocratic societies of pre-modern Europe, political pre-eminence, economic wealth, and cultural prestige did not coincide in a single social elite. Occupational separation by birth ensured that social groups lived in three types of relations to each other: segmentation, interdependence, and hierarchy. Occupationally divided social groups could not seek the same goods; and therefore, it reduced, if not entirely excluded, competition for wealth and power. Secondly, the caste order was based on a generally recognized *social* constitution, an authoritative allocation of social roles, rewards, and therefore life trajectories which governed the conduct of social groups in minute detail. Significantly, this authoritative allocation did not originate from political authority. Political rulers could not alter the rules of this social constitution, but were expected to uphold and administer its 'immutable' norms, and crucially, were themselves subject to its segmentally relevant rules. Consequently, in this social world the power of political rulers was limited to 'executive' functions: that is, to protect the social constitution, punish infringements, and return it to its order of normalcy. In this sense, political rulers did not have the 'legislative' authority to reconstitute this order, except in marginal ways. The idea of modern sovereignty therefore did not apply to the power of the political authority in this society.

However, there is an obvious objection at this point. Is this not an excessively Hindu view of political power? Since large parts of Indian society had been continually governed by Islamic rulers since the eleventh century, does this model apply to those areas? One of the most interesting historical questions about India's political past is the precise relation that Islamic imperial power established with the predominantly Hindu society over which it exercised control. Although Islamic religious doctrine was fundamentally different from Hinduism (e.g. over idolatry, monotheism, egalitarianism, etc.), in sociological terms (i.e. in the relation between *political* authority and the *social* constitution) Islam in India observed very similar principles, and tacitly accepted the restrictions the caste society placed on the 'legislative' functions of rulers. Thus, the coming of Islam was highly significant in other ways, but not in terms of the fundamental structure of the relation between political power and social order. It required a state of a very different sort, animated by very different intellectual principles of self-organization and endowed with new types of cognitive-statistical appliances, to alter this stable social constitution. The modern state is, by definition, the state which, because of its self-interpretation in terms of the principle of sovereignty, considers this invasive transformation of society possible.

III

Although the colonial system of states meant a subordination of other societies to some metropolitan European powers, the actual transactions of colonialism were extremely diverse. First, the European states themselves came from vastly different cultural and institutional contexts, and these differences were reflected in the system of political power each of them brought into their colonies. Secondly, much depended on exactly when a territory was brought under European control. Third, European powers followed entirely different projects in different colonies, and the experience of colonial rule in one part of the world often informed decisions about another: British rule in Africa, for instance, was very different from what it was in India. Finally, the exact nature of colonial rule depended not merely on what the colonial power was ideologically intent on doing, or instrumentally capable of achieving, but also the manner in which the colonized society deployed its own cultural and political resources in this encounter. Focusing on India therefore gives us a single story out of many diverse ones of

European colonial rule, and because of the strange intimacy that developed between India and Britain, it might portray European colonial domination in general in a misleadingly benevolent light. Not all groups in colonized countries responded to the arrival of European power and culture with the initial enthusiasm of India's elites. European powers did not direct the same amount of attention and energy towards the moral and social transformation of all their dominions. The sharing of at least abstract common political principles between the colonial rulers and the nationalist elite to produce an effective framework of political conflict was also rather unusual, as was the negotiated nature of the eventual withdrawal of British power.

The state established by British colonialism was a historical force of an untraditional kind. Even though its immediate instrument was a commercial company, the dominion established by British power occurred in an intellectual context which presupposed sovereignty as a definitional quality of state power.[4] Thus, when the British eventually turned India into a crown colony in 1858, the colonial state explicitly assumed the rights of sovereignty as understood in European discourses of the nineteenth century. Interestingly, as British colonial power did not enter India in the shape of state authority, the initial conflict was not in the form of a struggle between two states—the declining Mughal empire and the British crown. It is the peculiar constitution of society, and the relative externality of the state to the orders of caste practice, which allowed this to happen. By the early nineteenth century, British authorities already controlled much of commercial activity, military power, and quasi-political administrative apparatuses, and had a substantial influence on cultural life in several parts of India. When they finally ended the fiction of Mughal rule after the rebellion of 1857, Mughal authority was already purely nominal. But this first, and rather peculiar, stage in the establishment of British power, stretching over a century, is critical for an understanding of the special

[4] One of the most interesting accounts of this underlying connection between the commercial and political impulses in the Company's India was given in Burke's famous indictment of Warren Hastings before the House of Lords. Edmund Burke, 'On the Impeachment of Warren Hastings, 15–19 February 1788', in Burke 1998, pp. 31–8. The question of 'sovereignty' also figured prominently in discussions among British utilitarians and their critics about economic policy. For an excellent analysis, see Stokes 1959.

dynamics of British colonialism in India. In this stage, we must try to sketch out the contours of advancing colonial *power*, rather than describe the structure of the 'colonial *state*'.

British power, established initially through control over channels and instruments of commerce and revenue collection, and at the second step through the introduction of modern cultural apparatuses, slowly turned into a state of the modern kind—though its actual institutions were quite different from nineteenth-century European models. The most significant implication of this is that Indian opinion was always internally deeply divided about colonial rule. Older aristocracies that lost their power to the British were understandably hostile. Similarly, traditional Hindu holders of social authority and prestige, like conservative Brahmins, often looked at the new influences with hostility. Recent historical research has strongly underlined the fact that the British could establish their control over a large and diverse territory like India partly because they went along with historical trends that had already started in India in the eighteenth century, and for this reason they also drew substantial support from indigenous groups. Powerful commercial interests, aspirant political groups, and relatively modern professional elites produced by new educational institutions strongly supported the establishment of British rule. Eventually, this allowed British government in India to become an interesting arrangement administered by large groups of Indian elites who collaborated with British authority and ran the colony under British supervision.[5]

In the long term, the colonial state altered Indian society in two ways. The establishment of a new kind of state, with formal legal claims to sovereignty, was itself a major transformative project, which reversed the logic of limited political authority in the segmentary caste civilization. It established and familiarized the idea that the apparatuses of the state, especially its legislative organs, in British or Indian hands, could, in principle, judge social institutions critically, and formally

---

[5] For the new historical arguments suggesting this 'indigenous' force in favour of British success, see Bayly 1989, Washbrook 1988, and Stein 1985. Parallel arguments are advanced in Subrahmanyam 1990. For an excellent analysis of the contradictory impulses that shaped the early colonial state, see Washbrook 1999.

alter them by law. Some of the most fateful and long-lasting effects, however, were not introduced through political policies of the state, but through more indirect cultural changes that it induced through its administrative habits.[6] Administrative procedures, like the great statistical enterprises of the colonial regimes, though not political in themselves, nonetheless caused fundamental changes in social identities and their preparation for a new kind of politics. Surprisingly, the colonial administration changed identities by implanting cognitive practices which objectified communities, changing them from an earlier fuzzy or underspecified form to a modern enumerated one. Processes of enumeration of the social world, like mapping and the census, irreversibly altered social ontology by giving groups a new kind of agentive political identity.[7] This was not political agency in itself, but a precondition for the development of a political universe in which political agency could be imparted to large impersonal groups—like castes, ethnicities, or religious communities.

However, the colonial state was subject to contradictory impulses. It set in motion large information-gathering processes under the rationalist belief that, in order to rule such a large and complex society, officials had to know it accurately and exhaustively. This statistical project was not part of a state-directed agenda of wholesale social reform. One strand of administrative thinking advocated a state of deliberate inactivity, which would not meddle in social affairs that colonial rulers did not understand fully, and which might unwittingly create disaffection. Even in the case of a barbaric practice like sati (suttee)—the burning of widows on the funeral pyre of their deceased husbands—the initial response of the colonial regime was extremely cautious. Only the righteous indignation of the native reformers eventually pushed it into legislation banning it.[8] Apart from cultural scruples, the colonial state also mistrusted over-expansion of its activities on purely prudential grounds. British policy oscillated between an

---

[6] Recently, much work has been done on how the information order of colonial India was created, and how it underpinned colonial administration. See, for instance, Irschik 1994, and Bayly 1996.

[7] I have discussed this in greater detail in Kaviraj 1994. Cf. Appadurai 1996.

[8] For a detailed account of the intellectual debates around sati, see Mani, 1998.

urge towards reform, which wanted to restructure Indian society on rational lines, and a policy of restraint, which wanted to leave the social affairs of Indians alone. The self-limitation of the colonial state, justified at various times by arguments of financial prudence or cultural relativism, allowed a wide space for the development of a distinctive elite associational politics in nineteenth-century India. This initial ability to form associations, exercise group solidarity, pursue economic interests, and transact business with the colonial state gave the modern Indian elite the confidence to develop eventually larger projects of self-government, and led to the growth of Indian nationalism.

Ironically, the specific ideological culture in which the British colonial state operated played a part in the eventual growth of nationalist arguments in India. The time of the greatest expansion and power of British colonialism in India coincided with the time when principles of modern liberalism were being established in British political culture. The Indian empire thus witnessed all the internal contradictions of an imperialism which also sought to subscribe to liberal doctrine.[9] Liberal political theorists were arguing passionately against the substantial remnants of despotic power, and advocating dramatic expansion of citizens' freedom. Such principles sat uneasily with the demands of expanding empire. In the colonial context, liberal writers were often at pains to oppose precisely such extensions of freedom to colonial subjects. Educated Indians by now had gained considerable fluency in the theoretical arguments of liberalism and looked with interest at the practical extensions of suffrage. They were quick to convert to universalist liberal doctrine and demand their instant extension to India.

Liberal imperialism also produced a peculiar dynamics through the exchanges between Indian and British authors on the question of political morals. Indian intellectuals quickly realized that the best form of injustice was the injustice administered by liberals. The philosophical anthropology and procedural universalism of liberal doctrines required that political principles of liberty and equality should be declared as universal truths. Liberalism enunciated its principles in an abstract, impersonal, and universal form, but often made ungainly attempts to avoid their realization in practice. This was done in one of two

---

[9] For an excellent general treatment of this particular dilemma of liberal theory, see Mehta 1999. For the ideology of the British empire, see Armitage 2000.

ways—both unwittingly allowing nationalists to develop compelling counterarguments. In some contexts, the 'universal' principles were simply ignored in practice, which made it easy for nationalists to accuse the British of dishonesty, and to embarrass the administration by comparing the stated principles with actual practice. In other contexts, theorists like John Stuart Mill tried to produce a more serious intellectual argument using a stage theory of history, similar to that of the Scottish Enlightenment thinkers.[10] Mill's writings argued that representative institutions were incontrovertibly the best form of government, but incongruously counselled an indefinite postponement of their conferment on Indians. Although liberal institutions were, in the abstract, best for all mankind, they were not suitable for most of human societies until they had attained a required stage of civilization.[11] This ingenious argument saved the abstract universality of liberal ideals, but justified imperial rule for an indefinite future. Not surprisingly, this line of reasoning appeared more persuasive to the British than to the Indians. Yet this particular ideological configuration contributed subtly to the surprisingly amicable nature of the central political conflict in colonial India. The intellectual form of the British arguments subliminally acknowledged that denial of self-government was not right in principle, and could not be continued indefinitely. It also created a subtle sense of defensiveness, if not guilt, in the ideological defence of the empire. Interestingly, in their critique of British imperial rule Indian nationalists could appeal to the same principles. This sharing of principles, admittedly at a very abstract level, contributed to the slow but steady sequence of constitutional shifts, which eventually led to the transfer of power to Indians in 1947.

IV

After 1947, the defining structures of the Indian nation-state were produced by a combination of structural pressures and conjunctural

---

[10] Mill's arguments about India can be found in his *On Liberty*, introduction, especially p. 73, and his *Considerations on Representative Government*, chapters 16 and 17. His detailed comments on Indian government are collected in Mill 1990.

[11] One of the most famous cases of such arguments in J.S. Mill are in *On Liberty*, chapter 1, and *Considerations on Representative Government*, chapters 10 and 12.

openings. The state after Independence had a double and in some ways contradictory inheritance. It was a successor both to the British colonial state and to the movement of Indian nationalism. To combine the two sets of attributes—ideals, institutions, aspirations—that emerged from these contradictory legacies was not an easy task. Broadly, the legal institutions and coercive apparatuses of the state remained similar to the last stage of colonial rule—to the disappointment of those who expected a radical overhaul of the state. During its nationalist agitations, Congress had identified education, the police, and the bureaucracy as the three pillars of colonial domination, and made repeated promises to introduce radical changes in their functioning. In the event, when they assumed power, especially after the panic of Partition, they left these three apparatuses of persuasion and control entirely unreformed. On one point, however, a major transformation took place—though its full effects became apparent only after a certain historical interval. From the early decades of the twentieth century, the British authorities had cautiously introduced partial representative institutions.[12] Despite apprehensions about widespread illiteracy, the new state introduced universal franchise in a single dramatic move of inclusion.[13] The ideological discourse of nationalism had also created vast popular expectations from the state once it was taken over by the Congress, in sharp contrast with the rather limited objectives of the colonial state. Apart from the conventional responsibilities of the state in law and order, it was expected to play an enormous role in the ill-defined and constantly expanding field of 'development'.

The entire story of the state for the half-century after Independence can be seen in terms of two apparently contradictory trends.

[12] Major institutional changes were introduced several times in the first half of the twentieth century. The Montagu-Chelmsford reforms of 1919 began the processes of institutional change; further changes in the structure of government with Indian parties in the provincial legislatures and executives were introduced by the Government of India Act of 1935. The first elective governments took office in 1937. This act formed the main legal template for certain parts of the constitution adopted in 1950.

[13] Austin 1964, chapter 2, section 4, analyses the discussions about universal suffrage. More detailed treatment can be found in Rao 1964. An excellent analysis of the theoretical bases of democratic institutions can be found in Bhargava 2000.

Paradoxically, the Indian political world saw the simultaneous strengthening of two tendencies that can be schematically regarded as the logic of bureaucracy and the logic of democracy. The antecedents of both these trends can be found in the history of colonial rule. Since the middle of the nineteenth century, a process of gradual domination of society by modern state institutions had brought all significant social practices under its surveillance, supervision, and control. The colonial state also began a slow and cautious introduction of practices of representation—so that this increasing control could be seen not as the imposition of external rules of discipline, but the imposition of rules and demands generated by society itself. Both trends became more extensive and powerful after Independence.

Under British rule, the extension of bureaucracy was mainly sanctioned by a rhetoric of state efficiency; under nationalist leadership, this was replaced by the rhetoric of 'development'. For entirely fortuitous reasons, at the time of the state's foundation, Jawaharlal Nehru came to enjoy an extraordinary degree of freedom in shaping its institutions and basic policies. The death of Gandhi and Patel, who had very different ideological inclinations, left conservative sections of the Congress without effective leadership. Unopposed temporarily, Nehru imbued this state with a developmentalist and mildly redistributivist ideology. According to this political vision, the state was seen as the primary instrument of development, with extensive responsibilities in the direct management of production and redistribution.[14] In part, this was because the massive industrialization programme undertaken after Independence could not be financed or managed by private capital; in part, because private capitalist development was expected to worsen income inequality, while state-managed development could simultaneously contribute to redistribution of wealth. Eventually, this led to a massive expansion of the bureaucracy without a corresponding change in its culture. Rapid over-extension of the bureaucracy intensified its inefficiency, reduced observance of procedures, and this produced large zones of corruption and malpractice. By the late 1960s this led

---

[14] Chakrabarty 1987 provides a clear exposition of the economic objectives of the developmental state. Its historical development is analysed concisely but acutely in Bardhan 1985. Two careful, detailed analyses of the state's role in development can be found in Frankel 1978, and Rudolph and Rudolph 1987.

to the familiar paradox of the overextended state. It was expected to supervise all aspects of activity, from managing the army and running the administration to running the railways and the postal system and providing schools and hospitals. Its vast reach and responsibility resulted in a reduction of the reliability of social services. The state in contemporary India became ubiquitous, but also universally unreliable.

However, over the half century of its existence, subtle changes took place in the character of the developmental state itself; since the 1970s, its structures and practices have changed imperceptibly. Initially, during the Nehru years, the developmental state was seen primarily as an engine of production, specially active in the production of essential industrial capacities and in creating infrastructure. But the ideological justification of this constantly expanding state machinery was in terms of arguments of distributive justice. If the state managed heavy industries, the argument went, existing inequalities of income would not increase; and it would also act against the concentration of resources in a few private hands—classical Marxist arguments for socialist politics. In the first two decades after Independence, state institutions with the responsibility of establishing and running heavy industries performed with reasonable efficiency. They helped set up and run a considerable heavy industrial base driven by the current economic theory of self-reliance and import-substituting industrialization. By the early 1970s, a certain change in the character of state enterprises was discernible, and a corresponding change in their relation with political authority. 'The state sector', as it was called in India, came to control vast economic resources—through its gigantic, interconnected networks of financing, employment, and contracts emanating from both the productive and welfare activities of the state enterprises.

Nehru's government accorded to these enterprises a relative decisional and managerial autonomy to ensure technical correctness of decision-making. With the vast increase of their resources, however, political leaders and ministries began from the 1970s to seek more direct control of their operations. The government leadership under Indira Gandhi slowly abandoned the earlier Nehruvian aspiration of giving serious direction to the economy through directive state planning. Instead of being seen as segments of an internally coherent policy of development planning, these enterprises sank into uncontrolled bureaucratization, which increased unproductive activities, pushing them deeper into inefficiency. Anxiety over inefficiency made managements more dependent for their survival on the support of political leaders. The price the political class extracted for this support was indirect access to the use of these resources for political ends—for example, raising funds for the parties in power, or distribution of patronage. The huge economic bureaucracy of the developmental state increasingly had little to do with realistic redistributive objectives, but became utterly dependent on a disingenuous use of that rhetoric. The sizeable economic surplus under the state's control came to be used for illegitimate purposes by elected politicians who developed a vested interest in defending this large, overstretched, inefficient state.[15] From 1991, successive Indian governments have rather reluctantly begun some restructuring of the state under the general slogan of 'liberalization' of the economy. But compared to the swift and large-scale structural reforms carried out in other parts of Asia and Africa, liberalization in India has been remarkably slow. The logic of bureaucracy still pervades and dominates Indian political life.

The second undeniable historical feature of Indian political life has been the irresistible expansion of democracy. But the lines of its movement were at times surprisingly different from the history of European democracy in the nineteenth century. First, unlike the gradual, incremental development of the suffrage in most European states, democracy was introduced to India in a single, dramatic gesture of political inclusion. Although the colonial administration had slowly introduced representative institutions from the early twentieth century, the electorate at the last election under colonial administration was about 14 per cent of the adult population. The constitution adopted in 1950 installed universal adult suffrage in a country that was still 70 per cent illiterate. The new entrants into the arena of politics thus instantly outnumbered social elites already entrenched in representative institutions. This was likely to result in a conflict over representation, with entrant groups contesting the claim of elite politicians to 'represent' the entire nation—an eventuality that did happen, but after a considerable lapse of time. The probable reason for this comparatively placid introduction of an electoral revolution was that poor people

---

[15] For a serious attack on the basic principles of the developmental state, and an argument that it has slowed down economic growth, see Bhagwati 1993.

showed traditional habits of deference towards socially dominant groups. Similarly, it also took time for lower classes in a caste society, used to social repression, to understand the historic possibilities of the strategic use of the right to vote. For about two decades, although the poor and the disprivileged in Indian society had the formal right to vote, they actually left the arena of institutional politics entirely in the hands of the modernist elites. Paradoxically, the institutions of democratic government seemed to function with impeccably formal propriety precisely because levels of participation were low, and popular expectations from democratic government were limited. The usual problems of electoral politics—resource allocation on the basis of electoral pressure, which makes rational long-term decisions particularly difficult—did not affect Indian democratic government in the Nehru years.[16]

By the 1970s, however, the situation had changed significantly in two ways. Politicians of all parties had lost the inexhaustible fund of legitimacy that Nehru's generation had from their leadership in the national movement. The new generation of leaders, including Congress leaders like Indira Gandhi, had to acquire support in the short term by electoral promises of resource distribution. It was also clear that ordinary voters, especially the urban poor and the lower castes in the countryside, had learnt strategic use of the vote. They made greater demands on the political system, and politicians from these underprivileged groups began to emerge first in state assemblies, and later in parliament and national government. This somewhat delayed but decisive entry of the common people into the life of the state utterly transformed its character. Politics came to be practised increasingly in the vernacular—in two senses. Literally, much of political discourse was carried on in the vernacular, in contrast to the first decades when English was the mandatory language of high politics. But more significantly, after the 1970s, the political imagination of major social groups came to be shaped by a kind of conceptual vernacular as well, used by politicians who did not have the conventional education through the medium of English and whose political thinking was not determined by their knowledge of European historical precedents.

---

[16] The dialectic between government's ability to take long-term decisions and the insistence of electoral pressure is discussed in extensive detail in Rudolph and Rudolph 1987.

Nationalist leaders who had devised the constitution had expected democracy eventually to have wider social effects; but their expectations followed the familiar trajectories of European democracy. The introduction of modern democracy in Europe made the stark class inequalities of nineteenth-century capitalist society increasingly unsustainable. Radical leaders like Nehru had accordingly anticipated that, as ordinary Indians acquired a democratic consciousness, they would cease to identify themselves through traditional caste categories and demand greater economic equality. Democratic institutions would thus lead, in the long term, to modernist movements for the reduction of poverty. But what happened through half a century of democratic politics defied and confounded such expectations.[17] Democracy certainly led to vast revolutionary effects in the Indian context as well—but that historic change resembled Tocqueville's 'revolution' more than Marx's.[18] Democratic polities produced a fundamental transformation of Indian society—but not in terms of class. By contrast with Europe, the logic of democracy did not force changes of policy encouraging greater equality of income, but led to a real redistribution of dignity. The deep European influence on India's intellectuals made them subtly predisposed, irrespective of ideology, to underestimate the social presence of caste, and to underestimate the adaptive fecundity of traditions. Both liberals and socialists, who dominated the discourse of India's political world in the decades after Independence, expected that traditional forms of belonging and behaviour would disappear under the twin pressure of the economic logic of industrialization and the political logic of electoral democracy. Historically, the actual unfolding of modernity has proved enormously more complex.

The most comprehensive defining principle of India's social life before the coming of modern influences was undeniably the caste order. That order determined the individual's life chances, and its structural principles governed the relation between the collective bodies of castes in the social system. In all parts of India, despite regional variations, the expansion of economic modernity—urbanization and industrial

[17] I have sought to analyse this surprising turn in caste politics in 'Democracy and Social Inequality' in Frankel 2000.

[18] In fact, one of the major weaknesses of Indian Marxist writing about politics has been its reluctance to take the democratic upsurge seriously as a process of real, not illusory, social change.

development—led to a decline of caste observances in daily life. Hindu rules forbidding intermixture in marriage, social intercourse, and commensality lost their former ability to constrain individual behaviour and private lives. Ironically, in the public arenas of political life, by contrast, caste identities seem to have become much more assertive, defying modernist expectations. Caste affiliations have not broken down or faded in political life under the impact of electoral politics; the order of caste life has simply adapted to the operation of parliamentary democracy to produce highly effective large caste-based electoral coalitions.[19] Paradoxically, the historical demand of this form of caste politics is not the end of caste identity, but a democratic recognition of equality among self-recognizing caste groups—a state of affairs unthinkable according to the traditional grammar of caste behaviour.

The new caste politics therefore defies characterization in terms of the easy dichotomy of modernization theory.[20] It is not a wholly modern practice, since it is based on caste; equally, it is not wholly traditional, as it puts caste to an unprecedented modern use. An anomalous accompaniment of this development is the peculiar translation of the language of rights in contemporary Indian culture. In Indian society, despite the pressures of modernity, the process of sociological individuation has not gone very far. Consequently, although the universe of political discourse is ringing with unceasing demands for recognition of rights, rarely have these advocated the rights of atomistic liberal individuals. In a world made of very different principles of sociability—marked by the primacy of castes, regions, and communities—the strident new language of rights has sought to establish primarily the rights of contending groups. Most major radical demands in Indian politics are now for group equality rather than income equality between individuals—leading to a strange fading, from the discourse of one of the poorest societies of the world, of the distinctive arguments of socialism.

---

[19] M.N. Srinivas, the eminent Indian sociologist, who did pioneering work on the operation of caste practices in modern conditions, called these new configurations 'monster castes' to indicate that they are vast coalitions in size, but also that they defy the traditional segmentary logic of the caste system. Srinivas 1986.

[20] Scholars have pointed out these trends and their theoretically unsettling implications since the late 1960s. Cf. Rudolph and Rudolph 1968, and Kothari 1970.

The largest numbers of the Indian poor themselves seem to be more intent on removing degradation rather than poverty.[21]

It is not surprising that elite groups, who have most to lose from the assertion of demands of lower castes, have given large-scale support to a historical countermove made through the reassertion of religious identity. Hindu nationalist parties were relatively unsuccessful electorally in the period of Congress's hegemony. The Jana Sangh, the party of Hindu nationalism, had stable support among some social groups in particular regions of northern India, but it never came near threatening Congress dominance.[22] But in a climate of intensifying lower-caste assertion, their insinuation against the muddled secularism of the Congress—that it discriminated against the Hindus in return for secure voting support from the Muslim minority—attracted substantial upper-caste backing. Assisted by an inflammatory rhetoric of restitutive justice, centred on an old mosque allegedly built on a destroyed temple in the sixteenth century, the Hindu nationalist Bharatiya Janata Party (BJP), the successor to the Jana Sangh, made dramatic electoral gains in the elections in the 1990s. It finally emerged as the largest single party in parliament and has ruled India for five years with the support of volatile coalitions.[23] What is remarkable is that the BJP sought to fashion a response to the politics of lower-caste groups by appealing to the emotions of another form of community. Communitarianism in Indian politics takes complex and at times extremely unpleasant forms.[24]

---

[21] Communist parties in India had been traditionally reluctant to take up the cause of caste indignity as a central issue, preferring to focus on poverty and economic inequality. In the last decades, they have sought to adapt their agenda to the politics of the lower castes.

[22] For an excellent analysis of Hindu nationalist politics till the late 1960s, see Graham 1990.

[23] The fact that the BJP has come to power only as part of a coalition is highly significant: since some of its coalition partners do not share its strong anti-Muslim programme, it has imposed some moderation on its administration.

[24] There are several excellent studies of the recent growth of Hindu nationalism. See especially Jaffrelot 1994 for a detailed history. Hansen 1990 links the Hindu upsurge with a Tocquevillien understanding of democratization. Rajagopal 2000 analyses the associations between creating collective emotions and the use of semiotics and the media.

But democracy is a complex ideal which appeals equally to two types of political principles. On the one hand, it claims its legitimacy from the pursuit of conflict through established, transparent procedures, which ensure that no groups lose out finally and irreversibly, and so that they continue to follow their objectives through recursive electoral contests. On the other hand, it appeals to the principles of participation in both the deliberative and expressive forms. The politics of community assertion in India has created a potential conflict between these two principles. Political parties representing large communities with a strong sense of grievance have often regarded the procedures of liberal government as unjustified obstacles in their pursuit of justice. Procedures, which are central to the successful operation of democracy, can, as Indian experience shows, be threatened by some forms of participatory politics.

Another peculiarity of the story of modern politics in India is the simultaneous power of democracy and bureaucracy. Although theoretically, bureaucracy and democracy seem opposing tendencies—as the increased power and reach of the state seems to conflict, in principle, with democratic demands against it—this apparent paradox is not difficult to resolve. Democratic participation has increased ordinary people's expectations about the conditions and quality of life. In a society which does not generate enough wealth to enable interest groups in society to pursue their institutional aims with their own resources, all demands for amelioration—for hospitals, schools, roads—are directed at the state, which is the only possible source for the creation of collective goods. Thus the rise of democracy has reinforced the tendency towards a constant extension of the bureaucratic state.

For an understanding of how Europe affected the history of other cultures over the long term, the Indian story is significant for two reasons. A common pessimistic argument asserts that the 'export' of the state, with bounded territories and modern institutions of governance, to other parts of the world through European colonialism has largely failed, ending in most cases in disaster. It has forced people to live their lives, unsuccessfully, under unintelligible institutional frames, leading to increased tension and expanded capacities for violence. Eventually, the argument runs, such historical experiments have failed, leading in most cases to the common experience of state collapse. The Indian case encourages a more optimistic conclusion.[25] It shows that a country comprising nearly a fifth of the world's population has successfully mastered the techniques of establishing a modern state. Despite the complex demands on its ideological and material resources, India has not seen a collapse of its institutional structure leading to breakdown of minimal social order. Interestingly, although its state has been overstretched, it has managed to avoid bankruptcy and failure to provide basic services. India has avoided both the economic and the political forms of 'state collapse'.

Perhaps the most astonishing part of the Indian story has been the relative success of democracy. There are some familiar arguments in political theory which stress the economic or cultural 'conditions' for the success of democratic government. Either a certain level of prior economic growth, or an underlying cultural common sense which accords equal value to individuals, has been regarded as a necessary condition for the success of democratic institutions. The relative success of Indian democracy defies both arguments. In the politics of one of the poorest countries of the world, with a traditional order based on the pure principle of hierarchy, democracy has for half a century been a universally uncontested ideal. But the 'success of democracy' in India can mean two different things. In much of Western journalism, and in a part of academic analysis as well, the success of democracy simply means the uninterrupted continuance of electoral politics. Actually, however, the 'success' of Indian democracy ought to be viewed in Tocqueville's terms—as the historical development of a social force that has transformed fundamental social relations of everyday lives. It is true that the historical outcomes, the political trajectories of this story of democracy, have been quite different from the great European stories of democratic transformation. But that is hardly surprising. Formal institutions of democracy operate on the basis of a template of

---

[25] In comparisons of this kind, size matters. The pessimistic argument that states have failed in hundreds of cases should be weighed carefully against the fact that India, although representing a single state, accounts for a very large proportion of the non-Western world. Although one state, it is a powerful counterargument to the claim that modern states have failed outside the field of modern Western culture.

the specific sociabilities available in each society. If democracy achieves success in other non-European societies in future, their trajectories are more likely to resemble the Indian narrative than the European ones. It is impossible to predict the exact direction that this narrative of political transformation of a hierarchical society might take; but, despite the fact that it has happened in relative historical silence, without the spectacular violence that accompanied the American or French revolutions, it will rank as a story of one of the great transformations of modern times.

References

Al Biruni. 1914. *Al Biruni's India*. Transl. and ed. E.C. Sachau. London: Routledge and Kegan Paul.

Appadurai, A. 1966. Number in the Colonial Imagination. In *Orientalism and the Post-colonial Predicament*. Philadelphia: Pennsylvania University Press.

Armitage, D. 2000. *The Ideological Origins of the British Empire*. Cambridge: Cambridge University Press.

Austin, G. 1964. *The Indian Constitution: Cornerstone of a Nation*. Oxford: Clarendon Press.

Bardhan, P. 1985. *The Political Economy of Development in India*. Delhi: Oxford University Press.

Bayly, C.A. 1989. *Indian Society and the Making of the British Empire*. Cambridge: Cambridge University Press.

———. 1996. *Empire and Information*. Cambridge: Cambridge University Press.

Bhagwati, J. 1939. *India in Transition*. Oxford: Clarendon Press.

Bhargava, R. 2000. Democratic Vision of a New Republic: India 1950. In Francine Frankel *et al.* Eds. *Transforming India: Social and Political Dynamics of Democracy*. Delhi: Oxford University Press.

Burke, E. 1998. On the Impeachment of Warren Hastings, 15–19 February 1788. In B. Harlow and M. Carter. Eds. *Imperialism and Orientalism*. Oxford: Blackwell.

Chakrabarty, S. 1987. *Development Planning: The Indian Experience*. Oxford: Clarendon Press.

Dirks, N. 1986. *The Hollow Crown*. Ann Arbor: University of Michigan Press.

Frankel, F. 1978. *India's Political Economy*. Princeton: Princeton University Press.

Graham, B. 1990. *Hindu Nationalism and Indian Politics*. Cambridge: Cambridge University Press.

Guizot, F. 1997. *The History of Civilisation in Europe.* Transl. and ed. L. Seidentop. Harmondsworth: Penguin.
Hansen, T. 1999. *The Saffron Wave.* Princeton: Princeton University Press.
Irschik, D. 1994. *Dialogue and History.* Berkeley: University of California Press.
Jaffrelot, C. 1994. *The Hindu Nationalist Movement and Indian Politics.* New York: Columbia University Press.
Kaviraj, S. 1994. The Imaginary Institution of India. In G. Pandey and P. Chatterjee. Eds. *Subaltern Studies VII.* Delhi: Oxford University Press.
———. 2000a. Democracy and Social Inequality. In F. Frankel. Ed. *Transforming India.* Delhi: Oxford University Press.
———. 2000b. Modernity and Politics in India. *Daedalus.* Winter.
Kothari, R. Ed. 1970. *Caste in Indian Politics.* Delhi: Orient Longman.
Mani, L. 1998. *Contentious Traditions: The Debate on Sati in Colonial India.* Berkeley: University of California Press.
Mehta, U.S. 1999. *Liberalism and Empire: A Study in Nineteenth-century British Liberal Thought.* Chicago: University of Chicago Press.
Mill, J.S. 1962. *Utilitarianism, Liberty, Representative Government.* Ed. A.D. Lindsay. London: J.M. Dent.
———. 1990. *Writings on India. Collected Works of J.S. Mill,* vol. XXX. Ed. J.M. Robson, M. Moir, and Z. Moir. London: Routledge.
Rajagopal, A. 2000. *Politics After Television.* Cambridge: Cambridge University Press.
Rao, B. Shiva. Ed. 1964. *The Making of the Indian Constitution.* 4 vols. Delhi: Indian Institute of Public Administration.
Rudolph, L. and Rudolph, S.H. 1968. *The Modernity of Tradition.* Chicago: University of Chicago Press.
———. 1987. *In Pursuit of Lakshmi.* Chicago: University of Chicago Press.
Srinivas, M.N. 1986. Caste in Modern India. In idem. *Caste in Modern India and Other Essays.* Delhi: Oxford University Press.
Stein, B. 1985. State Formation Revisited. *Modern Asian Studies,* vol. 19, no. 3, December.
Stokes, E. 1959. *The English Utilitarians and India.* London: Oxford University Press.
Subrahmanyam, S. 1990. *Merchants, Markets and the State in Early Modern India.* Delhi: Oxford University Press.
Washbrook, D.A. 1988. Progress and Problems: South Asian Economic and Social History, 1720–1860. *Modern Asian Studies,* vol. 21, no. 4.
———. 1999. India, 1818–1860. In A. Porter. Ed. *Oxford History of the British Empire: The Nineteenth Century.* Oxford: Oxford University Press.

7

Government and Opposition: Fifty Years of Indian Independence

The General Elections in India

At the time of Independence Mahatma Gandhi suggested that the Indian National Congress, which he had successfully led till then, should be disbanded. As its function had been to produce a coalition towards achieving independence from British rule, its historical role was over. This was an entirely logical yet an entirely unpractical suggestion. Politicians active inside the Congress wished, not unnaturally, to turn their sacrifices into potential investments in an independent state. Independence was accompanied by Partition which degenerated into riots and massacre of civilians. There was no other political organization except the Congress to establish effective government. In any case, Congress was too successful a political organization to be dissolved purely by the power of argument. The Congress, therefore, turned from an independence movement into a governing party, a difficult transformation under all circumstances, and flourished. The historical significance of the eleventh general elections in India after Independence represents the actual realization of Gandhi's suggestion. India must now find a political structure which can function without the overwhelming presence of the Congress, a party universally reviled but, ironically, treated as indispensable.

The Long-term Context

What happened in these elections must be seen thus in the context of the place Congress has occupied in Indian democratic politics, both

First published in *Government and Opposition*, vol. 32, no. 1, Winter 1997, pp. 3–24.

in the long and the short term. After Independence Congress went through three phases of political evolution. In the first twenty years, under Jawaharlal Nehru, it enjoyed a secure if unspectacular dominance in Indian politics. Nehru's three election victories were never, considering his stature, of the utterly spectacular kind that Indira Gandhi achieved later. Congress never won a majority of votes.[1] Yet due to the system of winning by pluralities, it always won quite comfortably, both at the centre and in nearly all the states. Its electoral dominance in the political system was so overwhelming that opposition parties were forced to seek influence by forming coalitions with groups inside the Congress sharing their ideological or economic predilections.[2] Congress victories across the spectrum were an important element in India's democratic governance in the Nehru era. Nehru recognized the irreducibility of India's regional and social diversity and, in line with earlier Congress tradition, considered it proper that the political structure should allow this to be expressed rather than smothered. Accordingly, although in many respects India established a typical nation-state, its constitution sanctioned a distinctive two-tier nationalism which encouraged its citizens to be both Tamils/Bengalis/Gujaratis and Indians. Indeed, it was believed that there was no way of being an Indian pure and simple, without going through one of these identities.

Generally, Nehru's practical politics showed his belief that if state governments were strong, and handled state political problems with effectiveness, the result was a strong centre. The central government would then be relatively untroubled by regional political issues about which it knew less than the state politicians. This avoided a tendency towards centralization, although formally India appeared to be under the uncontested control of a single unassailable political party. The Congress Party was indispensable precisely because, due to its dominance, major issues of regional conflicts and their settlement were handled and solved inside the Congress. Congress, it was sometimes

---

[1] Congress's share of the vote has declined steadily from around 47.8 per cent at its peak in 1957 to 37.6 per cent in 1991, barring an unusual 48.1 per cent in 1984 after Indira Gandhi's death.

[2] This was famously called, after Rajni Kothari, the 'one-party dominant' Congress system.

argued, ruled India well precisely because it was internally diverse, like India. A better way of putting it would be to recognize that there was a duality in the nature of the Congress system: it was, at one level, rule by a single political party; but, in fact, inside, it was a coalition. Plural interests could seek and receive attention within it precisely because of its ideologically heterogeneous character; yet, the fact that these negotiations took place inside the institutional boundaries of a single party meant that the conflict of interests rarely exploded into overt political violence, or that the bitterness and disappointments they generated went out of control. Congress, because of its sociological diversity and the coalitional nature of its internal politics, developed a culture of negotiation and non-extremism. When interests were represented to its bodies, these were usually recognized, and promises made to further them; but this was rarely done with the decisiveness or total commitment characteristic of parties that were composed of single or more homogeneous interests. Congress thus followed characteristically moderate, unradical policies which irritated opinion at the two ends of the political spectrum, but left the bulk in the middle in a state of moderate contentment. From the early decades of the century it developed strong ties with the business community, yet it also expressed mild propensities towards reform and at least a formal obligation for distributive justice. It always sought support from the peasantry and working-class groups, promised them redistributive policies, yet never at the expense of expropriation of the propertied classes. Thus these social groups could provide Congress with support mixed always with a minor dissatisfaction at its lukewarmness about what they considered the evident justice of their sectional interest.

Indira Gandhi, when she entrenched herself in power after splitting the party in 1969, altered some of the basic features of this system of coalitional and negotiated democracy inside the Congress Party. Soon after she came to power, Congress fared badly in the fourth general elections in 1967, losing control over a large number of North Indian states. But she brought Congress back to power dramatically in 1971, with an unprecedented two-thirds majority in the central parliament.[3] This historical instance is of some significance, as it shows Congress's

---

[3] Interestingly, the difference in vote share was not very large, from 40.8 per cent in 1967 to 43.7 per cent in 1971.

peculiar ability to come back to power from seemingly hopeless situations, a feat she repeated in 1980.[4] However, the manner in which this victory was achieved, which installed Indira Gandhi in a position of unchallenged supremacy in Indian politics, altered the character of Indian democratic politics. She froze and stifled internal democracy inside Congress. Elections were never held for the state levels of the Congress organization; leaders were nominated from the centre. She appeared to think, since the initial challenge to her power had come from powerful state bosses inside the party, that the relation between state and central governments must always be a zero-sum game, irrespective of whether the state government was run by her own party or the opposition. In the more intense electoral contests during the 1970s and early 1980s, she often used an appeal to the sense of vulnerability of minorities wherever possible—Hindus in the states of Jammu and Kashmir and Punjab, Muslims who constituted a large and highly sensitive minority in Uttar Pradesh.

This strategy subtly but fatally altered the Congress claim to secularism. From a party under Nehru which would never use communal appeals for electoral advantage, it turned into one which used such appeals to all communities. Since it received support from *all* communities, it could hardly be called the party of anyone. But its electoral appeals and subsequent policies invited voters to look upon themselves in terms of their religious identities. This was obviously a dangerous game. The Congress, because of its historical legacies and internal character, could only use such appeals up to a point; others could use this in more extreme forms. That precisely happened in the states of Jammu and Kashmir, Punjab, and Uttar Pradesh in varying ways in the last decade.

The Congress Party did not lose its internal complexity and suppleness entirely under Indira Gandhi, but its internal hardening, decline in democracy, and increasingly divisive uses of electoral politics gave rise to widespread resentment in different regions. Indira Gandhi believed that the single solution to India's problems was centralization of power—inside the Congress, in its central leadership, ultimately in her own personal coterie. In parallel, in the federal system, power was

---

[4] In the elections held after the Emergency in 1977, Congress's vote share fell dramatically to 34.3 per cent.

to be concentrated in the centre. Yet, this seemed to run up against a historical trend in Indian democracy. One long-term effect of democratic mobilization was the entry and increased assertion of lower social groups in electoral politics. Since their cognitive horizons, the context in terms of which they thought about their own place in politics and their own interests, were limited and local, this led to a powerful surge for regional parties from the 1970s. Mrs Gandhi misread this development completely and sought to counter it with more frenetic centralization. In the 1970s and 1980s, the political system began to face new and more intransigent challenges from regional movements in Punjab, Assam, and later Kashmir. As she ran out of negotiative options in these political confrontations, the policy of centralization, when driven to desperation, always degenerated into the use of armed force. By the time Indira Gandhi was assassinated, the traditional Nehruvian Congress system—based on accommodation, negotiation, compromise—was in irreversible crisis.

The Short-term Context

The short rule of Rajiv Gandhi did nothing to reverse the trends of conflict. In some ways, his combination of inexperience and managerial arrogance, his 'modernist' contempt for the unpicturesque fixers of the old Congress system, helped exacerbate the crisis. His modernist rhetoric did not stop his administration from negotiating deals which aroused suspicion of large-scale bribery and corruption, and the systematic obstruction to legal inquiries did not dispel these doubts. Rajiv Gandhi also continued his mother's strategy of balancing one illegitimate concession to a sectarian demand by conceding another equally illegitimate. His concession to the most reactionary elements in the Muslim community in the Shah Bano case was 'balanced' in his short-sighted view by a concession to Hindu fundamentalists in the crisis over the Babri Masjid at Ayodhya. In the last phase, after the inconclusive general elections of 1991, India was ruled increasingly insecurely by a minority Congress government, under Narasimha Rao, which survived on support from some opposition parties.

However, there were some surprising features about the recently voted-out government of Narasimha Rao. Newspaper reports express admiration about his undying instinct for political survival. He came from a section of the Congress leadership which was put in the shade by the dynastic rule of Mrs Gandhi and Rajiv. As a result, some believed, when Rao came to power, that he might try to revive the earlier Nehruvian rules of party functioning and restore comparative rectitude in financial matters. These expectations were most rudely dispelled. Congress was riven by internal factionalism after Rajiv Gandhi's death, and a continuing devotion to the principles of dynastic rule by an elite which saw itself as modernist. Indeed, their simultaneous devotion to techniques of modern management and medieval monarchy is one of the great unsolved puzzles of modern Indian politics. Since Rao always felt threatened by powerful internal factions inside the Congress, his early enthusiasm for principles of open government and party democracy soon declined. Internal democratic elections within the Congress Party could provide entrenched and legitimized positions to some of his rivals. Corruption charges mounted and came too close for comfort, with Rao and his son implicated in some of the largest financial scams. There was considerable scepticism at first that his government would last its full term. In the event, he carried on successfully for an entire term of parliament with a minority government, which secured support from a few odd MPs by questionable means.

Yet there were two great achievements during the Rao regime. First, Rao's government ruled the country through a period in which the Hindu supremacist BJP (Bharatiya Janata Party) gained increasing influence through its stridently divisive campaigns. The BJP's predecessor, the Jana Sangh, had suffered electoral stagnation for a long time in the 1960s. Government attacks on its organization during the Emergency were sufficiently potent for it to join a coalition of forces in 1977 against Indira Gandhi. Even when it came out of the crumbling Janata coalition, it seemed inclined to revise its earlier image of Hindu extremism in favour of a centrist platform. But from the mid-1980s the BJP began a startling new campaign of Hindu extremism, using the central symbol of the Babri mosque. The new campaign was surprisingly successful, gathering support apparently from both urban-educated young Hindu voters and the rural population across North India. However, it was the success of the BJP which, paradoxically, ensured the survival of Rao's government.

The BJP campaign divided the country more deeply than ever before along a line of conflict between Hindu communalists and secular parties. Relatively leftist opposition parties, including the communists, were strongly opposed to the Rao government; but they were even more apprehensive of a BJP takeover. Between the two evils, they preferred Rao, and his government survived with the parliamentary support of parties who heartily detested him and the policies the Congress was implementing under his leadership. But like Rajiv Gandhi before him, Rao too showed signs of a strategy which would try to appease the creeping force of Hindu sentiment rather than fight it directly. At the time of the destruction of the Babri mosque by fundamentalist volunteers, the forces of the state were suspiciously absent; and after the demolition Rao showed even more peculiar indecision about the symbolic restoration of the structure. He was scrupulously ambiguous about whether a mosque or a temple would be built at the site of the Babri Masjid. It could thus be legitimately said that he acquiesced in the great symbolic humiliation of the Muslim community, probably with an eye on the Hindu vote.

Rao's regime accomplished something more striking. The Congress government under his leadership introduced some of the most radical economic measures in the history of independent India. Some unsure and faltering measures towards liberalizing the Indian economy had been taken under Indira and Rajiv Gandhi, somewhat more energetically under the latter, for he fancied himself as a technical-managerial leader who was at home in the advanced ideas of modern management. But despite his vast parliamentary majority Rajiv Gandhi's moves in this direction were indecisive and inconsistent. Astonishingly, Rao astutely turned his own parliamentary insecurity into an advantage. With a government which did not command a majority, Rao pushed through liberalizing reforms of an astonishingly radical nature—considering the historical evolution of India's political economy. He was in effect daring opposition parties to topple his administration. They could not do that for two separate reasons which became conjuncturally linked. Politically, they could not overturn his government for fear of putting power in the hands of the BJP. Economically, they feared that any other government, given the structural constraints of India's economy and its current crisis, would be forced to follow substantially similar policies. It was thus better from their point of view to allow the Congress to carry out these policies and make rhetorical noises in the opposition without offering any serious obstruction. The communists, who were the most likely opponents of liberalization, were obliged to introduce similar policies in their own captive state of West Bengal.

Rao's administration was noteworthy for one related feature. There was considerable instability in his cabinets, and large numbers of Congress leaders gained and lost cabinet posts. But Rao was remarkable in providing entirely steadfast support to his finance minister, Manmohan Singh, a former academic and bureaucrat and a complete outsider to the Congress Party machine. Precisely because Singh did not depend on support from any social group, or a particular constituency inside the Congress Party, he could force liberalizing policies through with a rare consistency and single-mindedness. This in part explains the great puzzle of the Rao phase in Indian politics: how could the weakest government in history carry out some of the most radically unpopular measures within the economy?

Election Issues

Consequently, two issues dominated the eleventh general elections. First, there was the proposal for unprecedented religious polarization of Indian politics coming from the Hindu communal forces. These included not only the BJP, but also some of its supporting organizations, such as the Vishwa Hindu Parishad (VHP), and its militant youth wing the Bajrang Dal—which played a key role in the actual demolition of the Babri mosque, and over which BJP politicians had rather inadequate control. Second, there was the fate, the pace, and the management of the liberalization programme. Psephology and market research have become increasingly sophisticated in recent years, and there is in addition to official electoral statistics a considerable wealth of material about voter intentions, exit polls, and general analysis of elections.

These elections were historically crucial in more than one way. The slow but steady decline of the electoral fortunes of the Congress since Rajiv Gandhi's time indicated that Indian politics was going through a period of transition, an interregnum between solid Congress rule and something to follow whose outlines were not yet quite clear. At this particular election, two crucial issues were raised for settlement by the electoral verdict: what should be the constitution of the Indian state, and what should be the fundamental structure of the Indian economy?

Should the design adopted in the Nehru era be revised, and in which direction? But as some of the shrewder observers realized, there was also another change.[5] Greater interest by the ordinary voter meant that local and state issues often intruded into the electoral struggle and complicated the nature of the questions the electorate thought they were voting about. Although elections to state assemblies were not being held at the same time, there was an obvious infusion of state issues and concerns in the voting. So, in a sense, it was two elections in one. At one level, the electorate was responding to the larger issues of the politico-economic constitution of modern India; at another, they were also responding to other, less general, less fundamental, but more immediate problems of social life. In most of North India, the central and local issues tended to coincide. The central problem was the relation between the two projected mobilizations: the BJP slogan to vote on the basis of *religion,* seeking to produce an unconquerable Hindu majority, and the anti-BJP slogan of voting in terms of the basic *caste* divisions within Hindu society, which isolates high-caste Hindus and produces a majority coalition of the middle and lower castes with the Muslim minority. Other regional contests also got interwoven with national issues. In West Bengal, for example, the election was an opportunity for interests discontented with uninterrupted Communist Party of India (Marxist)—CPI(M)—rule for twenty years to try out the option of either the Congress or the BJP. In Tamil Nadu, it similarly afforded an opportunity to a resentful electorate to show their hostility to the discredited film-star politician Jayalalitha. Through fifty years of capitalist economic integration, India has become a single unit for some significant purposes, e.g. economic policies. The same fifty years of federal democracy have also made India, equally effectively, a collection of discrete political and social regions, with their specific, diverse interests, imaginations, and conflicts. There is much avoidable disputation in academic literature about which of these pictures is true. This is the wrong way of asking the question. For, in fact, both are true; and the Indian political universe is complex and layered. The electorate's way of asserting this fact was to turn this election into a dual process of decision-making.

[5] For instance, Yogendra Yadav in his reports on the CSDS–ICSSR–India Today Surveys, reported in *India Today,* 31 May and 11 August 1996.

The Three Political Fronts

Before the elections, it was clear that there were four corners to the electoral contest: the Congress bloc, the bloc around the BJP, the combination of leftist and reformist parties (their combination was called the National Front), and mainly regional political groups with limited local objectives but often with intense support. The eventual results were not entirely surprising, though the major departure from earlier periods was the utter inability of the Congress to regroup and win back the support it had lost. Its inability to recover support was on account of several reasons. First, the Congress gradually disintegrated into factions. In sharp contrast to earlier splits, this time the faction in power did not offer the credible hope of winning office to attract ambitious politicians back into its fold. Congress had gone through a number of splits before without substantial damage. Although initially these splits had appeared ideological and irreparable, Congress politicians had fought for political advantage, not for high principles. Once the split went through and a clear winner emerged, followers of the losing faction had usually scuttled ship and been taken back into the party with easy generosity. The party had thus avoided the debilitating effects of real splits. On this occasion, however, no faction won convincingly. While Rao's group effectively controlled the resources of the government, others used the dynastic name of Indira Gandhi's family, and the considerable resources allegedly in its hands, to counteract Rao's moves. Congress remained organizationally deeply divided until the time of elections, as Rao formally expelled from the party intransigent leaders from dissenting factions who challenged his leadership.

Congress also lost support because of its policies. Although Rao made astute use of his vulnerability and turned it into a virtual advantage, in the nature of things this could last only for a short period, only as long as the peculiar circumstances continued. Liberalizing reforms in India were slow and circumspect in comparison to other countries; but they were, in the Indian context, quite radical. As the effects of liberalizing the economy started to bite, the discontent of social groups who suffered went against the Congress. Rao's indecision, or for some his deliberate inaction in the face of Hindu communal provocations, particularly the demolition of the Babri mosque, cost him dearly. Secular supporters of Congress among the Hindus, and the entire Muslim community, now saw Rao as unreliable, willing to barter away secularism for electoral gains. If his indecision was calculated to appeal to communal Hindus, it backfired. They had a much more reliable instrument of communal politics in the BJP, and found him unreliable for the opposite reasons. It appears that Rao's initial invocation of principles of rectitude injured his image deeply in the end. Evidently, this struck a chord in an electorate resentful of the increasing corruption and illicit wealth of the political class. Foreign agencies which supported and demanded the liberalization policies also emphasized the need to reduce corruption. Most interestingly, in a climate of the diminishing stature of and support for politicians, some supervisory institutions, particularly the Election Commission headed by T.N. Seshan (a man many saw as a maverick, deeply narcissist, and self-righteous bureaucrat), as well as some courts, began to show an oddly unexpected assertiveness. They laid down rules, which was not new, and threatened to implement them to the letter, which was. Politicians unused to such a strange climate—in which laws were suddenly meant not merely to be promulgated but also observed—fell easy and frequent victims to this flanking attack from a wholly unexpected adversary. Rao is suspected of having instigated court cases against most of his troublesome cabinet colleagues on charges of corruption; but unexpectedly, the long arm of the courts started coming uncomfortably close to his own person. His initial noises about corruption therefore tended to show him in a particularly unfavourable light.

The BJP always benefited from an impression it gave out of decisiveness and organization, though this was perhaps misplaced, or exaggerated to some degree. Certainly, compared to the Congress, the BJP was more united, particularly because it had the luxury of running practically no government policy except the gratuitously offensive idea of righting wrongs concerning mosques built in early medieval times. The Indian electorate needed some other, more contemporary problems, something other than disputes allegedly remaining unsettled from the eleventh century. However, there were great advantages in the BJP's invitation to amnesia; it kept controversies away from existing disputes and avoided alienating social groups who might have had potential conflicts of interest. The BJP had also managed without an economic policy for about forty years; now it showed signs of taking a nationalist stance against Congress's liberalizing reforms, trying to take over from Congress its now unused slogans about fighting to protect the country from foreign economic domination. Still, the unity of the BJP appeared an illusion. Immediately before it found unexpected success over the temple issues, it had slowly, out of frustration, steered towards a more centrist, less communal line. Politicians who supported that shift still form a sizeable section inside the party; and they prove peculiarly useful to the BJP when, occasionally, it has to deny charges of being a semi-fascist Hindu fundamentalist force. At such times, the BJP relies on these token figures and promotes a display of their moderation. More significantly, the BJP has also consistently followed a complex electoral strategy, seeking to influence one type of voter by an increasingly strident anti-Muslim strategy, and to another kind speaking a language of civility and urbane restraint, deploring the Congress's slide into corruption and incoherence. The Hindu communal side is also divided between two segments whose approach to politics is somewhat different. One group, mainly active in the BJP political party, looks at the anti-Muslim rhetoric instrumentally, as a vote-gathering technique. This group probably deplores the actual demolition of the mosque: a standing mosque was a potent vote-gathering issue, a demolished one is an ideological liability. But a more fanatical, religious group, based in the VHP, seriously wants to restart the unfinished 'religious' wars of medieval times. Their slogan, meant quite literally, is to destroy about two hundred mosques built, in their view, on destroyed Hindu temples by victorious Islamic rulers—a claim historians have treated with contempt. The political elements in the BJP must look at this extremist agenda with some discomfort, as this would completely disrupt the social fabric of everyday life in India. But these are potential rather than actual differences, and, compared to the Congress, the BJP obviously went into the elections in much better order. At least, in the short run, it benefited from the support of the Shiv Sena in Bombay which ruled the city and the state of Maharashtra through a mixture of populism and organized quasi-criminal violence.

Although in the 1960s it seemed that the only credible opposition to Nehru's Congress was the communist left, the scene has changed unrecognizably. Communists were fatally weakened by their internal squabbles of the 1960s, and were reduced to strange contentment at holding on to electoral power in the state of West Bengal. West Bengal,

Kerala, and Tripura—their fortresses in one sense— have also proved to be their prisons. Failing to expand out of their electoral strongholds, the communists have been forced increasingly into unstable alliances with other parties—with very different agendas and techniques of mobilization which, by radical acts of imaginative interpretation, they have construed as 'progressive'. Thus they have formed a stable but somewhat forlorn group of leftist parties, now reduced to utter historical incongruity after the fall of the Soviet bloc, unable to reimagine a socialist agenda for India. They do not produce much ideological conviction or attract idealistic youth support, as they once did. They speak like Stalinists but act like liberalizers, hardly a recipe for producing ideological conviction. The parties of the National Front, a title that mocks their transparently regional support, have recently used the appeals of lower-caste mobilizations as the only effective slogan against the BJP. The recent electoral history of Uttar Pradesh, the largest state in the federation, is a curious record of this struggle and its utterly startling twists. This has led mainly to a regional bi-party system where the BJP and lower-caste parties have controlled alternate governments, without decisive advantage. In a more recent phase, a party explicitly based on the support of the untouchables (Scheduled Castes), the Bahujan Samaj Party (BSP), went through a split and a dissident leader formed a short-lived administration with BJP support. Thus, although social groups play a fundamental part in the electoral arithmetic, purely electoral considerations of power can, at times, complicate these trends and produce coalitions, however short-lived, which are considered impossible in terms of the standard grammar of castes.

These transformations in Indian politics are happening not merely in the realignment of social groups and political parties. There are interesting signs of a shift in relations between political institutions. With the help of popular support, driven by exasperation with political corruption, some supervisory institutions like the courts and the election commission emerged to play a surprisingly assertive role. Coalition government, with minority administrations for the last decade, has reduced the dominance and the aura of invincibility that politicians like Indira or Rajiv Gandhi enjoyed, despite the widespread belief that they condoned corrupt deals. Since politicians, including central ministers, hardly command such parliamentary power, supervisory institutions have found some space to play their role more energetically. The Election Commission demanded that political parties must file returns of their expenditure, both as parties and as individual candidates, on pain of disqualification. Newspaper reports and eyewitness accounts supported the impression that in some areas at least the most egregious uses of money to influence voters were curbed during this election.

The Election Verdict

Given the short-term context, the election results were, not surprisingly, inconclusive. But they showed some interesting patterns, and might give some indications of longer historical trends. The BJP for the first time in the history of Independent India, pushed Congress aside and emerged as the single largest party. Congress came a close second, and the united front of the National Front parties and the Left came third. But smaller regional parties and independents captured a relatively large number of seats, likely to be crucial in the coalitional negotiations which must continue until the next election. One interesting feature of the polls was the strikingly close predictions by pre-election surveys. The poll conducted by the magazine *India Today* and the Centre for the Study of Developing Societies (CSDS) in Delhi came close to predicting the exact number of seats that major parties actually won. This might also show that electoral decisions are made well in advance, rather than on the spur of the moment by most voters, including the least literate.

Of the 543 seats in the Lok Sabha, the BJP won 194 seats with its allies. The Congress won 137 seats, the National Front parties and the Left taken together 179. Of the regional parties, some were quite significant not only for purposes of post-election coalition-building, but for showing the growing entrenchment of some regional political trends. The Shiv Sena continued to dominate the politics of Bombay city by the use of petty-bourgeois frustration and plebeian gangsterism; but its solid alliance with the BJP shows its attempt to widen out towards a more national perspective through Hindu nationalism. In Uttar Pradesh, important not only because of its size but also because the major flashpoint of the Ayodhya mosque controversy, the BSP made a fairly strong showing. But the split between the untouchable base of the BSP and the consolidation of the intermediate castes in the Samajwadi Party (SP) ensured a much better showing for the BJP, since the votes against its candidates were divided.

Party Profiles

Congress. The Congress did badly compared to earlier elections. Along with its allies, it won only 137 seats—far short of a majority in parliament. Taking all of India into account, Congress suffered a vote loss of about 8.4 per cent. Its all-India vote share fell from 36.5 per cent in the last elections in 1991 to 28.1 in this one. The Congress also suffered the ignominy of coming in third in several states, including the crucial states of Uttar Pradesh and Bihar. It came third in 144 parliamentary constituencies compared to 92 in 1991. In earlier elections as well, including ones in which Congress had scored its most dramatic victories, Congress's share of the vote remained around 40 to 45 per cent; the number of seats it actually won depended on the nature of the opposition it faced. With a wholly united opposition, it did badly— as in 1967. But this time its vote share fell so precipitously that it crossed a threshold. It is hard to build back into any serious electoral contention from this level of vote share. Yet it is interesting that in terms of vote share over the entire country, the Congress remains the largest single party. The major difference now is that its voting support is too thinly and widely scattered to give it much electoral advantage. It still remains the only party with support in all parts of India. Its support is not concentrated in a region, or in particular social constituencies, but has become too diluted to provide majorities in a sufficient number of seats.

The BJP. The largest single party in parliament turned out to be the BJP, which secured 160 seats on its own, 194 with its electoral allies: the Shiv Sena in Bombay, the Samata Party, the Haryana Vikas Party, and the Shiromani Akali Dal from Punjab. Its crucial gain was in Uttar Pradesh where it won 53 seats, turning the ultimate tally decisively in its favour. However, the vote share shows that if the anti-BJP vote had not been split, the party would have got far fewer seats. Although its all-India vote share was less than that of the Congress, at 23.5 per cent—up by 2.7 per cent on the last elections—its support was concentrated in the northern and western states, particularly the four large states of Uttar Pradesh, Madhya Pradesh, Bihar, and Maharashtra, with considerable strength in Rajasthan and Gujarat, which enabled it to turn this into a far higher number of seats. The CSDS study offers considerable insight into the sociology of voting in this election. Contrary to what some argued, the support for the BJP does not come exclusively from 'traditionalist' rural voters. Its support is strongest among the graduate, Hindu upper-caste males, primarily in urban centres. Among the really backward and exploited groups, like Dalits and the rural poor, its support is remarkably low. It thus represents a phenomenon of 'a revolt of the elite' rather than of the masses. It is also interesting that in opinion surveys about the viability of democracy, this group shows the greatest discontent about the way democracy has functioned.[6] Its support is also the greatest among the youth,[7] which evidently gives it greater dynamism, and occasionally aggression. With the support of youth, many of them unemployed or very lightly employed, it has got a huge reservoir of energy to draw upon, sometimes crucial in the politics of the streets between elections. From the statistics, it appears that the BJP has not been able to persuade Hindu voters to act as a solid single bloc. Twenty-nine per cent of Hindu respondents to the exit polls voted for the Congress in contrast to 27 per cent for the BJP. But this could be seriously misleading, as disaggregated state-level responses would surely show much higher voter support for the BJP in the North-West belt. But the most significant feature in the voting of religious communities is the clear evidence that Muslims, traditionally devoted supporters of the Congress, have moved solidly away towards the leftist or third parties wherever an option exists.

State and Regional Parties. Another interesting feature of the polls was that several regional parties, without any national aspirations, did remarkably well in their regions, showing that for their supporters at least the national elections were essentially a state-level poll. If we accept the idea that there were two distinct elections taking place within one, this shows a trend towards a greater regionalization of Indian politics. The four parties at the top of the table—the BJP, Congress, the Janata Dal, and the CPI(M)—are followed immediately by a roll of state parties. In fact, the Janata Dal and the CPI(M) are themselves somewhat complex cases, with national or universalist ideological

---

[6] Yogendra Yadav, 'How India Voted', *India Today,* 31 May 1996, p. 25.
[7] Ibid.

positions, but with actual support in specific regions. Like the Tamil Maanila Congress or TMC (20) and the Dravida Munnetra Kazhagam or DMK (17) in Tamilnadu, the SP (17) and the BSP (11) in Uttar Pradesh, the Telugu Desam (16) in Andhra Pradesh, and the Shiv Sena (15) in Maharashtra all have purely regional projects of political mobilization, and, considering the number of seats from these states, did extremely well. In some cases, their national allies probably leaned on their regionalist support to do well against their other national adversaries. It is difficult to say, for instance, whether the BJP needs the Shiv Sena more than the other way round. This might indicate that the 'national' messages of some large parties cannot communicate themselves to ordinary voters without translation into the relevant vernacular through these regional groups.

Leftists and the National Front. India's leftists lost their way after splits in the mid-1960s. After the split in the Communist Party, they never recovered their influence on political life as the most serious opposition to Nehru's Congress. The CPI(M), the segment which broke away from the parent party on the grounds of its revisionism and dedication to the 'electoral path to socialism', has itself been remarkably successful electorally. Though its declarations condemned bourgeois democracy as a sham, it showed itself particularly proficient in its intricacies, and has retained power in the state of West Bengal for decades. But its unbreakable grip on the West Bengal assembly has been counterbalanced by an inability to expand its base elsewhere. Since it is not preparing for an imminent revolution, at least for the time being, its electoral ineffectiveness in other states has forced it into alliances with the Janata Dal and other parties.

These were all breakaway factions from the Congress during the years of Indira Gandhi. Initially, their politics was indistinguishable from the Indira Congress, but gradually they found a distinctive strategy by supporting the intermediate and lower castes in their demands for high levels of job reservation on grounds of social justice. In the northern states of Uttar Pradesh and Bihar, their politics of caste mobilization, although divisive generally, has sometimes successfully split the Hindu community and prevented the success of the BJP. Not surprisingly, the BJP and these parties see each other as their main enemies. Due to personal rivalries between individual leaders, their project of uniting all the intermediate and lower-caste groups against the BJP could not be realized, leaving the BJP easy victors in Uttar Pradesh. But this group of parties is seriously undermined by several factors in its bid for power at the centre. First, most of these parties' objectives have been entirely regional, and they lack a credible national political platform. Second, they are troubled by factionalism between groups and their leaders to an extent not common even in the fractious world of Indian politics. There is also a serious underlying difference in the modernist, individualistic communist thinking about poverty and their deeply caste-based demands, which both sides opportunistically ignore at the time of electoral alliances.

Implications of the Election Results

The results were such that both sides could claim a kind of victory. The BJP had the moral satisfaction of emerging as the largest single party. The Congress and the United Front could equally claim to have defeated its campaign of Hindu fundamentalism. Despite its inconclusiveness the results reveal some interesting features of current Indian politics. Two facts stand out equally clearly and inconveniently. The first is that the supporters of the BJP constitute the largest single bloc of voters. If we take into account the fact that the BJP's national vote is not at all well spread, a feature that some commentators tend to welcome, it shows that in some parts of the country the support for the BJP is quite intense, and much higher than for any comparable political group. Democratic politics is not only about elections. Politics goes on between elections as well, and what happens during these intervals often determines outcomes of polls. Such concentration of support gives the BJP greater strategic power than other parties. It might not be able to win an election, but at least in those areas it can mobilize by far the largest groups on the streets. It is remarkable that other parties seem to have already lost the art of street mobilization to the BJP. Leftists who were experts in such mobilizations, mainly around economic demands, until the 1960s, seemed held back by fear of raising issues which might hurt the government in power. But the silence of others plays into the hands of the BJP which has mounted popular mobilizations to set the agenda of politics in its own terms. The measure of its success can be seen from the fact that even communists have been forced to concentrate on the 'fight against communalism' to the utter neglect of economic issues. This shows an implicit victory of the BJP in dragging the fight on to the terrain it prefers.

The second equally significant fact is that the majority of voters overall are opposed to the BJP and its brand of Hindu nationalism. Its provocations have alienated the Muslims and a large segment of lower-caste groups among the Hindus. This hostility is supplemented by the opposition it faces from those who would not like secular institutions to be undermined. Thus, even if the BJP is able to form governments in future, it would not be easy for it to rule. The two facts, taken together, do not make for much governmental stability in the near future. The BJP would find it impossible to rule because the coalition of forces against its simple majority would be too strong. The others would find it perhaps equally difficult to rule because their unity is merely a negative opposition to the BJP. Typically, such coalitions find it easy to win elections, but hard to carry on government. It is usual in such circumstances for the small groups in the middle to carry a lot of weight, though for short periods. Multi-party systems tend to have high turnover of governments due to shifting coalitions, and in the middle term Indian politics might go in that direction. In fact, for the last decade or more democratic politics in most Indian states has already acquired this multi-party coalitional character. What was true of the states is now coming to be true of the centre.

After the elections, however, the Indian president, a veteran Congress politician, stuck to formal propriety and called on the BJP to form a government. The BJP, in this position of relative weakness, chose to present Atal Bihari Vajpayee, a moderate, as its prime minister to project an uncharacteristic attitude of accommodation. Interestingly, however, even Vajpayee found no support from other parties; no one agreed to form a coalition with the BJP. As expected, Vajpayee's government was asked by the president to prove its majority in parliament, but failed—ending, for the time being, India's first experience of a Hindu majoritarian rule. Logically, the Congress should have been the next in line; but Rao would not have received support from the National and Left Front for a Congress-dominated coalition. Consequently, he settled for a coalition led by the NF-LF to be supported from the outside by the Congress. He can try to play these parties' game in reverse: they would take the blame for the policies of the government, and he can choose a time to topple the government when it becomes convenient. It seemed, despite defeat, a fairly advantageous position for the Congress, to set the terms within which the UF government's policies had to work, and to enjoy a comfortable invisible veto. However, immediately after the elections a host of cases pending against Rao in the courts have come down heavily on him, threatening even imprisonment, an unprecedented affair in Indian politics. Given the internal factionalism of the Congress and the dire difficulties of its veteran leader, Congress might lose coherence completely and fail to take advantage from its position of providing crucial support. Indeed, it might depend on the generosity and consideration of the government to avoid utter humiliation, inverting the relationship of dependence. Institutions like courts and the election commission, once released from their customary caution, are acting with increasing boldness. Restrictions placed by the commission on party expenditures have made it difficult for all parties to prepare for an immediate election. In such circumstances, the coalition government of Prime Minister Deve Gowda (a Janata Dal leader and former chief minister of Karnataka) might last for some time, not because of its skills but because of lack of initiative by others.

But the most significant problem of modern Indian politics, which these elections have placed at the centre of political life, is the question of a redefinition of Indian nationalism. Should India abandon its idea of a secular, democratic, pluralistic nationalism? Should it adopt the BJP's suggestion of a drastic revision into a nation that imagines itself as homogeneous, Hindu, and exclusivistic? These are two opposite strategies in the face of diversity. Both strategies have to take into account the various types of pluralities in Indian society—religion, caste, region, culture. The soft strategy seeks to find policies which would not exclude any segment entirely, or even impose sacrifices which would be found intolerable. It is the recognition of the soft strategy that imparts the irreducibly coalitional character to Indian politics. The hard strategy views diversity as a threat to the state, an impediment to economic development and political coherence, and tries to devise policies by means of which such plurality can be ground down into cultural uniformity by a reinvented anti-plural Hinduism. For the secular forces in Indian politics, the last election was not a triumph but a reprieve.

8

The Reversal of Orientalism: Bhudev Mukhopadhyay and the Project of Indigenist Social Theory

Sometimes titles say more than the works they name. Through all the cultural negligence of his writings, Bhudev Mukhopadhyay will be remembered for the unforgettable title of a rather inconsiderable literary work by him called *Swapnalabdha Bharatvarsher Itihas*.[1] Translated literally, this means 'a history of India received in a dream', an imaginary history.

It is difficult even to say what sort of writing this is. To call it a novel is to misclassify the work; it offers us no narrative pleasures. It is an extension, but in an intriguingly paradoxical form, of his serious reflection on Indian history. It is not a significant work in any ordinary sense; but in that phrase he has given expression to a most significant cultural fact: the desire for history. He has invented a name, not for a book, but for the intellectual enterprise of his age, his class, his people, the obsessive centre of their collective mentalité.

The concern of his history is, of course, a concern with something that is illimitable and ambiguous, and people relate to this urge differently because they read the 'problem of history' in different ways.[2] The construction he gave this question remains unique, and even unsurpassed: for he was the only social theorist that the celebrated age of the Bengal Renaissance produced; and his relation to the enterprises

---

First published in *Hinduism: Tradition and Reinterpretation*, ed. H. Stietencron and V. Dalmia (New Delhi: Sage, 1995).

[1] *Swapnalabdha* means 'received in a dream'. That text was published in 1895.

[2] I have discussed this in Kaviraj 1998: ch. 4.

of his times is complex. He is of it, but also against it. Indeed, there is a deep aristocratic aloofness in his stance which would have doubtless disapproved of the phrase as unworthy of a mature people, as revealing an ambition of inauthenticity, of having a desire for a second-hand history marked in the name itself. It is not surprising that in the chronicles of the Bengali intellect Bhudev is passed over in silence.

Yet there is something puzzling in this forgetting. Whatever their failings, Bengalis are not forgetful about their cultural history. Why does their collective boastfulness not have in it place for Bhudev? His passing into oblivion indicates something besides an internal censorship of the Bengal Renaissance or its dedication to European taxonomies of 'liberal, conservative, progressive'. It simply illustrates the trivial point that a history 'in general' is never written; histories are always written of conventionalized objects, narratives, searches, accounts of origins of some constituted historical entities to the exclusion of other possible ones.

Two such subjects dominate the writing of intellectual history in Bengal: the history of modern Bengali literature, and of nationalist ideology. Bhudev figures in both, but not as a central figure. He has always existed in that nondescript space where the shadows of these two narratives fall. In a literary history of Bengal he is wholly, and rightly, overshadowed by the creative versatility of Bankimchandra Chattopadhyay. What Bhudev did was also of course nationalist: but he was less interested in a construction of its ideological doctrines and mythical symbols than the historical reflection that must constitute its base. Indian nationalism neglected such reflection about history, and when it felt a serious need for this, it borrowed heavily from the existing Western ideological discourses. Bhudev was not even a good revivalist, for his Hinduism was too intellectual to satisfy more demagogic tastes.[3]

There was something extraordinary about this sudden irruption of history in the literary discourse of Bengal in the nineteenth century. And the question of history was asked with a strange desperation. They sought history in all possible forms, of which two were most common: seeking the factual history of peoples, and writing their imaginary

---

[3] Raychaudhuri 1988 is the first serious full-length study of Bhudev's ideas; and it places his criticism of European society next to Bankimchandra's.

history through historical novels. Irrespective of their skills, nearly all writers tried their hand at both forms. Bankimchandra, the incomparable writer of historical novels, also left behind intense, irritated, unfinished fragments on the history and anthropology of Bengalis. R.C. Dutt, the distinguished historian, wrote thinly veiled allegorical novels about Rajputs and Marathas. According to the trend of the times, Bhudev too tried his hand at both,[4] with less distinction: his chosen line was different from everyone else's. A true historical sense, he implied, could not be created by piling up factual material about the past, or merely finding convenient points from which to counterfactualize in fiction. History could be brought under cognitive, and then hopefully pragmatic, control only by seeking out deeper lines of design in its apparent chaos, often against its surface trends, by finding the causal context of the present in the past. History meant large historical reflection of this kind: philosophy of history, history brought under control by social theory. How does one find a social theory? It is his answer to this all-important question which sets him apart from his contemporaries and makes him so interesting.

Bhudev proposed a theory.[5] The distinction of his theory was that it was utterly different from the scrappy and imitative utilitarianism and positivism so common and fashionable among his generation in Calcutta.[6] Social theory, which was synonymous with large-scale historical reflection, was used by Europeans to bring under cognitive and pragmatic control their own and other societies: that was precisely what had to be done by Indians. Writers of Bhudev's generation seemed to him to have entirely misconstrued what this project entailed. It did not enjoin imitative thinking, the painstaking application of principles learnt from Western social theory to the recalcitrant material of Indian history. That was, paradoxically, to miss the point of doing theory. Theorists in Europe did not prove their erudition by applying tenets of Chinese philosophy or even ancient Greek concepts to their own unfolding historical experience. They sought to work out concepts of their own to understand that strange mixture of light and darkness in the history of the age of reason, the mixed record of an epoch

---

[4] Mukhopadhyay 1857, 1876.
[5] His social theory is contained in *Samajik Prabandha* (1892). All references to this text are to the 1981 edition.
[6] Dattagupta 1972.

constructed in the name of rationality, its successful deliberate acts and unintended consequences. Social theory was not an erudite academic discipline; it was essential for intelligent inhabitation within modernity. Through social theory a society tried to engage in self-reflection, see the present as history, and render clear to itself the meanings of the actions of its own members and of others who constituted their history. This argument required a social theory done through concepts of an indigenous tradition: historical and anthropological reflection about the self and the other, starting with a recognition of the contingency of these concepts themselves. I have labelled this project, which Bhudev outlined with admirable clarity, the idea of a reverse anthropology.

Every writer of this generation chose his own terrain for a personal battle with the West, and his own individual strategy.[7] Bhudev undertook the task of producing a rigorous theoretical justification of the principles of his own civilization against the invading forces of rationalist, colonial, Christian arguments, as well as those of indigenist Westernism. But what he defended turned out, on closer inspection, to be an interestingly indeterminate object. I have argued in a study of Bankimchandra that this generation decided quite early that 'we' should oppose British rule, but it took them some time to settle down to a common understanding of what this 'we' represented.[8] Even Bankimchandra had considerable hesitation in choosing his nation, but once his mind was made up he contributed most powerfully to the imagination and symbolization of itself. A more rigorous thinker, Bhudev spent some time on the conceptualization of this self. Instead of naming the nation Bharatvarsha, he used first an entirely neutral and logically formal place term, *swadesh*, one's own country, or *swajati*, one's own people. Swadesh and swajati carry the suggestions of indistinguishability and self-evidence implied by most self-terms. A person does not call himself by his name; for himself, he is in a peculiar way, unnameable. Apparently, the same holds for the inhabitants of a culture—it is as unnameable for them as all true selves are.

Early nationalism in India covered this uncertainty (its certainty that there is or should be a nation, but uncertainty about who its members are or would be) by the simple device of assuming an ideal

---

[7] See Raychaudhuri 1988 for a detailed discussion.
[8] I have discussed this elsewhere: Kaviraj 1992.

audience, by the pretence that to the people concerned the boundaries of this collective self are self-evidently clear. Bhudev did not take this simple and rhetoric recourse; he entered into a more serious process of defining who one's own people are.

The Bengali term *jati*, as Partha Chatterjee has argued, is a term of interesting ambiguities.[9] It can mean, first, simply a logical class. Of course, it can and did also mean social groups, notably, a caste, and was later extended to mean a nation. In traditional usage, it simply has the close, intimate, but indeterminate meaning of a community (in the ordinary English sense, not the more specialized sense of a *gemeinschaft*). The use of the term, frequent and inevitable as it is in any discourse of politics, conceals a political indeterminacy at the start of early nationalism. It is a crucial ambiguity about who will constitute this privileged community, its associational principle, its criteria of inclusion. This is obscured by the use of indigenous terms such as *swajati* or *swajatiya*, meaning 'like or of the self', which resist both naming and analysis. Who are the members of the community? The people of the same group: thus the self is identified by a reference to the group, and the group by the self. But nationalism must get out of the circularity of such an immediate consciousness of a pre-reflexively given self.

Contemporary India, Bhudev begins by asserting, lacks a sense of identity (*jatiya bhav*). Despite his caution, he uses the fundamental trope of nationalism in this passage by using the verb 'to lose' (*haraiyacche*) to indicate that absence (Mukhopadhyay [1892] 1981: 3). To use a distinction from *nyāya* logic, it is not a *prāgābhāva* but a *dhvānsābhāva*, not the absence of something before it has come into existence, but the absence after it has ceased to exist.[10] The fact that we miss it proves that sometime it must have been in hand. No nationalism can easily acknowledge the contingency of its origins, its constructedness. It usually pretends that it emerges teleologically from the mystic inner depths of an immemorial past, imposing on the historical record

---

[9] Chatterjee 1991.

[10] *Nyāyā* logic distinguishes between various types of *abhāva* (absence/negation): *prāgābhāva* means the non-existence of an entity before it has come into existence; *dhvānsābhāva*, the non-existence after it was destroyed; *anyonyābhāva*, the negation of X in Y, and vice versa; and *atyantābhāva*, an intrinsic absence.

an aggressive anachronistic organization of memory. To begin this anamnetic exercise, it is imperative to begin by asking what constitutes one's kind (jati)? Who should one consider as of the same kind as oneself, one's swajatiya?

The way Bhudev answers this question implicitly shows his belief regarding the character of the historical process, which is half deliberate at best. Swajatiyata, the matter of belonging to the same community or the same relevant class, is not a matter of intention, governed by principles of inclusion and exclusion, by deliberate, rationalist programmes. It is more like an organic sameness imposed on people living for a long time in the same environment, similar to the process of natural adaptation. Rationalist conceptions of culture are excessively constructivist, implying that single cultures are created by men and can be changed by them. Actually, cultures and languages exist above and beyond not only individual human beings, but also groups and generations, gradually changing, no doubt, through their actions, but by a logic they can hardly understand or direct. Swajatiyata is not an attribute conferred on a people by themselves or by others. It is a quality that comes to subsist in them by virtue of their sharing the same natural and historical world. Remarkably, in Bhudev's thought, the natural and material aspects of life are inextricable from its social ones. As inhabitants of the same natural conditions have similarities, the historical world creates similarity among people—in social or religious conduct, in speech and symbolism, and last, but not least, in material culture. Everyday practices create the most deep-seated similarity among people—the way they build houses, their food, dress, furniture, for these reveal their way of dealing with the material environment around them. When people see others who do similar things in these matters they consider them their swajatiya, i.e. similar to themselves (Mukhopadhyay [1892] 1981: 7). According to Indian logic, similarity is a term with a dual meaning. It can mean that objects A and B are directly similar, placed in a relation of identity or indiscernible resemblance. But even if A and B are not directly similar, they may exhibit a negative similarity. B may not be identical to A, but its difference from A may be negligible compared to its differences with C, D, E, etc. The application of this conception of *sādṛśya* to Indian society reveals an important fact. Two types of similarity can be found in the Indian social order: the direct similarity among the Hindus, but also a wider circle of negative similarity between them and other religious communities (ibid.) Sharing the same nature and same history has created a quality of *samaduhkhasukhatā* among them, a commonality of happiness and suffering (ibid.: 10). Colonial ideology in British India denies this samadukhasukhata of people belonging to different religious communities. Are they right, or are non-Hindus swajatiya?

Hindus and Others

In the conceptual language Bhudev is using here, both natural objects and social beings can be said to have their own *swadharma* (i.e. the collection of properties or attributes which make them what they are), the basis of their differentiation from other objects in the world. However, unlike natural objects, human beings, because of the gift of volition, can change their selfhood (*swabhava*). Changing religion is like changing one's social being (swadharma). Apparently, this raises great difficulties in a *jatiya bhava* common among the Hindus.[11]

Swajatiyata comes from inhabiting the same history; it is not a matter of formal faith alone. The census declares that one-fifth of Indians are Muslims, but it is characteristic of the census enumeration that its statistics cannot take into account the stratification and historical complexity of identities it counts. It thus tends to deny Indian society a map or taxonomy that denies history. From an external view, Indian Muslims would seem to share beliefs or religious conduct with other Islamic societies. But in fact they have a greater similarity to Hindus than to Muslims elsewhere (ibid.: 12).

Indeed, converts to other religions are tied to Hindus by both types of similarity, direct and negative. Essential properties are originary

---

[11] Bhudev complains that British historians are using history to divide Indian communities: 'Now there is a new and more significant reason for maintaining and intensifying the division between Hindus and Muslims. Many English historians suggest, explicitly at times, through hints at others, that the Muslims perpetrated unspeakable oppression on Hindus when they held political power. Thus, English historians are sowing a seed of deep resentment against Muslims in the minds of Hindus. This kind of resentment against Muslims and the Islamic religion among modern English educated youth—one would not have found half of that in traditional cultivated Brahmins who were often educated in Persian' (Mukhopadhyay [1892] 1981: 14).

ones. These people were converted to Islam, and if the prior argument that historical attributes are neither created nor destroyed by intentionality is correct, there would remain indelible vestiges of Hinduism carried over into the practice of their new faith. Indian Muslims are tolerant, despite their religious injunctions. In relation to religion they accept their general neighbourliness with Hindus. Their material practices are in any case indistinct from those of Hindus of the same region. Second, in India religious distinctions have a peculiar way of transformation: what originated as religious distinctions of faith usually get changed into relatively self-regulating castes within the loose structure of Hindu society. Religions profess an ideology of uninfringable distinctions; in practice, however, they enter into unavoidable processes of transaction and exchange. Islam in India is thus quite different from Islam elsewhere, both in doctrine and in internal social practices.

Historically, Muslim rule did not counteract the long-term tendencies of Indian civilization. Actually, Muslim rule furthered the process of unification implicit in earlier history. By creating a stable, centralized empire, by imposing identical laws relating to land and administration, by creating the new common language of Hindustani which was intelligible to all Indians, Muslim rule contributed significantly to the emergence of an inchoate consciousness of community among Indians (ibid.: 14ff). This argument is extended to Christians through an anecdote in which a South Indian Christian tells Bhudev with firm conviction: 'we are Brahmins by caste and Christian by faith . . . what we changed was only our religion, not the caste to which we have traditionally belonged' (ibid.: 19). Also, Christianity represented even less of a threat to swajatiyata on account of a cardinal difference between Islam and Christianity in matters of conversion. After conversion, Islam treated all its adherents as equals; but the more the converted Christians and Anglo-Indians sidled up to the British, the more the latter moved away to keep their distance. The Englishman suffered from a congenital inability to make an *apan* out of a *par* (ibid.: 17). By the grace of God, India was saved from colonization by the Portuguese or the French, and the terrible effect of their easy intermarriage and promiscuity (ibid.: 17). Another distinct segment of the Indian population, the tribals, were also coming into a slow historical subsumption inside the Hindu world. A *jatiya bhav* was thus already coming into being in India, not through the creation of a common pattern of customs and beliefs (as in the USA) but by a mutual recognition of these contiguous and interplaying identities.

Does Indian Society have a History?

Clearly, this argument invokes a logic of history and appeals to a kind of historical consciousness among Indians. But the difficulty was that Western scholarship seemed to have conclusively proved that Indians, especially Hindus, were notoriously lacking in historical consciousness.

Every society requires a minimal sense of continuity through some form of organization of collective memory. All societies have a sense of their past, but they organize and represent this in varying ways. 'The style of composition of all literature tends to differ from one people to another' (ibid.: 20). History thus differs in terms of form. It is insensitivity to other forms of historical perception which often creates the illusion that most societies do not have either the curiosity or the implements necessary for a knowledge of their own past. Ontologically, the past is an inescapable dimension of all societies; 'history' is only one of its forms of possible representation. It is only a privileging of history, a local and regional form of social remembrance, into a universal rational norm which makes it appear that other societies suffer from a radical absence. The arrangement of memory in Hindu society is different from the European conventions of history writing; and it is essential to understand its internal principles.

Understanding the past requires an explanatory framework. A chronology, a mere temporal sequence of incidents, hardly merits the title of history. Among the Tatars and the Turanians, we are told, there were well-established traditions of chronicling events; still, these are hardly signs of their possessing historical consciousness. To simply indicate that one event followed another is not to explain why they happened in that order: 'Chronological sequence is a coarse substitute for causality' (ibid.: 21). Arabic and Judaic cultures also have such chronicles, but these are governed by the 'cognitively irresponsible' doctrine that every event is a direct expression of god's intentions—a doctrine that destroys serious history by absolving the enquirer of the responsibility of explaining anything.

Contrary to Orientalist doctrine, Indian writers have been more perspicuous on this point than other cultures. Causality is a concept that can be read in many ways. A shallow reading simply conceives of cause as the event prior in time. A more complex one would regard it as a configuration of circumstances necessary for the consequent *ananyatha siddhi* (literally: 'could not have happened otherwise', indicating an 'if' clause; ibid.: 22). In fact, the second notion subsumes the first by distinguishing between two strands of causal force—first, the peculiar configuration of circumstances left from the past, or the entire gamut of causal pressures stemming from the past whether perceived or not (called the *praktana*), and second a line of deliberate action directed at this horizon (*purushakara*), i.e. application of intelligence and force guided by a sense of what is right (*dharma sahakrta*; ibid.: 22–3). The Hindu construction of the historical is also guided by the distinction, common to all branches of classical philosophy, between actual and real, between factuality and truth, which can often assume a poetic form. The poetic accounts of historical reality and the world are true in this sense: their point is not to give a reliable account of factual sequences, but to present to its readers the essential order of things (ibid.: 23). Tagore gave this distinction a powerful expression in his famous poem on the birth of poetry. To Valmiki, dazzled by the gift of poetry, but unsure about what to write, Narada says, significantly, with a smile:

> *narad kahila hasi sei satya ja rachibe tumi ghate ja ta sab satya nahe.*
> *kabi taba manobhumi ramer janamsthan ayodhyar cheye satya jeno*
>
> What you create will be the truth; for all that happens is not what truth is. Poet, know that the land of your mind is truer than the land of Rama's birth, Ayodhya.[12]

The Puranas, though poetic and fabulous, contain therefore a certain resolution of the people's historical experience.[13] As long as these texts survive, they offer the Indian people a representation of their past, a collective memory. To understand any object is to consider

---

[12] *Bhasha o Chhanda*, in Thakur 1963, 5: 97.

[13] Simply because the historical texts of Indians are not composed according to the conventions of Greek or European writing of history, it is not appropriate to assert that Indians have no history. Thus, the idea that the absence of historical texts indicates a lack of national consciousness does not apply to India. There are entirely different kinds of histories of the nature of our society.

its reality or nature, its *prakrti*. 'To estimate what an object is likely to be in future, we must judge if what exists is in harmony with the forces of nature. It is nature alone that is permanent. What she favours survives and expands, what she disfavours wanes to eventual destruction' (ibid.: 16). Thus, it is necessary to analyse the nature of Indian society through an analysis of its historical logic and the intellectual representations of that nature as congealed in self-images.

The essential logic of Indian history, in that sense its reality or its truth, is a trend towards gradual unification of its diverse elements through mutual awareness (ibid.: 29), Muslim conquests in India, despite frictions at the surface of political incidents, actually aided this tendency. Muslim rulers simply carried on this trend through the unintended results of their no doubt more narrowly conceived, selfishly deliberate plans (ibid.: 28). The dominion of the British too, amusingly, has not escaped this cunning of reason peculiar to Indian history. By introducing economic and administrative unification on an unprecedented scale, the British have simply created the preconditions for the emergence of a *jatiya bhav*. Hindus must swim with this tide of history and not uncomprehendingly oppose British rule. To decide what must be welcomed in the British dominion and what must be opposed, Indians need more explicit, conscious historical self-reflection. Hindu society must act according to its own nature (ibid.: 29). In a world which has moved to self-consciousness, which holds the self up to itself as an object of reflection and analysis, Hindu society must do the same, to come to terms with modernity's imperative of self-reflection. It must make a transition from telling stories about itself to a theory of its social order, from Purana to historical sociology.

The Sociology of the Self: The Structure of Hindu Society

The puranic way of self-consciousness, adequate traditionally, is no longer so because the world has changed irreversibly. Bhudev acknowledges that in European ideas there is an inextricable connection between social theory and the anthropological enterprise. Knowledge of the self is possible only through a supplementary, if asymmetric, knowledge of the other. By defining itself dialectically, European knowledge has practically forced other societies to do the same through a similar, if not identical, duality. For Hindu society, too, knowledge of the self is imbricated with knowledge of the other. Unlike more chauvinistic contemporaries, Bhudev considers a theory of European modernity essential for the historical survival of Hinduism. This must be isomorphic with the European anthropological exercise, but essayed from the other side. European social theory emerged through an attempt to think through the travails of modernity, making the modern historical world intelligible by degrees. In doing this, social theory began with concepts of ordinary practical life and refined them into theoretical concepts. Once a theoretical structure emerged through an interconnected pattern of such concepts, it was applied to other societies to understand their difference. This gave Europe not merely knowledge of other social worlds in a manner consonant with its needs, it also gave its notion of the self greater definition. To work with social theory, or historical reflection, means repeating this process. A Hindu social theory must be distilled out of the concepts of traditional philosophy and everyday practical concepts, its structure must be built up. Afterwards, the concepts of this social theory should enable Indians to grasp the truth of European modernity 'from their side', with their concepts. The intellectual task was not to master European history through its own concepts of self-reflection, but through 'ours'. Some truths of a society appear only to the eye of an outsider; Indians must therefore produce a Hindu historical sociology of European modernity, in a strict reversal of the Weberian project, an exact mirror image, with the logical places of the self and the other interchanged. A knowledge of the self is prior to the knowledge of the other; philosophies of history precede the emergence of anthropology. The journey must have three parts: first, a sociology of Hindu India; second, a theory of European modernity; and finally, a consideration of what might emerge through the crossing of these two trajectories in the India of the nineteenth century.

European culture is dominated by evolutionist thinking. But Orientalists forget to apply one of its great criteria to their analysis of India. A primary function of any social order is to ensure its survival, and the durability of its primary social organization. Hindu society shows extraordinary strength in this regard: 'those ancient Egyptian, Assyrian, Persian, Greek and Roman societies long since passed into oblivion. Hindu society continues unruptured and undestroyed' (ibid.: 31). What features of the social order ensure this durability?

Commonly, European writers begin their histories with a falsehood—that England conquered India by force of arms. It might be more realistic, Bhudev suggests, to say that the Indian people placed themselves under British dominion (ibid.: 32). By contrast, Muslim rulers had truly conquered India by military force: and this happened because Hindu society had placed military skills in the province of a separate and special caste. Hindu society could do that because it did not consider warfare a particularly significant task which should be practised by all members of society. Historically, whenever Indian society has made common cause, it has succeeded against military attacks, but it does not do so as a rule. This simply reveals a principle of Hindu social ordering—the marginality of the state. Inner governance is what keeps Hindu communities in their proper order, rather than the everyday menace of political power. As the state is not central to its existence, Hindu society can show a certain indifference even at times of great military turmoil. At times of war, when political storms of succession or control tear apart the upper layers of society, the ordinary business of productive work, of agriculture and commerce, can continue in its customary rhythm. There is an imperturbable normality in this society that continues despite wars, conquests, the rise and fall of kings and dynasties. Hindu social organization is peculiarly antimartial, peaceable, self-ordered. Consequently, it is a society that is easy to conquer but impossible to dominate.

This, surprisingly, inverts the explanation as to why British conquest happened. It is a fact that can be explained by reference to Hindu social principles rather than to the invincible superiority of European arms or rationalist knowledge. Military success, in any case, is hardly an infallible criterion of cultural superiority. Ignorant Spartans inflicted defeat on the highly cultured people of Athens, the barbaric Macedonians on the rest of Greece, wild Tartars on the civilized Chinese, and hordes of German tribesmen on the great Roman empire. 'Those who lose a war are therefore proved inferior—is a doctrine of the unsubtle, unworthy of men of discernment' (ibid.: 33).

Hindu society is ruled by dharma; but it is essential to explicate what this means. Religion is not superstitious fancifulness, or even a predominantly moral order; it has fundamentally a cognitive relation with the world: 'Religious texts are those works which provide answers to questions men cannot refrain from asking about the external world of nature and the inner world of their consciousness' (ibid.: 36). One of the central questions of this kind, says Bhudev, is 'why is there so much difference; so much inequality in the world, and why is there so much inequality among men?' (ibid.: 36). Surprisingly, the Hindu caste order provides a credible answer to this basic puzzle. Hindu seers sought to answer this question by reference to the ubiquitous perception of causality in all intelligible events. Time is divided into its tripartite form in the interest of causal explanation—*bhuta, bhavishyat*, and *vartaman*. Any event in the present can be said to have been brought about by causalities lodged in the past, and would similarly produce effect in the future, the *parakala*. Clearly, there is an asymmetry between the three *kalas* (times), in that it is only the present which can be clearly seen. There is a haziness that inevitably attends the human picture of the past and the future—though the haziness is due to different reasons in the two cases. The circumstances of individuals are different precisely due to the forces of causation in the past; and in future the present chain of acts would equally have its effects. Hindu religious thought, according to Bhudev, is rooted in this recognition of the ubiquity of causal chains: nothing in our experience is uncaused, not merely in the world of nature, but also in the social condition of human beings. Thus, what a person is undergoing at present must have been caused by previous acts in the past, perhaps a past that stretches beyond this birth into a previous life. For Bhudev, an attraction of this moral belief is that it inspires endeavour and induces discipline. Present suffering is merely the result of past misdeeds, screened off by our birth. Present good conduct, by the same logic, would cause later happiness, even if delayed by a birth or two. 'A traditional Hindu thus has no cause for dissatisfied agitation. His traditionalism makes him peaceable: for how can one resent the enjoyment of the fruits of one's own acts.' Since *parakala* is determined by acts in the *ihakala*, the present, this also sufficiently excites his endeavour to do good. Indeed, good conduct is in one's own extended interest (ibid.: 36). Bhudev does not analyse Buddhist thought as its principles are basically similar to those of Hinduism.

Christianity arises from a different way of looking at the ontology of the past. It does not acknowledge the *praktana*, the causal power of the past. Men sometimes confer on the processes of nature their own characteristic of self-conscious activity. In Christianity, this is shown in the parable of creation on the model of bringing things into existence by naming and speech. As they do not believe in the *praktana*, Christians cannot be peaceable, satisfied, or resigned: 'Their societies resemble battlefields between the various groups which constitute them' (ibid.: 38). Christians believe in *parakala*; but their thinking is affected by the excessive subjectivism of their religion, and what happens then is referred to the arbitrary will of an omnipotent god. Subtly, by interpretation, Bhudev confers on Christianity features reminiscent of Weber's notion of a magical religion; and because of the Hindu dedication to causality he reserves for it the title of a rationalist religiosity, an amazing inversion of the demonstrations of Western *Religionsoziologie*: 'Egotism is the most powerful emotion in the minds of ordinary Europeans; no other society is composed of people as immoral, indomitable/ungovernable, irrational and egotistic' (ibid.: 39). Islam partly resembles Christianity but tempers it by its own distinctive passion for equality: 'Egalitarianism is an idea with great charm. It is here that the strength of the Islamic religion lies. In the whole world, the Muslim is the only true believer in equality. Equality, consequently, is the primary principle of all Islamic societies' (ibid.: 41). Evidently, this sociology of religion violates all taxonomies commonly built up by European social theory. It becomes necessary then to submit the principles of European social science to a more general critical examination.

Critique of Western Social Theory

Science enjoys great prestige in European intellectual cultures. European scholars claim to apply scientific principles in their comparative study of societies, 'But science is not produced by the mere invocation of its name' (ibid.: 41). Unprincipled and unreal science is, in fact, more dangerous because it enhances the ignorance of the unlearned. European science often suggests correlations between the physical attributes of a country and the social organization of its people—a reference probably to Buckle's theories—'but European historical science is yet dreaming about such scientificity' (ibid.: 43). In fact, this kind of tenuous and vulgar natural determinism is shown by Bhudev to have a surface and a deep structure. Only on its surface, or at the level of subjective intentions, does it make an effort towards scientific inference; at a deeper level, it is simply wilfully libellous towards Indian society. To express disbelief in this pseudo-scientific literature is not to disbelieve science or the powers of the causal explanation of social facts; it is merely separating real from fraudulent science. Actually, the science of society has achieved only fragmentary, disjointed, and crude principles of such causal understanding, and in fact Europeans are bringing science itself into disrepute by putting it at the service of their respective national histories and their internal prejudices.

Bhudev's treatise takes up for disproof some common naturalistic hypotheses suggesting the inferiority of Indians. First, he tackles the climatic determinism claiming heat and excessive fertility of the soil as being hindrances to Indian exertion and civilization. Second, he turns towards dietary theories which maintain that rice is insufficiently nutritious and that vegetarianism leads to biological degeneration of the race. To deduce subtle social principles from such general geographical facts is 'erroneous and laughable' (ibid.: 46). Interestingly, the only European science that seems more credible to him is racial physiology: that proves for him the fact that Indian society is based on racial divisions, and its interdictions are meant to preserve racial purity.

Historical sociology in Europe is so undeveloped because it depends fatally on analogical reasoning, a simple transference by analogy of ideas from natural to social science. As these ideas are allegorical, such reasoning is slippery and easily swallowed by the unwary. European theorists often see all relations as contractual, including such arrangements as marriage. Some treat the family as the atom of society; others compare the body politic with the body or an organism subject to the cyclical process of birth, youth, decline, and death, with the predictable corollary that European society is seen in a state of youthful vigour whereas other societies are in a state of infancy or decline, requiring European superintendence. It is interesting to note that, unlike most of his contemporaries, Bhudev is simultaneously critical of both the mechanical-atomistic and organicist constructions of society. A careful examination shows both these allegories to be misleading: to try to judge which one is better is a waste of time.

Indeed, if we insist on analogies, Hindu thought offers a superior one: by analogy the body of a society can be compared to a divine body (*devasharira*): it has no temporal origin or end; as long as it exists, it shows a youthful functionality (gods never age, they are *sthirayauvana*); and every society has a specific nature according to its historic prime function (ibid.: 50).

The priority of society over the individual is a patent fact to be accepted in any serious reflection about society, but not in the form in which this idea has been cast in European organicism. Hindu thinking analogically puts it into the otherwise inexplicable concept of a *daiva rna* (a debt to the gods)—a feeling of debt or thankfulness to one's own society which is to be paid back in rituals and good work.[14] European writers advance another equally untenable idea through analogical reasoning: a society that has lost political sovereignty is considered destroyed because it will fail to take serious decisions such as those relating to war and peace. Again, this is untrue and it is used in the service of colonial control. The loss of political sovereignty does not indicate the death of a society; and if society survives, the recovery of its political power is always possible.

By assuming that the relation between society and the individual is always antagonistic, European theory falls into overgeneralization, turning a contingent historical principle of European modernity into a universal human requirement. Yet Bhudev recognizes that there should be a distinction between the relation between men, and between societies. Though social solidarity is based on a feeling of community among men, the relation between societies is usually unfriendly, irrespective of their forms. At the heart of the argument lies a strange Hindu Malthusianism. Successful social organization leads to paradoxical and, in some ways, self-defeating results. It leads to an increase in population, resulting in the scarcity of goods; thus, the social principles in all social forms must strike a balance between population and productivity/sustenance. A labour theory of property reduces waste and kindles activity and enterprise. Property rights change historically; there is no form of property that can be considered either universal or natural for mankind, or in all circumstances superior to others (ibid.: 52). Indeed, the evolution of the right to property follows a historical logic. Initially, the right to property rests with the social group, the clan or community, a situation that Europeans often confuse with slavery. Certainly, this creates a condition in which individuals cannot enjoy rights, but it is substantially different from slavery in European history. 'Uncle Tom is tortured by his masters, the slaves of Asia—Sabaktagin, Qutabuddin, Iltutmish—succeed them to their

---

[14] Bhudev's discussion about the religious relations with the ancestors is similar to some elements of Durkheim's sociology of religion.

thrones' (ibid.: 53). European history gradually evolved into the modern form of property rights, in which private property was the natural form of possession of material goods. Yet this theory is philosophically flawed and inconsistent with its premises. If labour alone is considered the justifiable basis of property, then individual possession becomes wholly untenable. According to this theory, no one can claim any title to literally any property, for each social object involves the complex expenditure of various people's labour. All societies tend to expand at the expense of others, but not with equal aggressiveness. Agrarian and pastoral societies also seek expansion, because they too suffer from their own specific forms of scarcity, but that is fundamentally different from the peculiar aggressiveness of European commercial civilization (ibid.: 60). Bhudev shrewdly discovers a tendency towards an equalization of modernity among the European nations. Consequently, the most likely outcome of national rivalry in Europe was that European nations would maintain a tense peace amongst themselves by devising rules of international law which would keep their internal conflicts under control in Europe, but push these conflicts outside towards the colonial periphery. Europeans would thus enjoy the fruits of an artificial peace, while the rest of the world would have to suffer the unbridled destructiveness of modern warfare, not for any fault of its own. Uncontrollable aggression and the internal disorder of European commercialism would be directed outwards in the form of a militaristic colonialism.

The Theory of the Other: Occidentalism

To counteract the historical effects of colonialism does not imply contemplating rebellion against British rule, at least not yet. Colonialism is not merely a structure of economic extraction; it requires as a condition of success a habitual obedience of the colonized to the cognitive forms produced by Western rationalism. Rationalism's central theses about how societies are known are entirely different from earlier thinking. These earlier forms of knowledge assumed that every social form necessarily gave rise to some self-knowledge around a conceptual structure adequate for living within its special intricacies. Outsiders wrote about them as mere spectators or reporters, performing the thankless task of translating, always inadequately, between two internal languages of description, identification, making sense, and making do, which must remain incommensurable to some degree. This was captured in the image of the traveller, with its associations of transience, externality, fallibility, without any claim to a knowledge superior to that of the insiders. Rationalist thought had ended this image of communication between societies and their accounts of themselves. The new theory placed knowledge of societies in a clear hierarchy, internal knowledge being inferior to Western theory analysing other cultures. Of course, the reverse of this did not hold. Pictures of Western societies produced by other cultures were irredeemably false. The internal knowledge of European societies produced by European social theory was adequate for understanding them, but this was not true of the internal knowledge of other cultures. The external knowledge of the West alone was able to reveal their truth. European knowledge about itself (social theory) and the other (anthropology) could be countered only by a strictly symmetrical construction. Hindu society does not have a developed sociology: but that is hardly surprising. Neither had Europe till a hundred years earlier. Social science is an implement for coping with modernity and its strange and unprecedented puzzlements. Although Hindu thought did not have a sociology ready at hand, its concepts could be used to work out a sociology, and then analyse European history through its conceptual grid. This was no less than a project of an anthropology in reverse. Bhudev sets out to capture the essence of Westernnness (*pashchatya bhav*; ibid.: 65 ff.). His enterprise carries the inescapable marks of the immoderateness of the colonial encounter: it speaks with the polite insolence of a high civilization, using a subtle play of indigenous concepts to partly understand, partly misconstrue, and partly denigrate the culture of the other.

The whole of Western civilization is being transformed by a capitalist modernity; but Bhudev's knowledge of history is too profound to allow him to overlook its internal diversities. He recognizes that neither the structure nor the exact sequence of development of modernity is the same in different European societies. But the West, though not homogeneous, comes to be known in India through the instrumentality of British power. The first task, accordingly, is to compare the principles of social organization in India and Britain. In one of his passages this contrast is worked out with great vividness:

The nature of Hindu society is peaceability, of the English an energetic pursuit of material prosperity. Hindu society is primarily agrarian, the English mainly industrial and commercial. Hindu society recognises collective ownership of property, the English has a strong preference for primogeniture and private ownership. In Hindu society early marriage is the rule, in the English relatively late marriage. Hindu society controls itself by internal governance, English society confers sovereignty on the state to keep itself under control. On Indian soil these two societies with different constitutions have come to meet in conflict. The English are energetic, skillful, conceited and grasping/rapacious/greedy. The Hindu is hardworking, peace-loving, obedient, and contented. Considering these attributes, it seems clear that all that the Hindu has to learn from the British is simply his technological virtuosity, nothing more. Indeed, it would be good for him if he were to learn nothing else. (Ibid.: 65)

Thus the two societies are destined for each other in a perverse fashion; for no other society had perfected the principles of altruism as Hindu society had, and no other had refined egotism to the extent the English had. It would have been better if this encounter had changed the British character instead of the Indian (ibid.: 66). Colonialism was gradually imposing the principles of British life on Indian culture. To the educated classes in India, the British had become the measure of all things.

Constituents of Western Modernity

The strange paradox in all this was that while 'we were, out of our illimitable regard for the British, constantly devising ways for turning our society into a second England, European philosophers were insistently warning us about the fact that Europe is increasingly overwhelmed by discontent, and would very soon perhaps witness terrible social disorder' (ibid.: 69). To understand why Europe has reached the present state, and which among its principles are applicable to Indian society, we must analyse the complex fact of Westernism (*pashchatya bhav*) into its constituent elements. Bhudev lists these elements as egotism, evolutionism, egalitarianism, materialism (*aihikata*), libertarianism/liberalism, scientific culture, and political constitutionalism (ibid.: 70).

All knowledge of the world begins from a sense of the self. Consciousness always implicates a knowledge of the self whose knowledge it is, an awareness that the Hindu shastras referred to as *pratibodhaviditatva*. But the sense of the non-self is equally natural and primary, and these are inextricable. However, although all knowledge implies knowledge of the self, different cultures construct diverse conceptions of what the self is. Hindus have an exceptionally open conception of the self (*swartha*) because it is advaitic, i.e. non-dualistic. Hindus acknowledge the eventual impossibility of a distinction between the self and the non-self because of the ubiquitous existence of internal relations. Bhudev admits that there is no single or general 'European' theory of the self. Social philosophy in the West is riven by disputes on the most fundamental questions. French theory after Rousseau has taught that human beings ought to live for others (*pararthe*). English writers usually object that one must live for and love the self even if one has to live for others' sake. Englishmen are constitutionally selfish (ibid.: 71); but the selfishness of English social thought is covered by a remarkable conceit. The English blithely equate what is good for them with what is good for the world. By contrast, the Hindu is a natural practitioner of hermeneutics, with a natural inclination and ability to sense what is on the other's mind (*parachittagnata*; ibid.: 73). British social theory is thus wholly opposed to Hindu thought, while German reflection is not; and Bhudev's favourites among German thinkers are Hegel and Schopenhauer.

Indians have a deeply cyclical conception of the movement of the universe; and Bhudev does not miss the connection between political quietism and a metaphysical assurance that everything that has disappeared would return once more, and everything triumphant must suffer decline. Nothing reinforces the European belief in their own superiority more than the idea of evolution in history. 'The scientific-minded European does not desist from abusing people; he will try to substantiate his epithets by scientific evidence' (ibid.: 75). Science is engaged in a constant search for more general causal laws, and the subsumption of these into ever larger wholes. Evolutionism, a theory invented to explain facts of animal life, its complexity and differentiation, must, according to this view, be extended to encompass human affairs. However, its extension to human history led to two unwarranted conclusions: (a) that modern men are biologically superior to their ancient ancestors, and (b) Europeans are correspondingly superior to people of other societies. Imperialist expansion simply illustrates the dominion of the fittest.

Bhudev, interestingly, does not attack evolutionary theories in general, only their illegitimate extension to society and historical explanation. Science simply provides explanations of processes, the evidence for which is obtained through observation. 'Science has nothing to say about improvement or decline. Science says that organisms transform themselves gradually to adapt to their environment. There is nothing in science to claim that this change is by definition development' (ibid.: 75). Historical evidence about human progress is very mixed and contestable, and always relative to discordant standards of measurement. Political economy, which Bhudev calls 'the skeletal frame of European social science' (ibid.: 77), also offers very mixed evidence on the matter of progress. Technological progress is not accompanied by increased contentment in society—the final goal of all social arrangement. Rather, it has led to the threat of the most intense social discontent and disorder. 'The forces which contribute to the advance of society also contribute, as it were, to its destruction . . . Thus nowhere do we see rectilinear paths; all paths are circular, turns of the wheel of time' (ibid.: 78).

The idea of human progress is, however, not rejected as entirely unfounded. To be sustained, it has to be philosophically grounded in a different style. No other part of nature, except man, manifests the crucial attribute of self-consciousness. Due to this capacity of self-reflexion, and recursive consideration of their actions, human beings alone are able to take action directed towards their collective life. Of course, the world of man must be seen as part of the world of nature which is governed by circular patterns, but if there were to be an exception to this rule it is likely to happen in the human world. Human affairs are held together and directed by collective practical ideals. Societies have to be compared, and the proposals of reform of one society in the image of another must be judged by a consideration of the ideals around which social forms are organized. Conservatism means simply considering new proposals for social reform with care, comparing them critically with older forms of social behaviour (ibid.: 80). Replacing everything old in society simply because it is old is no evidence of critical thought. The uncritical acceptance of older ideals is as harmful as obsessive imitativeness of practices that are new. The question is how to compare societies organized on different principles of practical reason and ideals of moral conduct.

In determining the stage of development of societies, the criterion must be more complex than a simple indicator of technical progress. After a long discussion Bhudev concludes that the state of the social order in Europe is one-sided and declining, and that of India is stagnant—thus the choice is much less clear than commonly supposed: 'Real improvement of society is not caused by mere technical progress, or the capacity to produce cheap goods, or by excessive accumulation of material wealth, by extension of formal political equality, and certainly not by self-glorification' (ibid.: 82). Religious conceptions of the world can be theoretically divided into two types: naturalistic and mentalist. In naturalistic religions, god is attributeless, in mentalist ones he has attributes. In the first, the path to god lies through knowledge, in the second through devotion. Hinduism and Buddhism are examples of naturalistic religious forms. Islam and Christianity are both idealistic systems. In the first group, salvation depends on the rules of causality applied to the individual's own actions; in the second, it depends wholly on the will of god. In the first, the Almighty is seen as sinless (*apapabiddha*), eternal and pervasive in all creation; the second type sees him as possessing the qualities of omnipotence, omniscience, and mercifulness. On most other points, too, naturalistic religions are superior on a scale of rationality; idealistic faiths are superior on one count alone: the question of equality (ibid.: 84).

The idea of equality should be handled with great care. There is no equality in nature, in a strict sense. What we encounter are similarities and resemblances; the limited intelligence of man often reads it wrongly as equality, because there is some resemblance between the ideas of equality and resemblance. The idea of equality has undeniably produced some wonderful historical results; and it could be justified, even if it is philosophically flawed, on the ground of its social usefulness. A sense of equality among men restricts arbitrary power and is naturally attractive to the underprivileged. There are, however, serious shortcomings in the ways in which the idea of equality has been outlined by Western social theory and developed by the events of European political history.

However, European declarations of equality should not be taken at face value, argues Bhudev, echoing radical critiques, because the equality that is professed is an equality of opportunity, not of condition. This could be called affording every individual an equal right to be unequal with others. Its actual effects on society have been disastrous. For, while it does not create a real equality of conditions, it irreversibly undermines hierarchies of all kinds, even though some of these are eminently justifiable. European modernity shows a distaste for all hierarchy in the name of a false egalitarianism. It destroys hierarchies of knowledge, skills, morals, status; yet it leaves untouched a new hierarchy, the least defensible, the inequality of wealth. America, with its frenetic and dedicated commercialism, shows the more cultured and aristocratic European societies the image of their common future.

Societies based on cultures of naturalistic religions look at the question of equality in a completely different way. They accept inequality as an ineradicable fact of nature, but seek to ensure that hierarchies are more justifiable than the inequality of wealth. Hierarchy is an internally complex principle; its different forms have a countervailing relationship; and it is not measured or rewarded by material returns. The *Manusmrti* puts the case in the following manner:

vittam vandhurvayah karma vidya bhavati panchami
etani manyasthanani gariyoryadyaduttaram[15]

Manu mentions five different criteria for precedence: wealth, family, age, achievement, and knowledge, but takes care to add that these are to be seen as a hierarchical order. Wealth certainly helps people acquire a certain social precedence, but the least considerable of all.

It is commonly believed, Bhudev goes on to argue, that Indian culture is otherworldly, and the Western by contrast attends to the demands of rationality in the affairs of this world. Bhudev accepts this as true, but with an air of deprecation entirely uncharacteristic for his times. Indian *shastric* thought saw *pravrtti* and *nivrtti* as the dual springs of all human acts (ibid.: 90), but this complex theory was gradually simplified into a theory of two paths of life, one of a hedonistic

---

[15] Mukhopadhyay [1892] 1981: 87, quoting from *Manusmrti*.

domesticity, the other of a totally distinct path of renunciation. For him, this is a wholly unwelcome development, and it is in the interest of colonial ideology that Western theorists sometimes speak approvingly of the deep immaterialism of Indian culture and the spiritual inclination of the Indian intellect. What were supposed to be two forces in the original theory governing pragmatic acts were transformed into a division between two paths, one of ineffectual holiness and the other of vulgar acquisitiveness without moral control. In fact, all acts are produced by an interplay between pravrtti and nivrtti. *Ayana*, movement, is despite its apparent simplicity a dual act, consisting of a step forward indicating exertion, and then of resting before the next step can be taken. All activity in life should be seen accordingly as a combination of exerting and pausing, without which there would be loss of internal balance. Of the two, the *shastrakaras* realized that nivrtti was the weaker instinct, and emphasized it more in their advice on human conduct. However, it is wrong to conclude from this that the primary ideal of Hindu life is renunciation. Even the *Kathopanishad*, one of its basic texts, says about the relation between the *aihika* and the *paramarthika* that they are inextricable—*yadeveha tadamutra, yadamutra tadanviha* (ibid.: 90). Indeed, for Bhudev, the notion of the *paraloukika* should be taken to mean, literally, 'relating to people who come after', that is, simply as an injunction not to act with a generational selfishness, but to act in a way that does not reduce the chance of happiness of generations still unborn (ibid.: 92). Western theory teaches egotism not only for individuals, but also for generations. Enlightened self-interest implies an understanding of the ways in which the interests of others are inextricably connected with one's own, so that to injure others is really to injure the self. The idea of nondualism teaches that such *bhedabuddhi* is destructive; and in the calculation of interest even the interests of the future should be taken into account. Utilitarian individualism is hardly a new theory for Indians; its tenets are exactly similar to those of some *lokayatika* philosophies, and the answers to its aspirations are already contained in *advaitism*. Contrary to the Western overemphasis on autonomy, it must be seen that all societies are created by the meeting of the forces of autonomy and community. The principal task of political theory is to indicate ways of striking a rational balance between these two.

The difference between European and Indian societies in their basic principles becomes clear from the way the relation between the rulers and the people is arranged.[16] Europe has a hierarchical organization of power in which all spheres of social life are brought under the control of a single central organization called the state. Bhudev recognizes that the historical changes in Europe tend towards a decline of absolutism and spread of constitutional principles. He does not favour Indians learning even constitutionalism from Europeans, though in its proper context it is a wholly welcome development. In Indian society the relation between the rulers and the subjects is governed by a different principle. Indian society recognizes what could be called a sociological separation of powers, instead of concentrating all powers in the state and then trying to restrain it by Montesquieuan devices. In India each element of society exercises some power of self-governance, and everyday life is not submitted to the state for either inspection or guidance. Most significantly, the structure of everyday life is not open to the state to alter through legislation. Sovereignty is thus a deeply misleading concept to apply to Indian society: it simply does not recognize a site for this function. The function of creating and maintaining order, centralized into the notion of sovereignty in Europe, is distributed among various elements of the social structure; but that is not to be construed as an absence of something vital which is to be supplied by British rule. Kings had the power to govern individuals, but not to control and through legislation reorder society, the *devasharira* composed of *iha* and *parakala*, i.e. present and future generations, and consequently their power of law-making in the Western sense was strictly limited. The principles of Indian statecraft are not translatable into the Austinian language of sovereignty. Bhudev is, therefore, sceptical about state-centred projects for reforming Indian society.

If one particular force in society comes to acquire excessive dominance, it gives rise to countervailing action. Social theorists in the West sought to curb the excessive powers of absolutism by means of contractarian theories of government. Under this scheme, the power of the ruler was kept in check by the organized power of the people. It is only recently that Europeans have developed a notion of fiduciary power. The Indian social system considered power fiduciary in any case. Each group was confined within its segmental constitution, and these were kept in place by a constitution of society laid down in the religious

---

[16] The argument about the relation between society and political authority is outlined in Mukhopadhyay [1892] 1981: 119–25.

order. Religious power was always superior to political power in India, while in Europe the power of the clergy was always derived and backed up by the power of the state. This was possible due to some peculiarities of the functionaries who administered the religious order in Indian society.

1. They were *grhasthas*, and part of ordinary domesticity, not segregated into a separate monastic order.

2. As they did not have a single establishment, they were able to express diversity and grievances.

3. Economically, they did not depend on the ruler's munificence, because their property was beyond despoliation by royal writs.

Finally, Indian society was ordered by internal governance rather than royal power. To refer to Brahmins as a theocracy was, therefore, entirely misleading. With this, Bhudev's rejection of current diffusionist justifications of colonial rule is complete. Some features of European modernity are, on inspection, found undesirable. Others are commendable, but really not new to Indian culture. Some, which are both commendable and new, like scientific reasoning, are not being imparted to Indian society through colonial rule.

Contest between the Self and the Other: Possible Results of British Rule

Unlike the earlier experience of Muslim rule, British colonialism was a process of immense significance. The rise of Islamic dynasties, despite the extent of their conquests in India, did nothing to alter the basic rules of operation of the Indian social structure. During British colonial rule, these organizing principles gradually came under the dominance of another society (ibid.: 130). It was, therefore, essential to make long-term historical judgements about what this might hold in store for India in future: 'British dominion over India is an event unparalleled in the history of mankind. Never have so few people from such a small country been able to rule over such a large empire so far away from their home' (ibid.: 130). But the conflict between India and Britain should not be seen as a record of confrontations between individuals and battles between armies. What was unfolding in India was a contest between two ways of ordering human society.

Of course, history had seen large empires before, but the modern British empire was special in several ways. The Roman and Russian empires were undoubtedly of vast extent, but these were agrarian empires and geographically contiguous (*ekachakra*); the British empire was a commercial empire and discontinuous (*bahuchakra*; ibid.: 130). The reason for the British conquest of India was not British power, but their possession of a reason at once more subtle and significant. British dominion lay in the logic of Indian history: it came more out of the inevitable logic of Indian history than of England's expansion. For this strange reason, Bhudev sympathizes with historians like Seeley who claimed that the empire was created in a state of absentmindedness (ibid.: 130). For Bhudev this expresses a vital truth, though in a distorted form. It was the logic of Indian history which chose, out of all the available political actors at the end of Mughal rule, the British as the protagonists best suited to take this logic forward. For him, too, British rule was the unconscious tool of history, but history of a very different tendency. It is now that we are able to understand the import of the earlier quizzical claim that the British did not conquer India, it placed itself in their hands. Indian unity was primarily a cultural idea during the ancient period. Muslim rule introduced significant institutional elements into this cultural process, especially the administrative structures, and the creation of the minimal common language in Hindustani. British rule simply carried forward this logic of unity by creating preconditions for the translation of this cultural unity into a more self-conscious political sense of the self. Indian history could thus be seen as a great narrative of the rising of a culture to self-consciousness.

British rule had created an indestructible and uninterrupted political order, a network of communication which brought different regions into contact. British presence deterred external attacks, and finally provided India with a single centre of governance (ibid.: 132ff.). All these, though introduced by the British, were real preconditions for the emergence of a political identity for India: only colonialism could create the preconditions for nationalism. This, however, did not minimize the basic faults of British rule. First, alien rule could produce only the preconditions, not the identity itself. Second, colonial authorities were trying to impose on Indian society a fundamentally alien logic of political governance. By explicit declaration, the colonial government had assumed all legislative, executive, and judicial powers, a state of things quite unintelligible to Indian people, and therefore unlikely to be workable in the final analysis. The traditional rulers of

India had not enjoyed sovereignty in the Western sense of the concept: they had executive powers in full measure, very restricted judicial powers, but no legislative authority in terms of having the capacity to reorder basic social arrangements and relations among groups. Western political life was based on conflict between opposing social forces in a common public realm (ibid.: 136ff.). Traditional India did not have such a common public realm in the strict sense; it contained groups living in their own public arenas, avoiding contact with others rather than settling conflicts by appeal to a common sovereign. It was due to this incomprehension that the political initiatives of colonial authorities had brought forth peculiar and unintended consequences.

What are the lines of historical possibility in such a case? The first is that the British would gradually understand the logic of Indian social form and accept these—which was unlikely: the British only liked others' lands, not others' customs (ibid.: 144). The second possibility was the reverse: the British would assimilate Indians entirely and create a new people, as had happened in Latin America. But the history of the US shows why that could not happen—the logic of British imperialism was very different from the Iberian (ibid.: 144–5). Thus, the most likely possibility was that unassimilated Indians and the unmixing British would face each other for quite some time, and we would have to wait and see what might result from this.

In Indian languages it is customary to speak of the past, future, and present in that sequence, which, though apparently counterintuitive, indicates a necessary explanatory order. To decide what one must do in the present one must consider not only the past but also future prospects, because both are in different ways contexts or ingredients for the present (ibid.: 153).

Judging the future course of events has to be done through a somewhat complex procedure, because of the inextricability of the future of two societies in a colonial world. First, the future course of European history has to be analysed, and since Europe controls the colonies, we can then judge how far that course would be able to impose its logic on all the other societies under its control. Western social theories have given rise to conflicting pictures of the future; and in Bhudev's mind there is a close connection between explanatory and normative thinking in these theories. The conceptions of the future in European theory are wholly materialistic and show the usual immodesty of rationalist ideas.

Bhudev suggests a different periodization of European history: from early times to the fall of Rome, from the fall of Rome to the French Revolution, and the new age that the Revolution has ushered in (ibid.: 162). Societies, we have been told earlier, have to be judged according to their constitutive social ideals. Premodern societies gave rise to a number of ideals, but these are considered too utopian by present-day writers. After the Revolution new ideologies have arisen which revealed interesting possibilities about future history. Curiously for someone with such pronounced conservative sympathies, Bhudev shows a peculiar admiration for the Revolution: 'the great lesson of the French Revolution is that societies should be run for enhancing the welfare of their people' (ibid.: 163). But, like everything in modern Europe, this great principle has been won, not by the power of self-regulating morality, or dharma, but by social conflict. These welcome changes have been brought about by the destructive and malignant force of egalitarianism. Bhudev notes several paradoxes about the revolutionary process: it displays the conceit of a deliberate rational reconstruction of the social order; but the actual progress of the Revolution showed that such rationality was, in fact, impossible. Second, though launched in the name of equality, the Revolution did not end social inequality but only changed it. It replaced the inequality of status with an equally unjust inequality of wealth (ibid.: 163). The society that emerged from it was, therefore, one of extreme contradiction. This was partly because social groups did not enjoy equality. More fundamentally, this society was troubled because there was a contradiction between its formal principles of equality and the actual inequality of the social condition. It led to the illimitable power of men of property and to the grinding poverty of working people. And the peoples of the rest of the world suffered at the hands of this civilization as it was driven to find markets for its products outside because of low demand at home.

It is not surprising, according to Bhudev, that social theorists have suggested the eradication of inequality through socialist projects. His summary of its principles is astonishingly succinct and appropriate: 'The right to property should be vested in society rather than the individual. If individuals should not own property, let ownership be given to society as a whole. What we all produce should be given to society; which in return should maintain all its members. We should work according to our ability, and enjoy according to our needs' (ibid.: 164).

Indeed, the socialist doctrine appears to him better grounded philosophically than egotistic individualism, which claims that labour is the basis of property. If that premise is strictly applied, nothing can belong to any individual because of the ineradicable sociality of all created things. There is always the implicit existence of others' labour in one's own (ibid.: 168). Since socialist principles are better grounded than individualist or utilitarian ethics, it is likely that in the immediate future Europe might see the rise of powerful socialist movements. Yet, for outsiders like him, it is meaningless to dispute whether socialism or individualism is the right theory. In fact, it would be idle to seek Europe's future in the deliberate visions of these theoretical systems. True, ideological thinking can influence historical trajectories because they govern the initiatives of people, but the connection between historical paths and social designs is considerably more complex. To express it in more modern terminology, although men with a common ideology may pursue common rational plans, they are rarely able to force history to follow them—if there is any rationality in the historical process that exists over and beyond such collective plans of action. Real progress never takes place through such impulses.[17] All that was valuable in an earlier epoch lies sublated in the new truth that emerges; and the new truth does not take part in the earlier contests; it simply gets away from the plane of the earlier conflict. This has the additional advantage, in his view, that no earlier truth is rejected or wasted. The collective history of humanity follows an implicit law of economy; it never wastes any social experience that is really valuable.

This bears a strong resemblance to the Hegelian theory of history, and Bhudev may have been influenced by German idealism; this way of looking at history appeared to Bhudev compatible with his own reading of Hindu thought, for his historical reasoning derived from its basic concepts. Bhudev ends his discussion by deprecating the utopian constructivism of contemporary European social theory; the supposition underlying many modern ideologies that human societies could be shaped like clay on the potter's wheel (ibid.: 166). Rationalism does not understand that societies have no origin; they can be changed, as evidence shows, but only by understanding their logic of construction and development and acting with it.

[17] Ibid.: 165. He calls these impulses *jhonk*.

Colonialism has linked the destiny of India with Europe; it is likely that British administrators will use Indian society as a laboratory for their social theories and models, and treat it precisely as potter's clay. Bhudev did not expect such simplistic reforms to succeed; they would only scratch the outer shell of society. Political power always bore an external relation to social relations in India; and since the state did not create the caste order, it could not destroy it either. The British were unlikely to succeed in their attempt to break down Indian society as Latin American society had been broken. They would, however, try to enhance their control over Indian life by instituting more intricate and intensive economic controls. Already, there were alarming signs of this extension: formerly the British were contented with occupying official positions in the state; in the second half of the nineteenth century they were gradually penetrating the spheres of trade and commerce. As it turned out, Bhudev grossly underestimated the ingenuity of the indigenous business community, who were soon to outclass the British in their application of the Protestant ethic. However, at the time, it must have appeared like a threatening extension of the logic of subjugation from the political to the productive sphere (ibid.: 257).

What is to be Done?

What was to be done? Bhudev advises a repeat of the classical strategy of Hinduism, a strategy of withdrawal. Social activities and initiatives should be withdrawn from the public realm of the colonial state. Because whatever is rendered public in this sense, immediately becomes amenable to colonial control. Indians should also try to heighten their sense of community, and this incudes a rebuke to Bankimchandra Chattopadhyay for his sharp attack on Indian zamindars.[18] This will merely split the ranks of the swajatiya and 'make the adversary chuckle with pleasure'.

Historically, the great strength of Hindu society had been its principles of internal governance. The present historical task, however, was not the mere survival of Hindu religion but a revitalization of Indian society. Religion has three internal levels: a level of high

[18] Ibid.: 212. Though Bhudev does not mention any name, it is a reasonable guess that this was a criticism of Bankim's celebrated essay on the condition of the peasantry in Bengal (*Bangadesher Krshak*).

philosophic doctrine, a level of rules of conduct which introduces moral order in society, and a third level of *achara*, or everyday rituals and practice (ibid.: 77). Hinduism must generate a self-reflexive theory and seriously reflect on its historical state. The high philosophy of Hinduism was the most exalted in the world and was therefore impossible to undermine, even by British colonialism. Its moral order was organized around the principle of marginalizing the state, and was unlikely to fall under legislative attacks from colonial power. Achara was the least significant part of religious life and could be adjusted to the needs of the times. The main threat to the Hindu order was not from direct missionary attacks on the Hindu faith, but through the gradually spreading effect of English education, a slow nibbling away at the roots of the conceptual structure of traditional society. This was reflected in the gradual decline of the vernacular languages among a people that had lost their religion—a shrewd use of the idea that every language contains within itself a conception of the world (ibid.: 185ff). Conversely, this conception can retreat and take shelter in the recesses of language. Language can be put to various political uses. The obstinate use of vernaculars in internal communication among Indians—either in the regional vernacular or Hindi—could impart a peculiar secrecy to social and political life, and withdraw them from the realm of public law which the colonial administration was seeking to establish. Bhudev suggests a strategy of non-cooperation through language.

Bhudev's work clearly reveals the peculiarity of his own intellect and the climate of his times; but it also displays a limitation of Hindu thought in general, its tendency towards an ineradicable contemplativeness. Its riches are in its intellectual acuity, fashioning a sociology of Hindu society and applying its principles for a sociology of European modernity. Yet Bhudev's pragmatic advice amounted to a passive form of *netrpratiksha*, waiting for a leader to emerge in the historical process. He had not guessed badly even in this regard. As Raychaudhuri (1988) has suggested, the image of the leader he was waiting for strongly fitted the man who was to emerge in twenty years' time.

What Bhudev essayed, nothing less than a social theory, was not attempted by anyone after him in quite the same fashion. Later nationalists, who felt the need for a social theory to make sense of their historical world, mostly relied on Western systems with simple adaptations to the climate. Of course, he was not alone in being alone. Suffering from intellectual loneliness appears to be the cross of all thinkers of some originality. The more interesting question is how they inhabit their loneliness—what they attempt and accomplish inside the peculiar privacy afforded them by general disapproval.

By his own declaration, Bhudev was a man of tradition. This is one of the reasons why he is consistently neglected by modernist chroniclers of the nationalist movement who saw a defence of tradition as an unmitigated evil. Bhudev offered to defend the most disreputable aspects of Hindu society, including the caste system (ibid.: 192ff); nor did he conceal his contempt for the imitative, inconsequential, modernism of reformers. He constantly emphasized an idea that is now more easily grasped—that in the inverted world of colonialism, it took more courage and ingenuity to be a conservative than to be a common reformer. It was the conservative who displayed in greater measure what is taken to be the unfailing mark of intellectual radicalism, the courage to think against the grain of history. Against both traditionalists and modernists, Bhudev showed a deep sense of the historicity of traditions, despite their own pretence of immutability. Traditions survive, despite their own delusions, by coming to terms with the unprecedented and surprising in their history. He was advising Hindus to do this with a lucid self-consciousness, not through grudging, surreptitious, unreflected change. It required an agenda of reflexivity—understanding their own history in the past, and the new, external, unwanted, but still unavoidable history in which colonialism has placed them. This rejected traditional forms of traditionalism because they resisted self-analysis, and denigrated as unwelcome any curiosity about the modern history of Europe.

In devising this very innovative traditionalism, Bhudev had to take some unprecedented intellectual steps. *Samaj*, the concept Bhudev uses so centrally, is a concept of great indeterminacy in traditional thought and social practice. In traditional discourse, a reference to one's samaj would be context dependent and highly variable: it could mean anything from neighbourhood, village, religious group, to caste, sect. Bhudev's theoretical performance, despite its clear intention of offering a defence of Hindu society, must restructure its internal logic of concepts in quite a fundamental fashion. To speak of samaj in the old indeterminate way would have been inadequate for his purposes:

through his argument he coined a Bengali equivalent of the abstract modern conception of society, very different, conceptually, from the earlier indeterminate way of thinking of one's community, of one's samaj. His thought is, therefore, as much an extension of Hindu theory towards unaccustomed questions as a subtle violation of its internal order.

In this essay I have analysed only one of Bhudev's texts, *Samajik Prabandha*, partly because it is the principal site of his social theorizing. But his intellectual portrait cannot be complete without a supplement, a study of his other, more quizzical, work, *Swapnalabdha Bharatvarsher Itihas*. That text describes a most extraordinary dream, in which the content entirely violates the customary expectations one has of a dream narrative. In a dream of astonishing clarity and consistency, he describes in great, often tiresome, detail the social constitution of India under an imagined un-British rule, twisting the line of Indian history away from what had actually happened. This shows the insistence of his social thinking; even in his dreams he is constantly constructing social and political forms. Of particular interest is the time in which the story unfolds, a dreamtime that is half past, half future, the indescribable time of historical desire. The formal structure, argument, and pretences of that work are entirely different from the one I have analysed here; but it is also an extension of the same enterprise in another style.

References

Chatterjee, Partha. 1991. 'Many Uses of Jati'. Paper presented at a seminar on Terms of Political Discourse in India, Bhubaneshwar.

Dattagupta, Bela. 1972. *Sociology in India*. Calcutta: Centre for Sociological Research.

Kaviraj, Sudipta. 1992. The Imaginary Institution of India. In Partha Chatterjee and Gyanendra Pandey. Eds. *Subaltern Studies VII*. Delhi: Oxford University Press.

———. 1998. *The Unhappy Consciousness: Bankimchandra Chattopadhyaya and the Formation of Nationalist Discourse in India*. Delhi: Oxford University Press.

Mukhopadhyay, Bhudev. 1857. *Anguriyabinimay*.

———. 1876. *Pushpanjali*.

———. 1895. *Swapnalabdha Bharatvarsher Itihas*.

———. [1982] 1981. *Samajik Prabandha*. Ed. Jahnabi Kumar Chakrabarti. Calcutta: Paschimbanga Rajya Pustak Parshad.

Raychaudhuri, Tapan. 1988. *Europe Reconsidered*. Delhi: Oxford University Press.

Thakur, Rabindranath. 1963. *Bhasha o Chhanda*. In *Rabindrarachanabali* (Collected Works), Vol. 5. Calcutta: Visvabharati.

Index

Acharya, P. 202
administrative histories 48
American development theory 36
anachronism 40; and periodization 171–6
Anandamangal 137n
Anderson, Benedict 19, 109, 189
anti-colonial: consciousness 101–10; early 94–101, 177, 180, 197, 203; protest and 57, 94
Arabic culture: chronicles of 262; language and Muslim rule 134
Arendt, H. 123
Asiatic Society 61
Assam: linguistic determination in 158; movement 238; problem 163
atman 77
Austin, J.L. 177
Ayodhya mosque controversy 247; *see also* Babri Masjid

Babri Masjid: crisis 238; demolition of 240, 241, 243
Bahujan Samaj Party (BSP) 246, 247–8, 250
Bajrang Dal 241
Barrier, N.G. 99
Bengal: conquest of 51; Renaissance 254, 255; speech community in 147
Bengali: *bhadralok* 74, 97, 107, 128, 135n; British empire and 182–3; claim to distinction 98; culture 97, 108; dialect 147; Europeanization of 76; historical literature 141; *jati* 107, 182; language 127, 128, 142, 143, 146–7 190, 192; literature 255; Marxism 3; 'nation' 74; identity and 107; norm-language of 146; political rights and 128; Utilitarianism and 196; Vaishnavism 139; writing 73, 145, 149
bhakti: cult 213; Hinduism 140; literature 138; movements 139
Bakhtin, M. 49, 86
Bharatiya Janata Party (BJP) 229, 240, 241, 243, 245, 246, 248–9, 251, 252; communal politics of 244; electoral allies of 248; influence of 239; Shiv Sena's support to 250; vote on religion and 242; victory in elections 247
Bhargava, Rajeev 8
Bhavabhuti, *Uttararamacharita* of 138n
bilingualism 152–3
Bose, Subhas Chandra 119
boundaries 142, 169, 183–4
Bourdieu, P. 47
bourgeois: political order in Europe 80; sciences 2
Brahmins/Brahminism 131, 132, 213
British: colonial administration 63, 66, 101, 145–6, 220; conquest and 14–15; historiography 46;

identities and 219; Indian society and 51, 57, 64, 143, 218; legitimization of 48, 61–2, 103–4, 195; linguistic identity and 143–50; policy 15; political discourse on 59, 197; power in India 197, 218, 281; public opinion 43, 60; reforms and 92; significance of 280; social affairs and 219; social theory 274
Buddhism/Buddhist 139, 192, 213, 276
bureaucracy 25, 223, 225, 230

capitalism/capitalist 17, 26, 80, 124, 198, 202, 212
caste: barriers 131–2; divisions 242; hierarchies 133n; identities 228; mobilizations 250; orders 215, 227, 228; politics 228; system 11, 96, 97, 214, 287
causality 262–3
census 99
Chaitanya, avatar of Krishna 138–9
Chaitanyabhagavat 139
Chaitanyacharitamrita 139
Chakrabarti, Mukundaram 136n
Chandidas 139
Chandimangal 136n
Chandra, B. 101
Chatterjee, Bankimchandra: see under Chattopadhyay, Bankimchandra
Chatterjee, Partha 8, 34, 37, 77, 88, 258
Chattopadhyay, Bankimchandra 42n, 72, 73, 74, 75, 77, 101, 104, 105, 106–7, 109, 146, 147, 148, 149, 182, 183, 186, 187, 196, 197, 255, 256, 257, 285
Christianity 145, 261, 267–8, 276
civil society 10, 25
civilization 72, 103

Clive, Robert 60
coalition governments 246
Cohn, Bernard 65
collective: action 70, 133, 199; self-determination 21, 183
colonial: culture 66, 67; discourse 50, 76, 78–80, 205; economy 105–6; education 93; historiography 43; institutional system 144; intelligentsia 71; laws and rules 144; modernity 4, 15–20, 103; rationalism 43, 203; reconstruction of Indian society 81; social transformation 145; state in India 39, 41, 51, 218
colonialism 5, 10, 20, 21, 40–1, 43, 178, 271, 273, 285; cultural invasion of 76; cultural strategy of 92–3; hegemonic discourse of 58; nationalism and 121–2, 176–7, 179; opposition to 177–80, 200
common sense 80; Gramscian theory of 63; orbits of 160
communal/communalism 13, 251
Communist Party 250; —of India (CPI-M) 242, 249, 250; governments in Kerala, Tripura, and West Bengal 245, 250
communists: during 'people's war' phase 115–16; insurgency and 24; opposition to liberalization 240–1; support to British war effort 119n
communitarianism 229
community 13–14, 56; assertion and politics of 230; cognitive identification of 55; enumerated 187–201; fuzzy 56, 57, 80, 95, 193–4; identity and 188; primordial 190; traditional and modern 56

Index

Congress Party 27, 94, 101, 170, 171, 222, 234, 249, 250, 253; advent of 110; anti-Congress trends 119; decline in electoral fortunes of 241; early stages of 118–19; factionalism in 239, 243; India's relationship with the Soviet Union and 25; Indian nationalism and 20, 115; Indira Gandhi and 120, 237; Jawaharlal Nehru and 25; leadership of 24, 223; liberalization policies of 244, 245; linguistic provisions and 157; loss in elections of 247; Moderates and Extremists in 88; Muslim support to 229; policies of 236; secularism and 237; split in 236
Constituent Assembly 24; ideological conflicts in 26–7; national language and 155–6
constitution (Indian) 154, 225
Cromwellian revolution 90
culture/cultural: bilingualism and 151; British intrusion and 91–3; colonial 72, 93; composite 13, 121, 150; conflict 155; Gandhi and 115; homogenization of 150; identity 169n; Indian society and 92; Jawaharlal Nehru and 161; organizations 92; process of 159; rationalist concept of 259; space of 19; transformation and 93; unity and 34

Danto, A.C. 186
decolonization, societies after 211
democracy/democratic 22, 30, 165, 223, 225, 230; formal institutions of 227, 231–2; Indian politics and 6; mobilization and 238; politics and 251, 252; poverty and 161; success of 211–12, 231–2
dependency theory 37
Derozio, Henry Louis Vivian 67
Derrida, Jacques 129
de Swann, Abram 152
de Tocqueville, A. 90, 122, 124, 211, 227 231
Deuskar, Sakharam Ganesh 92
development 29, 117, 222, 223, 224
dharma, Hindu society and rule of 266
dialects 97, 142, 192
Dilthey, W. 93
discourse 85, 86, 87, 168–9
discursive space 50
Discovery of India, The 150–1
Disraeli, B. 183
distributive justice 161, 224
Dravida Munnetra Kazhagam (DMK) 250
Dunn, John 8, 36, 37
dusri parampara 137
Dutt, R.C. 75, 256
Dutt, R.P. 88

East India Company 51–2, 217n; economic growth 27, 161; rent extraction by 63
economic planning 28, 117
economic reforms 17, 240; *see also* liberalization
economy of India 97, 241
education 18, 93, 160, 162
egotism 268, 278
elite/elites: consensus 26; discourse of 29, 134; in nationalist movement 152
election: issues 241–2; revolution 225; verdict 247–8, 251–3
Election Commission 244, 247
electoral politics 31, 226

Emergency (the Indian) 31, 120n, 237n, 239
English: education 152, 286; language 146, 156, 226
Enlightenment 15, 41, 62, 196, 202
enumeration (as classification) 18, 70, 99, 180, 194, 198–9, 219, 260
Europe/European: capitalism 28; colonial rule and 216–17, 230; culture and 131, 265; democracy and 225, 227; Enlightenment and 11; equality and 277; Indian society and 89–91; history of 24, 210, 270–1, 283; missionaries and 145; modernity and 94, 212, 265, 277; narratives of 69; nationalism and 149; rationalism and 41, 63, 73, 91; romanticism and 104; science and 268; social theory and 36, 265; social transformation in 211; societies and 210, 272; suffrage in 225
evolutionary theories 274–5

Fadnavis, Nana 100
financial scams 239
Five Year Plan, Second 25
food shortages 28
Forward Bloc 119
Foucault, M. 37, 86, 125, 179, 179n, 208
Fox, R.G. 95, 125, 142n, 166
French Revolution 90, 170n, 283

Gadamer, Hans Georg 129, 129n, 166, 171n, 172, 184, 208
Gandhi, Indira 117, 119, 121, 163, 226, 236, 239, 243, 250; assassination of 238; centralization of power under 238; Congress under 120; electoral moves of 32; Emergency under 31; leadership and 224, 237
Gandhi, Mahatma 77, 100, 113, 115, 172, 211, 223, 234; discourse of 23; on modernity 35; nationalism of 111–12, 115; politics of 113–14
Gandhi–Irwin Pact 88
Gandhi, Rajiv 238, 239, 240, 241, 246
Gellner, E. 96, 121, 141, 184, 185, 189, 191, 198, 208
gemeinschaft 13, 94, 95, 188, 189, 199, 258
Germany, unification of 90
gesellschaft 13, 94, 95, 188, 189, 190, 199
Government of India Act of 1935 222n
Gowda, Deve 253
Gramsci, Antonio 50, 71, 79, 80, 92, 99, 175
Guha, R. 8, 67, 82, 124, 125
Guizot, Francois 210

Harishchandra, Bharatendu 159n
Haryana Vikas Party 248
Hastings, Warren 60, 217n
heavy industry, state-managed 224
Hegel, G.W.F. 4; theory of history 284
hegemony 47, 48, 66–82 *passim*
Hindi 142; chauvinism and 163; demand for replacement of English and 164; as national language 155, 159; as official language 156; standardization of 158
Hindu: caste order 267; extemism 239; history and 263; majoritarianism 164, 252; Muslim rulers and 54;

—nationalism 229n, 247;
nationalist parties 229; others
and 260-2; social ordering
53, 266; social theory
265; society 214, 264–8;
—tradition 77
Hinduism 138, 140, 169, 261, 276, 285–6
Hindustani (language) 159, 281
history/historical/historicism/
historiography 2, 3, 46, 66–82,
86–7, 116, 123, 127, 170, 172,
174, 176, 184–7, 206, 207, 269

identity: enumerated 219; formation
147, 258; reconfiguration of
164
ideology/ideological 87–8, 102, 170
illiteracy 19, 99, 154, 222
'imagined community' 109, 186–7
'imaginary histories' 74
imperial/imperialism: 9, 105, 220;
historiography and 68–71;
naturalism and 73
import-substituting industrialization
224
income, inequalities in 29, 224
Indian: antiquity 181, 190, 192;
colonialism 94–5, 213, 218,
278–9; culture 130, 131; history
73, 74; intellectuals 90–1, 220;
nationalism 5, 6, 7, 20, 26–31,
40, 78, 88, 106, 107 148n, 149,
156, 168, 170–1, 190, 204, 222,
253, 257
Indian National Congress: see
Congress
Indianness 160, 175, 181
Indus Valley civilization 184, 185
industrial/industrialization 25, 30,
32, 223, 224, 227–8
inequality 277, 283

institution/institutional 16, 32, 34, 214
Islam/Islamic 54, 214, 261, 276;
conversion to 135; culture 15,
135; dynasties 214, 215; equality
in 268; religious doctrines of 216
Italian nationalism 175

Jainism 213
Jan Sangh 229, 239
Janata coalition 239
Janata Dal 164, 249, 250
jati system 12, 258
Jayadeva 139–41
Jayalalitha, J. 242
Jnanandas 139
Judaic culture, chronicles of 262

Kashiramdas, *Mahabharata* of 136
Kashmir movement 238
Kasim, Mir 100
Kathopanishad 278
Kaviraj, Krishnadas, *Chaitanya-charitamrita* of 139
Kayasthas 1, 35
Keynesian economics 27
Khadi boli (language) 159
Khilnani, Sunil 8
knowledge 62, 274
Koselleck, R. 41n, 66, 83, 122, 125
Kothari, Rajni 8n, 22, 22n, 26, 38, 228n, 233, 235n

language 35–6, 86, 97, 282, 286;
alterations in 134; colonialist and
vernacular 177; composite 5;
culture and 259; debate in
Constituent Assembly on 155;
in a fuzzy world 141–3; and
historical formation of identities
127; 'internal economy' of
129–41; and politics 155–65;

region and 191; rights 164;
social functions of 127
Left parties 250
Lenin, V.I. 3, 116
liberalism 17, 21, 220
'liberalization' 225, 240, 243–5
linguistic: colonialism and 141–50;
communities 96; identities 148;
region and 192; separatism 163
literacy 131–4
Locke, John 63
Lytton, Lord 64

MacIntyre, Alasdair 200, 200n, 208
Madan, T.N. 22, 22n, 32, 32n, 34, 38
Madras Presidency 157
Mahabharata 136
Maine, Henry 196
majoritarianism 164–5, 262
Mandal Commission 161n
Mangalkavyas, of Bengal 136, 169
Manusmrti 277
Mao Tse Tung 3
Marx, Karl 1, 3, 33, 122, 189, 201, 202, 227
Marxism 1, 3, 28, 116, 117
middle class 4, 20, 68, 72, 152
Mill, John Stuart 60, 221
minority rights 27, 30
modernity 9–11, 105, 122–3, 145, 212; civilization of 106; in Europe 90–1; Gandhi on 35; nationalist thinking on 197, 202–6; and subjection 16; and tradition 104
modernization theory 10, 228
Mohenjodaro 185
Montagu–Chelmsford reforms (1919) 222n
Montesquieu, C.S. 65, 83, 196, 279
Mughal empire 15, 63, 217

Mukhopadhyay, Bhudev 42n, 74, 75, 259, 269; and indigenist social theory 254, 256; *Samajik Prabandha* of 288; *Swapnalabdha Bharatvarsher Itihas* of 254, 288
Müller, Max 72
Munshi-Ayyangar formula 156
Muslim: Arabic and Persian languages and 134; community 242, 244, 26; rule in India 261, 264, 266, 281; stable rule of 135; structure of society and 53

nada (form of sound) 130
Nagel, Thomas 180
Nandy, Ashis 8, 22, 34, 34n, 38
Naoroji, Dadabhai 21
Napoleon 90
Narayan, Jayaprakash 117
narrative/narratives 180, 200, 206; of colonial rule 46; of contract 201–2; empowering 151; nationalist 87
nation-building 185, 188; boundaries of 194; community and 199; objectivity of 200; region and 190; relation with earlier identities 189–90; states and 199, 214, 221
national community, discovery of 176–84
National Front 243, 246, 247, 250, 252
nationalism 6, 167, 174, 197, 199; colonialism and 121–2; discourse of 77, 85, 88–9, 98, 110–17; Gandhi and 115; modern 189; narratives of 200, 202; Nehru and 7, 101, 117, 120, 122; political thinking of 117; since Independence 117–24; syllogistic

Index

structure of 20–6; understanding 40
nationalist: diglossia 150–4; discourse 87, 88, 173; ideology 7, 121, 197; movement 23–4, 81, 106, 119–20, 150, 151, 155, 189, 213
naturalist religion 276, 277
Nazism 90
Nehru, Jawaharlal 21, 22–4, 32, 71, 76, 100, 116, 151, 155, 157, 183, 201, 223, 226, 227, 242, 245; achievements under 27; democracy of 28; development policy of 159, 224; *Discovery of India* of 150; economic policies under 27; election victories under 235; institutional pattern and 26; linguistic reorganization of states and 158; on modern elite class 23–4; narratives of 78; nationalism of 7, 101, 117, 120, 122; socialism and 27
Nehru, Motilal 186

occidentalism 271–3
official/national language 155
Olson, Mancur 199
oral incantations 138
Orient, conception of 65, 68
Orientalism 105, 205
Orientalist constructions 37
Oriya (language) 143
other/otherness 68, 69; self and 280–5; theory of 271–3
Owen, Robert 60

paradhinata 173
paraloukika, notion of 278
Partition (of India) 157, 222, 234
Patel, Sardar 25, 223

patriotism 5, 7, 174, 198
peasants revolts 129
Permanent Settlement 144
Persian (language) 134
planning, state 25, 224
Planning Commission 27
Plassey, Battle of 51
political: compliance 48–9; diagnosis 31–6; history 173; identity 148; power 5, 49, 215–16; relations 41; theory 36
politics 6, 85, 86, 212–13, 219; in colonial society 177; discourse of 228; evolution of 160; language and 155–65; in the vernacular 226
Pollock, Sheldon 8
Popper, Karl 3
poverty 29, 32, 227
power: discourse of 39; state 48; structure of 47
printing 146
primordial communities 190
property rights 17, 270, 271, 283
public realm 58n
public/state sector 27, 224
publicity 58n; concept of 49; notion of 50
Punjab 163, 238
Punjabi (language) 149n
Punjabi *suba*, demand for 158
Puranas 263

ramarajya 187n
Ramayana 136, 138n
Ramcharitmanas 136, 137
Rani of Jhansi 100
Ranjit Singh 102
Rao, P.V. Narasimha 238, 239, 239–41, 243, 244, 252
rational social theory 123
rationalism/rationalistic 55, 76–7,

81, 145, 198, 271, 284; colonial narrative 68; culture 67; discourse 54–5, 81; modernity 21, 54; in politics 59
Raychaudhuri, Tapan 286
region/regional: autonomy movement of 1950s 29; identities 148; and language 193; and nation 98–9, 190, 191; national identities and 98; political— 99; vernacular cultures and 110
religion/religious: developments and languages 135; identities 229; in India 261; power and 280; rationality of 103
reservations 250
revolt of 1857 57, 64, 72, 94, 195, 217
rights 27, 32, 228; equality of 17; to protest 164; to vote 226
Roman empire 280–1
Rousseau, J. 178
Roy, D.L. 189n
Roy, M.N. 88, 124
Roy, Ram Mohan 100, 134n
Russian empire 280–1

Saberwal, Satish 8
Said, Edward 65, 205
Samajik Prabandha 288
Samajwadi Party (SP) 248, 250
Samata Party 248
Sanatana dharma 132, 133
Sanskrit (language) 134, 135, 140, 146, 191
Sarkar, Jadunath 72
Satavahanas, history of 185–6
Sathyamurthy, T.V. 85
sati, practice of 219
Schopenhauer 274
Seal, Anil 64, 182
secular/secularism 25, 30, 100

self, Hindu concept of 264–5, 274, 280–5
Seshan, T.N. 244
Shah Bano case 238
Shaivas 143
Shiromani Akali Dal, Punjab 248
Shiv Sena, Maharashtra 245, 247, 248, 250
Singh, Manmohan 241
Singh, Namwar 137
Skinner, Quentin 8
slavery 270
social: action 57, 145; change 10, 22, 28, 105; conduct 132; democracy 27, 117; hierarchy 11, 80; identity 95, 127, 200; justice 25, 250; ontology 60, 99; organizations 203; power 214; relations 52, 61, 64; science 2, 4, 43; theory 77, 121, 201, 204, 256, 257; Western theory 205, 256, 268–71, 276, 282
socialism 27, 90, 116
socialist ideology/principles 116, 224, 284
society: development in 276; discursive type of 23; history of Indian 262–4; individual's relation with 270; language communities in 97; modern conception of 288; political division and 23; segmentation of 97; and space for 44–61; and the state 9, 12, 18; structure of Hindu 52–3; traditional construction of 11–15
Soviet Union 25, 118
Srinivas, M.N. 228n
state-building 151; concept of 49; formation 5; linguistic reorganization of 157, 158; meaning of 10; power of 279;

Index

and regional parties 249–50; and society 9, 18, 80; space of 11; structure of 44–61
statecraft, principles of Indian 279
structuralism 86
subordinate groups 2, 4, 134
subaltern cultures 81
Swadharma 260
Swadesh 257
Swajati 257, 258, 259
Swajatiyata 258, 259, 260
Swapnalabdha Bharatvarsher Itihas 254, 288

Tagore, Abanindranath 202
Tagore, Rabindranath 72, 128, 187, 263
Tamil Maanila Congress (TMC) 250
Tamil Nadu, voting pattern in 242
Tara Chand 119
Telugu Desam, Andhra Pradesh 250
'Third World' 36, 37, 211
Tilak, Bal Gangadhar 111
Tipu Sultan 100, 102
Tocquevelle: *see under* de Tocqueville
Tönnies, Ferdinand 13, 94, 188, 188n, 209
tradition/traditional: collective selves and 180; culture and 19; Hindu society and 80; ritual prohibitions and 52; social space in 52; historicity of 287; society and 11
transfer of power (1947) 221
Tulsidas, *Ramcharitamanas* of 136

United Front (government of) 251, 253
universal adult suffrage 21, 222, 225

Urdu (language) 149n, 158, 159, 163
Utilitarian/Utilitarianism 103–4, 195, 196, 278
Uttararamacharita 138n

Vais(h)nava/Vais(h)navism 56, 57, 138–140, 143, 193
Vajpayee, Atal Bihari 252
Valmiki 263; *Ramayana* of 138n
Vande Mataram 108, 147
vernacular: education 162; languages 98–9, 135, 140, 226 ; literary discourse 75; literature 136–7, 141
Vidyapati 140, 141, 193
Vidyasagar 146
Vidyasundarkavya 137n
Vishwa Hindu Parishad (VHP) 241, 245
Vivekananda, Swami 72
Volosinov, V.N. 86, 87
Voltaire 65
Vrindavandas, *Chaitanyabhagavat* of 139

Weber, Max 33, 122, 188, 213, 268
West Bengal 242
Western: civilization 272; cultural tradition 129; education 55, 61, 63, 67, 90; intelligentsia and 110–11, 192; modernity 204, 273–80; rationalism 65, 271
Whiggism 172
Wittgenstein, L. 47
written cultures 130, 132

'Young Bengal' movement 102

GPSR Authorized Representative: Easy Access System Europe, Mustamäe tee 50, 10621 Tallinn, Estonia, gpsr.requests@easproject.com

www.ingramcontent.com/pod-product-compliance
Lightning Source LLC
Chambersburg PA
CBHW031546300426
44111CB00006BA/191